You Thought I Was Dead

You Thought I Was Dead

MY LIFE of CELEBRITIES, SEX, and CHAMPAGNE

Mamie Van Doren

A PERMUTED PRESS BOOK
ISBN: 979-8-89565-323-4
ISBN (eBook): 979-8-89565-324-1

You Thought I Was Dead:
My Life of Celebrities, Sex, and Champagne

Cover design by Cody Corcoran
Cover photo by Alan Mercer

This is a work of nonfiction. All people, locations, events, and situations are portrayed to the best of the author's memory.

This book, as well as any other Permuted Press publications, may be purchased in bulk quantities at a special discounted rate. Contact orders@permutedpress.com for more information.

Permuted Press
New York • Nashville
permutedpress.com

Published in the United States of America
1 2 3 4 5 6 7 8 9 10

This book is dedicated to my beloved husband, Thomas Dixon; my son, Perry Anthony; Vietnam veteran, John "Rusty" Huddleston; the brave Vietnam veterans who survived the war; and those who did not.

A special dedication to Lilimae, my white German Shepherd angel who was by my side throughout the writing of this book. Though she did not live to see its publication, she is always in my heart and her spirit dwells in every page.

PEACE

Contents

Introduction

The Girl Who Invented Rock and Roll

In many ways, rock and roll invented *me*. Of all the different facets of my career, the most exciting for me has been rock and roll. The teenage movies that I starred in—*Untamed Youth, Girls Town,* and *Running Wild*—featured a new, wild-sounding brand of music that some thought would be a temporary fad, like the mambo or calypso, but it would in fact become the music that changed the world. I was the first woman to perform rock and roll music on the silver screen, and, along with those teen-exploitation movies that have now become cult classics, it came to define me in many ways.

I worked alongside legendary rock and roll pioneers like Eddie Cochran, Paul Anka, Bill Haley & His Comets, Conway Twitty, and Jerry Lee Lewis. Ironically, I married Ray Anthony, a very successful orchestra leader, who at the high point of his career was the bestselling band leader at Capitol Records. The rise in popularity of rock and roll music became the force that ultimately muted the big band sound.

I have always loved jazz, blues, bebop, and boogie-woogie. As a teenager, I hung out in East LA jazz clubs like the Club Oasis, where on any night you might hear Lionel Hampton, Thelonious Monk, Lena Horne, or Dinah Washington.

When I was growing up, my parents and I often spent time in Vegas. (This was the 1940s, long before the Vegas Strip was a glamorous sprawl of neon distractions dedicated to separating rubes from their money and leaving them smiling. Back then, there were a few scattered hotels and a handful of casinos. They still separated rubes like my dad from their money but left them weeping in the parking lot.) We usually stayed at the El Rancho Vegas where Lena Horne worked. I watched her every night and did my best to imitate her when I sang. But, c'mon, seriously, who could ever equal the incomparable Lena?

I moved my singing career to the back burner when I got my contract with Universal Studios. I had taken scene-study classes and appeared in plays at showcase theaters, but I was largely untrained as an actor. Universal had a highly regarded talent school, and before the ink was dry on my contract, I enrolled in as many of the classes as I could.

Clark Gable was the reason I was cast in *Teacher's Pet* to begin with. He had seen me in the Warner Brothers commissary when I was filming *Born Reckless* with Howard Koch and told *Teacher's Pet* producer William Perlberg that he wanted me for the role of the nightclub singer. Gable would later tell me that I reminded him of Carole Lombard—something Dorothy Lamour once told me too.

When I made *Teacher's Pet*, I felt fortunate to work with a director like George Seaton, who took the time to help me create the character of Peggy DeFore.

Peggy DeFore was a brash young nightclub singer who is Gable's main squeeze until he meets Doris Day's character. I had really good scenes with Gable, including one where I throw myself into his arms and kiss him on the mouth. The difference in our ages was obvious—it looked like a kidnapping—so the scene was cut from the movie.

What Ever Happened to Mamie?

Well, admit it. That's what you were thinking when you picked up this book. How old is she? Is she still alive?

Okay, here's the deal. I am alive and kicking. As of this writing (spring of 2024), I am ninety-three. Think of that. I am at the threshold of age.

You Thought I Was Dead has been a decade in the making, give or take. I made a couple of false starts, setting it aside each time because it didn't feel right. Then I had one of those transcendent moments: a birthday with a zero in it. It occurred to me that this ride I've been on may not last forever. I still had some secrets to tell, so it was time to start writing.

My autobiography, *Playing the Field*, published by Putnam in 1987, was more or less traditional. The story line was linear and followed the rules. There were a good many deletions made by stodgy old Putnam from my original manuscript. Some of those stories survived their exile to my desk drawer and are included in this book. Other stories herein are, if not secrets, unwritten by me until now, though I may have told some of them over a cocktail somewhere. If you weren't there, they'll be new to you. Unlike *Playing the Field,* this book is not strictly linear in its timeline. Some chapters may overlap in time. I trust the reader will be able to sort them out. Time is linear, but life circles back on itself. We often do two things at once.

In here you will find superb cartoons by the expressionist artist Stephen B. Whatley introducing each chapter. My whimsical concept for this book was to include cartoons dramatizing scenes and characters central to certain stories—a sort of graphic-novel-style memoir. Stephen and I stumbled onto each other on Facebook. He sent me the wonderful cartoon strip retrospective of my career and leading men at the beginning of this introduction. It was kismet—the artist perfectly suited to my concept. Stephen signed on to do the cartoons that introduce each chapter.

You can read all about Stephen's career in his bio in these pages. I promise you that in addition to being a gifted expressionist painter and sensational cartoonist, Stephen is an insightful and smart collaborator and one of the most compassionate people I've ever known.

One of the few people in Hollywood that I never met was the legendary Frank Capra. In the course of his long career, he directed fifty-four films with the biggest Hollywood stars of his day, including Jimmy Stewart in the perennial *It's a Wonderful Life* and *Mr. Smith Goes to Washington* and Clark Gable in *It Happened One Night*. Capra also directed my idol, Jean Harlow, in *Platinum Blonde* in 1931, the year I was born.

I always admired Capra's work, which catches the essence of what we think of as America. As a little girl in Sioux City, Iowa, I grew up watching his movies from the front row of the Orpheum Theatre. During those hard years of the Depression, when my mother and father both worked, the movie theater was my daycare center, and all those glamorous actors and actresses were my babysitters.

In 2011, I got an email from a San Diego college professor named Al Greenberg asking if I would speak to him on the phone about Frank Capra's opinion of me as an actress. I get a lot of emails from people who want to make contact. I am lucky to have the nicest fans in the world, and I really do love meeting them, but I usually don't reply because there are simply not enough hours in the day to do it all. However, it was an intriguing email since I had no idea Capra was even aware of me, much less had an opinion of me, so I gave him my phone number.

Professor Greenberg taught a unique course to foreign-born students, using contemporary American popular culture—movies, literature, autobiographies, interviews, and written correspondence—to give them a sense of the spirit of America. Greenberg's approach exposed his students to American history, arts, and government by acquainting them with the personalities who participated in them.

In the course of our conversation, Professor Greenberg told me he had developed a close relationship with Frank Capra in the 1960s in Palm Desert, California, where Capra had retired. Greenberg and his wife often socialized with Capra and his wife, Lou, and with the Hollywood luminaries with whom Capra was acquainted, like Jimmy Stewart, Frank Sinatra, Billy Wilder, and John Huston.

Capra often screened his films for Greenberg while reflecting on his experiences in Hollywood and the movie business. Capra felt that the Hollywood establishment was often blind in recognizing new talent. He told Greenberg of an unknown actress who had been turned down by other studios and directors. However, when Capra saw her screen test, he detected a spark of real talent. Capra would help develop her into a major star and make five films with her. Her name was Barbara Stanwyck.

According to Professor Greenberg, Capra continued in his retirement to follow the careers of the stars he had worked with over the years. When *Teacher's Pet* was released in 1958, Capra had made a point of seeing this newest film starring his old friend, Clark Gable. Discussing the movie over lunch with Professor Greenberg one day, Capra observed that Gable was still the major force on screen he had always been.

"Then Capra surprised me," Professor Greenberg said, "by saying that the actress who played Gable's girlfriend, Mamie Van Doren, was quite talented and could be used to a greater extent in films."

Capra explained that the most important quality an actor can have is believability. If you don't believe the person on screen is the character they are portraying, you don't have much of a performance. "And Mamie," Capra went on to say, "pulled off the role of the giddy nightclub performer quite well."

Greenberg concluded, "Coming from a director who was rated by film historians as one of the top five of all time, [that] is quite a compliment."

I couldn't agree more.

I took my acting craft very seriously, even when the fates brought me movie scripts that were not exactly works of art and directors who were far from being heirs to Capra's skill and talent. It was up to me, most of the time, to craft a performance that was somehow believable.

I am both blessed and burdened with total recall. It is often painful to remember *everything*. A dog barking, the smell of Pan Stik makeup, the sight of a summer sunset, or an old photograph—it's easy to feel haunted, and you just want to shut it off. But, I am thankful for the long life I've had and for being able to remember the details and set them down for you.

There are funny stories in here. And there are sad ones too. I have tried to tell them honestly, and, where I can, with good humor. Some stories—no, make that *many* stories—involve sex. Imagine that! I make no apologies for my sexual adventures. Jack Kerouac said, "My fault, my failure, is not in the passions I have, but in my lack of control of them." I'll live by that one.

I am happy you've chosen to spend some time with me. As you will see, my life has been messy, exciting, sad, difficult, and utterly amazing. I hope you enjoy reading about it as much as I have enjoyed living it.

Stephen B. Whatley

Stephen B. Whatley on location in London in June 1999, painting Changing The Guard at Buckingham Palace (Oil on canvas, 40 x 40in) commissioned by The Royal Collection of HM The Queen. The Royal Collection © 1999 Her Majesty Queen Elizabeth II.

Stephen B. Whatley is a British expressionist painter whose major commissions include architectural paintings for public institutions including BBC Heritage and The Royal Collection Trust of HM Queen Elizabeth II. He has been presented to HM The Queen and HRH The Duke of Edinburgh in recognition of his work for The Royal Collection and Historic Royal Palaces.

Born in London in 1965, he studied at the Ipswich and Norwich Schools of Art and the University of London. He has exhibited in solo and group exhibitions since 1988. His work is in private and public collections worldwide. Whatley's portrait of Barack Obama was published in *TIME* magazine in 2009, and his many portrait sitters include: actors Dame Judi Dench, Dame Julie Walters, and Sir Ian McKellen and barrister and human rights activist, Michael Mansfield KC.

His thirty paintings commissioned by the Tower of London in 2000 are showcased throughout Tower Hill Underpass at Tower Hill, London—a permanent public art exhibit viewed daily by the public every year.

www.stephenbwhatley.com

Chapter One

From South Dakota to Hollywoodland

"As long as I am the 'platinum blonde,' as long as I appear in décolleté gowns and sexy love scenes, as long as I am Jean Harlow, I am going to be discussed. It is the price that my kind of screen character pays for her fame, her MGM contract. I have always tried to be truthful and frank with the public about Jean Harlow. It is the least I can do."

—JEAN HARLOW

"I want that color hair," said the little girl, pointing to the picture on the front page of the Sioux City Journal, *one of Sioux City, Iowa's two newspapers.*

The paper was spread out on the long table of the rooming house where the little girl lived for three weeks that summer with her parents. The rooming house charged one dollar a day for each person, including a clean, safe place to sleep and three meals a day. (The little girl was delighted because three meals were not something she was accustomed to.) The breakfast dishes were cleared to make room for the newspaper with the front page picture that would change the little girl's life. The headline read: "Jean Harlow Dies."

The little girl was me. I was six. It was a warm summer day, on Tuesday, June 8, 1937. Jean Harlow had died the day before, but the news was just getting to Sioux City. I stared transfixed at the newspaper. The platinum blonde woman was the most beautiful thing I'd ever seen. I felt an eerie connection to that face. I began to cry.

"Why did she die?" I sobbed. "She's so beautiful."

One of the two ladies who owned the boarding house put a hand on my shoulder.

"It's all right, honey. It's says she had been sick."

"Who was she?"

"An actress in Hollywood. She was a big movie star."

I had never seen anything like her. I wanted to wrap myself in the beautiful pictures of Jean Harlow on the big newspaper page and make her a part of me. I poured over her pictures until the paper was taken away. I wandered outside into the yard still full of the aura of the pictures of Jean Harlow.

Sitting under a tree in the front yard of the rooming house, I pretended that I was her, touching my hair that I wished was snowy platinum like hers. I suddenly *felt* Jean Harlow in a visceral way—a curious sensation in my head. It would have frightened my grandmother back on the farm, who harbored the idea I might be a witch. I saw something unfolding.

The MGM wardrobe department smelled of dry-cleaning solvent, mothballs, and old clothes. The high ceilings of the cavernous building were hung with racks of costumes: pirates, soldiers, kings, queens, priests, cowboys, elves, Indians, and southern belles. Huge storage drawers were filled with shirts, blouses, trousers, scarves, ties, belts, suspenders, and wigs.

A blonde woman, whose name is Mamie, opened the wig drawer and rummaged through the contents. At the bottom, among the redheads, dishwater blondes, and brunettes, she found a platinum blonde wig. The hair was soft and fine, a natural towhead. Written inside the headband were the words: "Jean Harlow." She tried on the wig. It was a little small, but she fit it over her head. She looked in a mirror and touched the wig. She smiled, feeling the connection.

I blinked and the vision was gone. I didn't know what or who I had seen, but a part of me recognized it all. What I had seen faded after a few moments, leaving me with a pleasantly empty feeling.

Then, I pretended Jean Harlow was my mother and got lost in the fantasy. My mother was beautiful in her own right but not goddess-beautiful like Harlow, who had an elegance that could hold a six-year-old spellbound.

I wanted to talk to someone who might understand. I thought of my summer playmate, Nancy Clark, who lived a short distance up the street from the rooming house in a lovely large home with a yard and shade trees. I had been secretly envious of Nancy's flaming red hair and green eyes, but now I was yearning for platinum hair like Harlow. Nancy and I loved to roller skate. I had a cheap pair of skates that strapped onto my shoes, and Nancy had a real pair of skates. Together we raced up and down the neighborhood sidewalks, occasionally skating out into the street when there was no traffic. Her parents were always nice to me, seeming to realize that I was a lonely kid whose home life was something less than perfect.

I was roused from my reverie by five women carrying suitcases, chattering as they came down the front steps of the rooming house. They walked past me under my tree and loaded their luggage into an old automobile. I walked over to them and asked the woman getting behind the wheel where they were going.

"To California," she replied. "Hollywood."

"I've heard of Hollywood," I said, recalling what the rooming house owner had told me that morning. "Where's California?"

"A very long way from here. It's on the Pacific Ocean."

"Ocean?" I was trying to process all this new information.

"Yes," the woman said, "and there are palm trees and a desert and it's always warm."

"Warm?" I thought about the God-awful freezing winters I'd endured in my short life on my grandparents' South Dakota farm where I lived because my young and wild parents were too irresponsible to take on raising me—except for three-week vacations like this one in Sioux City.

I dreaded going back to the loneliness of the farm.

I had never seen a palm tree or an ocean, but there was a determination forming in my six-year-old mind to go there and see them.

"What's in Hollywood?"

"They make movies there, honey. Movie stars live there."

"Like Jean Harlow?"

"Yes. What a shame she died. She was so beautiful."

"Very beautiful," I agreed, saddened again.

I heard my mother's voice calling. "Jo! Jo, you'd better come inside now."

"Can I go with you?" I abruptly asked the woman, who was starting her car.

All the women laughed not unkindly. "No, sweetie," the woman said. "You'd better go to your mother."

"I promise I won't be any trouble."

"Bye-bye, baby." She put the car in gear, smiled at me, and drove away.

My mother was waiting in the doorway to the rooming house. I watched the car disappear around a corner and shouldered my disappointment. I kicked at the dirt and walked reluctantly to my mother. The precious three weeks with my parents were almost up. This coming Sunday I would return to my grandparents and their farm in South

Dakota with no running water, no electricity, and a drafty outhouse full of spiders.

"Who was that you were talking to?" she asked.

"Just some women who were going to California."

She shook her head. "They'll be lucky to get there in that jalopy."

"Can we go to California? She said there were palm trees and a desert."

"Your father has a good job here, Jo. He couldn't leave that."

I had heard many times that jobs were hard to come by. I couldn't fully grasp what that meant, but I knew we never had any money. Only what my dad earned as a truck mechanic. If we splurged on ice cream on a Friday night at a nickel apiece, it seemed to me like something sent from heaven.

"Maybe someday we could go?" I asked hopefully.

"I don't see how, Jo. Unless something really bad happens. You'd better come in and take a bath. It'll be dinnertime soon."

At the mention of a bath, I brightened. "Okay!"

I loved the rooming house's big bathtub. I skipped through the doorway and up the stairs to the bathroom. Baths were a weekly thing on the farm. Because the water had to be hauled from the cistern and heated on the black iron stove, the smallest and youngest—me—bathed in everyone else's tepid water. I felt dirty the whole time I was on the farm. When I got to the rooming house, I soaked in the tub for as long as I could. The dirt I scrubbed off my skin floated to the surface of the bathwater like an oil slick.

It rained that Friday night, but it didn't stop my parents from indulging in their usual weekend bender. The two women who owned the rooming house kindly looked after me while Mom and Dad went to a nearby tavern called The Tap and drank themselves into a stupor. Often, they'd fight when they came home drunk. I stayed far away from them.

I was asleep when they came in that night, but I was awakened in the wee hours by a dog barking and crying. Dogs were strictly forbidden in the boarding house, so I went looking for the source of the sound. I followed it downstairs and outside the front door. There, in the steady rain, I saw a small dog tied to the tree I had sat under. I dashed through the downpour and untied him. He was a Boston Bull puppy with a little stub of a tail wagging so hard his whole rear end danced. I picked him up and carried him inside the rooming house.

I stood at the bottom of the stairs dripping wet, wondering what to do. The rooming house rules were "No Dogs Allowed," but my heart told me to ignore the rules this once. I could feel the dog's heart racing. I held him close to shush his whimpering, terrified that someone would hear him. I raced up the stairs with the dog in my arms and ducked into my room. I dried the two of us, and we dove shivering under the covers.

The next morning my mother angrily woke me. "What on Earth are you doing? You know no dogs are allowed here."

"He was tied to a tree outside, and it was pouring rain. The poor thing was crying for help. I don't know how he got there."

"He got there," my mother snapped, "because we put him there. We bought him from some guy at The Tap last night for five dollars."

I clapped my hands and scooped him up in my arms. "Then he's ours? He's so cute!"

"Well, he's going back outside. They don't allow dogs."

"It's still raining! He can't stay out in the rain!"

"Well, he can't stay in here or we'll all be out in the rain."

"No." I set my jaw. "If he goes out, I go with him."

My father walked in at that moment. "Jo, don't sass your mother back. That dog can't be in this boarding house. It's against the rules."

"I'm not sassing, Daddy. It's a fact. If the rules say he can't stay, then I won't stay either."

My father turned to my mother. "Lucille, get me a couple aspirins, will you? I've got a pounding headache." He turned back to me. "We'll do this, Jo: We'll hide him until the rain stops, then he's got to go outside."

"Daddy, why did you get him if you knew that dogs weren't allowed?"

He turned away and followed my mother back to their room to get his aspirin. The answer to my question was, of course, he was too drunk the night before to know what he was doing.

"Does he have a name?" I shouted after them.

My mother rushed back to my doorway. "Shush! Not so loud. His name is Bobo."

When the rain stopped that afternoon, my father came to enforce Bobo's exile to the front yard.

Bobo looked at me with big, inquisitive eyes. I held him tightly in my arms.

"I'm going with him," I said stubbornly.

"You can stay outside with him until dinnertime," he said. "But don't get too attached to him. We'll have to find him a good home."

I carried Bobo outside. Out of earshot of my father, I said, "We've already found him a good home. And he's going to stay."

I took the rope they'd used to tie Bobo to the tree and fashioned a loosely knotted leash. Together, we set off to walk around the neighborhood. When we were out of sight of the rooming house, I sat on the curb with Bobo in my lap. He licked my face with his little pink tongue. I kissed him on the nose and held him close.

"No one's going to take you away from me, I promise. I love you, Bobo." He licked my face again in agreement. "And you love me too, right?" Another lick. "Then it's settled. I'm going back to the farm in a couple of days, and you're going with me."

I stood up from the curb. "C'mon, Bobo, let's go meet my friend Nancy."

Bobo walked beside me as we made our way in the opposite direction of the rooming house.

Nancy's mother answered the door when I knocked. She smiled down at Bobo and me.

"Hi, Joanie, who's your friend?"

"His name's Bobo, Mrs. Clark. Is Nancy here?"

"Yes, come on in. Where'd you get Bobo?"

"My dad bought him off someone at The Tap. We're hiding because they don't allow dogs at the rooming house."

Mrs. Clark nodded. "I see. I'll go get Nancy. You and Bobo make yourselves at home."

The house had a large living room with a comfortable sofa and chairs. I sat on the sofa, and Bobo jumped deftly onto my lap.

"You stay in my lap, Bobo. I'm sure they don't want you on their furniture."

Nancy bounced into the room a moment later.

"Hey, I hear you've got a dog! What's his name?"

"Bobo. Isn't he cute?"

She picked up Bobo and hugged him. "I'll say."

Bobo gave her a grateful lick and started to squirm.

"He wants to go to you," Nancy said, handing him back. "I'll be right back, Joanie." She disappeared into the hallway and came back a moment later holding a pretty red dog collar and leash. "My dog died three months ago. Take these for Bobo."

"I'm sorry, Nancy. Thank you, but what if you get another dog?"

"I'll get another leash and collar. Bobo needs that one now instead of that ugly rope."

I put the collar on him. It was a little large for his puppy neck, but I tightened it enough to be secure. He'd certainly grow into it.

"It's beautiful on him," said Nancy.

"Listen, Nancy, I've got a problem."

I explained my predicament—how I got Bobo out of the rainstorm after my parents had left him outside, and that he wasn't allowed to stay in the rooming house, and that they wanted to turn him outside again and find another home for him.

"It's not fair," Nancy said, frowning.

"I don't know what to do, but I'm not leaving Bobo outside. They're sending me back to the farm on Sunday and he's going with me whether they like it or not. But in the meantime, what do I do?"

"Do your parents know you're here?"

"No, but it's getting close to dinnertime," I said, glancing out a window. "They'll start to wonder where I am."

"Come on up to my room," she said, guiding me toward the stairs. "Quietly. You need a hideout."

We tiptoed into Nancy's room and closed the door. Her room was not large but tidy and pleasant, girlish without being fussy. I could see the sun setting and the twilight growing through the window drapes.

"You can't hide me here for long, Nancy. You'll get in trouble."

She tossed her red hair to one side. "We'll see about that. They're going to be looking for you soon."

"Yes, but they'll come here. They know we're friends. They'll come here and ask your mother if she's seen me."

"You and Bobo can hide in the closet. I'll tell my mom that you left."

"Nancy, I can't ask you to lie for me."

"You don't have to. I'm doing it on my own. What're friends for?"

Tears welled up in my eyes. "I can't thank you enough, Nancy."

Nancy grinned. "You and Bobo better get in the closet. I heard the doorbell ring."

Bobo and I got in among the shoes and dresses. Nancy closed the door. I heard her mother call up the stairs, "Nancy, come down here for a minute."

She left the room and went downstairs. I couldn't hear what was happening. I was frightened. I hugged Bobo tightly. After a couple more minutes, I heard the door to Nancy's room open. She opened the closet door and smiled.

"It was one of the women who owns the rooming house. Everyone's searching the neighborhood for you. I told them you left here with your dog just before dark."

"Thank you, Nancy. I'd better go back and let them find me."

Bobo and I got out of the closet. "Thank you again for the collar and leash. It looks so good on him." I stopped at the door. "Nancy, if they make me give up Bobo, will you take him? This would be the best home he could have."

"I'll keep him until you come back."

We hugged. "Thank you."

I turned toward the door, just as Nancy's mother walked into the room.

"You two scamps. I thought Nancy's little performance downstairs was a little too convincing. What's going on?"

I stammered out an explanation of how I got Bobo, and my parents' threat that he'd have to stay outside, and that I might not be able to keep him. Mrs. Clark nodded and sat on Nancy's bed. She looked at us sternly.

"You girls have put me in an awkward position. I lied to that woman because I didn't know you were here, Joanie. And, Nancy, you told an absolutely bald-faced lie that Joanie had left here before dark. If they find out you were hiding here, I'll look like a perfect fool, and the two of you will look like a couple of cheap phonies."

"I'm sorry, Mrs. Clark," I said contritely.

"I'm sorry too, Mom," said Nancy.

I went on, "I'll leave if you want me to. It's just that Bobo's so little and helpless. He's just a puppy. If you'd seen him out there tied to a tree and crying in the rain, you'd have—"

Mrs. Clark held up her hand. "Stop! You're right, I would have." She smiled. "Well, since you've included me in your little plot, let's make sure you get back to the rooming house without anyone seeing you leave here."

I ran to her and threw my arms around her neck. "Thank you, Mrs. Clark."

She patted my shoulder. "I'm glad I can help, Joanie. C'mon, let's go downstairs. Nancy, go outside and find out where the searchers are. When they've moved on to other areas, Joanie and Bobo can make a dash for the rooming house. Once you're out there, you're on your own, Joanie."

"I understand, Mrs. Clark. We'll be fine."

Nancy went outside briefly and returned. "They've moved on up the hill. The coast looks clear."

"Then I'm off. There's no way I can make this up to you both—"

Nancy embraced me and kissed my cheek. Her mother did the same. "Go."

I half walked and half ran back toward the rooming house. I could hear people shouting, "Joanie! Joanie!" in the distance. Bobo was having a hard time keeping up on his little stubby legs, so I carried him the rest of the way.

I reached the rooming house in time to run into my mother coming out the front door.

"Good God, Jo, where have you been? We've been worried sick. The whole rooming house has been searching for you. We thought you'd been kidnapped."

It had been only four years since the sensational kidnapping of the twenty-month-old son of the world-famous aviator, Charles Lindbergh. The tragedy of the Lindbergh baby became an enduring part of American history. A missing child evoked fear of a similar tragedy.

"I'm fine, Mother. Bobo and I went for a long walk."

"We looked all over for you. Where were you?"

I shrugged. "We found a good place to hide."

"You should get a licking for putting us through this," my mother said angrily.

I squared my shoulders defiantly. "I told you that if Bobo had to go outside, I was going with him. I meant it."

My mother gave me an exasperated look. "Well, I've got good news for you, Jo. The ladies who own the rooming house said that you can keep Bobo inside until you leave on Sunday."

I hugged Bobo, then I hugged my mother. "Oh, thank you so much! And he's going back to the farm with me."

Mother hesitated a moment. "Yes. Your grandmother will have a fit, but, yes, he can go back with you."

I kissed Bobo on the nose. "Hear that, Bobo? You're going to be a farm dog. But first you'll have to meet Jack."

On Sunday, Bobo's little nose was working overtime as we followed the long dirt driveway up to the farmhouse. The smells of the farm were familiar to my nose: freshly plowed ground, horse manure, hay, the pigs over by the barn, bread baking in the kitchen, and the outhouse on a small rise behind the farmhouse.

Jack, my grandfather's big black German Shepherd, ran toward us barking. Jack was the farm's chief security guard. If strangers approached, Jack would sound the alarm, then confront the stranger with hackles raised and teeth bared. Jack ruled the roost on the farm. He lived outdoors for all but the snowiest months, when he took refuge in the barn with the horses and the milk cows.

Because Jack was so tough and independent, I was concerned whether he and Bobo would get along. When Jack recognized us, he stopped barking and started wagging his tail. I got out of the car holding Bobo, and Jack immediately came over to investigate.

"Good boy, Jack," I said, scratching his ears. "Be nice to Bobo."

Jack looked agreeable, so I put Bobo on the ground. Bobo made a little puppy "woof," jumped up, and licked Jack on the mouth. Jack made a friendly "harumpf!" and dropped to his tummy. Bobo politely turned his rear end to be sniffed. In a matter of moments, the two became friends and wandered off together as if they'd known each other all their lives. Chickens in the yard regarded Bobo curiously. Bobo had never seen a chicken before and was very suspicious.

"Looks like those two are going to be pals," my grandfather said.

I said goodbye to my parents. They dutifully kissed me, handed over my battered little cardboard suitcase, and reminded me to behave myself.

"Mind your grandma, Jo," my mother said.

I nodded, tears welling. "I will, Mother. I'll miss you and Daddy."

"We'll miss you too," she said.

But I knew they would not. The moment they drove away from the farmhouse, they would scarcely think of me at all. As they disappeared down the road back to Sioux City, I felt the familiar ache of being unwanted.

My grandfather walked toward me and smiled.

"What's your dog's name?"

"Bobo, Pa. He's just a puppy. Really sweet."

"Make sure he doesn't mess in the house," my grandmother warned.

"Oh, I will, Dah, I promise. Bobo," I called, "c'mon."

Bobo scampered over, followed by his new comrade, Jack.

My grandfather hugged me. "Welcome back, Joanie."

"You'd better get washed up," my grandmother said. "It'll be dinnertime soon. And keep that dog off the bed. He can't sleep with you."

"Yes, Dah."

As I walked toward the farmhouse, I passed my grandparents' ancient car and my mother's older brother popped out of the back seat.

"Hello, stranger. Glad to see you back, Joanie." He took a step toward me and held out his arms. I sidestepped the embrace and went inside the house.

My mother's younger sisters, Myrna and Norma, were inside packing suitcases. They looked up for a moment and greeted me distractedly.

"What are you doing?" I asked.

"We're packing, can't you see?" Norma said. "We're going to the Black Hills to see the faces."

"What faces?"

"Mount Rushmore, where the four president's faces are carved into the side of the mountain."

"Really?" I was suddenly thrilled at the prospect. "That sounds like fun."

The two of them exchanged glances.

"Oh, yes," said Myrna.

"I need to get ready," I chirped happily.

Bobo and I dashed up the stairs to the bedroom I shared with my grandmother. My grandmother was a stern authoritarian. She slept in a large bed on one side of the room. My grandfather and Cliff slept in the same bed in the other upstairs bedroom, with a window that looked over the front of the house. I slept on a cot near the window in my grandmother's room. It was cold sleeping there in the wintertime. On the coldest nights, my grandmother would heat flat irons on the big wood-burning kitchen stove, wrap them in towels, and tuck them in my bed to keep me warm.

That night there was excited talk at the dinner table about the trip to the Black Hills. How long would it take to get there? How long would they stay? What would they eat at roadside picnics along the way? Everyone was happy.

Bobo sat next to my chair wagging his little stump of a tail and waiting for handouts.

"Don't feed that dog from the table, Joanie."

"Okay, Dah, but he's hungry."

Just then Pa asked her to pass the bread. When she looked away, I slipped Bobo some of my dinner. Pa winked at me and added, "And the butter too, please."

She handed the butter down the table, and I slipped Bobo another morsel.

That night I went to sleep early in anticipation of setting off for the Black Hills. The next morning, everyone was up at daybreak bustling about, loading the car and packing three days' worth of picnic lunches. I had my little cardboard suitcase packed, and I carried it down to the kitchen.

Everyone was outside packing the car. I went out into the yard with Bobo at my heels. He bounded across the yard and jumped into the car.

"Where can I put my suitcase, Dah?"

"Get that dog out of the car," Dah snapped. "He's not going and neither are you."

I stopped in my tracks. "What?"

"You're not going with us. There's no room."

Myrna chimed in from the other end side of the car. "You're too little. And you're too much trouble."

"I won't be any trouble. Bobo and I won't take up much room. And we won't eat much either. We can take care of ourselves."

"No. You have to stay here with your grandpa."

I dropped my suitcase and began to cry.

"I don't understand, Dah. Why would you do this to me? What have I done?"

My grandmother stood implacable, arms folded. "This trip is for grownups. You're too young to appreciate it."

"I am not." I clenched my fists. "This is a terrible thing you're doing to me. It's not fair and it's mean." My temper was about to get out of control. "All of you are just plain mean."

Pa looked away. Myrna and Norma avoided my gaze. Cliff shrugged and kept packing the car.

"Watch your mouth, Joanie." Dah warned. "You're asking for a licking."

"I don't care. It wouldn't be the first time you've given me a licking for nothing. Bobo, come on, let's go inside and leave these bad people." At the front steps, I turned around. "If Bobo couldn't go, I wouldn't go anyway. I hope it rains every day and you have a miserable time!"

My tears broke through my anger, and I ran sobbing into the house, Bobo scurried after me. I ran upstairs and threw myself on my grandmother's bed. I buried my head in her pillow. Bobo stood by the bed wailing with me. I picked him up and cuddled him next to me. We wept together.

I half expected Dah to relent and send someone to get me. Or come herself to give me the whipping she promised. But the car doors slammed, the motor started, and they drove away. It was silent except for my sniffling and the barnyard sounds of chickens clucking, a horse whinnying, and the metallic creak of the windmill.

Pa came into the bedroom carrying my suitcase. He put it on the floor and sat beside me on the bed.

"Well, it's just you and me for a couple of days, Joanie." He tried to sound cheerful. "And Bobo and Jack, of course." He put an arm around me.

"Oh, Pa, why did they do this to me? I just got home. I've been good. Dah always acts like I'm some kind of pest."

He patted my arm. "I know, Joanie. You know how your grandma is."

***

I knew. But at that early age, I had not yet solved the puzzle that was my grandmother. I did not understand the day she sent me to school with a temperature of 102 over my protests that I felt too sick. I was five years old, and it was a two-mile walk through deep snow and a snowstorm. When I reached the little country school, I was shivering uncontrollably and collapsed in the doorway. The teacher was my great aunt Hazel from my father's side of the family. She immediately recognized that I was in distress. She left the rest of her students, loaded me into her car, and drove me home. When we got to the farmhouse, she woke my grandmother, who had gone back to bed. Aunt Hazel insisted that my grandmother put me to bed and keep me warm.

"No more school until she feels well," she chided Dah. "And give her more food. She's too skinny."

***

Pa and I must have played dozens of games of Chinese checkers that weekend. I won every one. To this day, I don't know if I was that good at Chinese checkers or if Pa let a sad and lonely little girl win to make her happy.

Every day, I kept watch on the road leading to the farm. By some fluke, they might decide to come home early, and I wanted to be the first to see them.

As revenge against Dah, Bobo and I slept in her bed. It was cozy and warm. But no matter how cold the night or how terrible my nightmare, she had never tucked me in with her.

Late one night, I was awakened by Jack's loud barking. Bobo yipped at the sound of his friend outside. I was frightened and ran to my grandfather's bedroom. We went to the window and looked out into the yard. Pa picked up the shotgun that always leaned next to the window, opened the breech to make sure it was loaded, and snapped it closed with a loud click. We could make out Jack in the faint moonlight barking in the direction of the barn. Suddenly, a small animal darted past, and he took off after it.

"A skunk," Pa said. We both chuckled in relief. "Old Jack loves those skunks."

"He's going to smell bad in the morning," I added.

"That's for sure," he said, returning the shotgun to its place by the window. "Good thing your grandma ain't here."

"Sorry I woke you, Pa. I got scared when I heard Jack barking. I was afraid it was like that time those men drove up in front, and you and Jack scared them away."

"You remember that, Joanie? You couldn't have been more than three."

"It was right after my third birthday, Pa. I remember it real good."

***

The hand-cranked phone on the wall had rung two short rings and two long rings—the danger signal from one farm to the next along the party line.

Pa and Cliff hurried to the upstairs window where the shotgun and rifle were kept ready in case of trouble, like gangsters on the lam from the big cities coming to steal money and chickens. Small farms scattered across the prairies of South Dakota and Iowa were easy pickings for provisions and provided ideal hiding places for outlaws.

Before long, a car turned off the main road and drove slowly up the dirt track toward the farmhouse. Jack started barking like crazy, his hackles standing high and his teeth bared. He meant business.

The car stopped in front of the farmhouse, the engine running. The windows rolled down. From my hiding place next to the bedroom window, I could see that there were six men inside.

Pa whispered, "Jesus, Cliff, I think that's John Dillinger and his gang."

"Looks like 'em," Cliff said. "I seen their pictures in the *Argus Leader*. They've been robbing banks all over."

Pa and Cliff stuck their guns out the bedroom window. Pa yelled down, "Whatever you're after, you ain't going to find it here. And you'd better not get out of that car. My dog will get ya."

One of the men in the car aimed his gun at Jack.

"And if you shoot my dog, you'll be dead meat. My son here's a crack shot."

The man on the driver's side held a submachine gun out of the car. "You think you can outshoot one of these, old man?"

"Guess we'll just have to find out," Cliff shouted down.

The men in the car laughed, but the gun disappeared inside. They rolled up the windows and put the car in gear. They turned around and drove slowly back to the main road, followed by Jack, still barking. The car disappeared in the direction of Sioux Falls, and Jack came loping back to the farmhouse, wagging his tail and looking very pleased with himself.

The following week, on March 6, 1934, exactly one month after my third birthday, the Security National Bank in Sioux Falls was held up in broad daylight by the Dillinger gang. Far from being the easy mark Dillinger imagined the small-town bank would be, the robbery was a disaster. The gang members got trigger-happy. Baby Face Nelson fired his submachine gun through the bank's plate glass window and wounded a policeman. The Sioux Falls police got involved and more shots were fired. Hostages were taken so the bank robbers could escape; Dillinger and one of his gang members, John Hamilton, were wounded. They managed to escape with $50,000.

***

"You really told them off that night, Pa," I said.

"Don't know where I found the courage. We were lucky they didn't shoot all of us," he said. "But they made me mad when they threatened Jack. Thank goodness there was nothing like that tonight."

We both sniffed the air and laughed. I wrinkled my nose. "Just a scared skunk."

Sunday afternoon the family returned from the Black Hills. I caught sight of the car from the upstairs window just as it turned onto the dirt driveway.

"They're home, Pa!" I shouted, running down the stairs. Bobo kept up with me as we both dashed into the yard to greet them.

My aunts Myrna and Norma got out first. Bobo immediately jumped into the back seat. I was astonished that such a little dog could jump so high. I hugged Myrna and Norma, who were both chattering about the sights they had seen.

"The faces were so huge," Norma gushed. "And they look absolutely like the presidents. You wouldn't have believed your eyes."

I wanted to say, "The two of you made sure I didn't have the chance to not believe my eyes."

But I kept my mouth shut.

My grandmother got out of the car and strode toward the house. "Joanie, get that dog out of the car. He's on the back seat where I like to sit. I hope you and your grandfather kept the fire burning in the kitchen stove."

"We did," Pa said from the front porch. He gave Dah a peck on the cheek as she went into the house. She ignored it and kept walking.

Cliff finished unpacking the car and went to the barn to milk the cow. The usual routine settled over the farm: Dah in the kitchen, Pa and Cliff in the barn, Myrna and Norma bantering back and forth, and me, clutching to a little girl's seemingly hopeless fantasies of being a movie star.

***

The giant austere building on the outskirts of Sioux Falls was an orphanage. When we drove into town a couple of times a month, my grandmother always pointed it out as we went past. "See the orphanage? That's where you'll end up if you're not good."

The sight of the gray stone building sent shivers through my body. The prospect of being imprisoned with the forlorn children we saw playing in the dirt in the front yard gave me nightmares.

As I grew older and more adventurous, my grandmother and I often clashed. My grandmother issued orders like a drill sergeant, and I was not a child who enjoyed being told what to do.

It was a great joy for me when Colleen, my first cousin on my father's side of the family, came to visit on weekends. She was a pretty girl a year younger than me, and we became fast friends and partners in little escapades. On one of Colleen's Sunday visits, I decided it would be a good idea for us to go for a ride on my grandfather's plow horse, Molly. None of the adults were paying attention to us, so Colleen and I snuck off to the barn, armed with a few carrots to bribe Molly.

Colleen looked at Molly and said, "She's so tall. How are we going to get on her back?"

Molly must have been seventeen hands tall and looked like a huge gray mountain. She gratefully ate a carrot and eyed Colleen and me, as if to say, "How are you two going to do this?"

"Watch," I said.

I maneuvered Molly to the side of her stall, climbed the wooden slats, and jumped onto her back.

"See? It's easy. C'mon, Colleen."

She climbed the side of the stall the way I did. I extended a hand and pulled her onto Molly's back.

"Hold on around my waist, Colleen," I said, grabbing a double handful of Molly's mane. I gave the big horse some encouragement with my heels. "C'mon old girl, let's go."

Molly walked slowly out of her stall and through the barn door. I steered her up the driveway, and we turned onto the main road. I leaned over her neck and handed her another carrot. Colleen and I were chattering, not caring where we were going, just enjoying the ride, while Molly stepped softly and surely to make sure we were safe.

Just then, my grandfather and Cliff came rattling up the road in the old Chevy. Pa slammed on the brakes.

"What in the Sam Hill are you two doing with that horse?"

"Hi, Pa. We're going for a ride."

He jumped out of the car. "Jesus, Mary, and Joseph, get down off there before you break your necks, or worse."

"It's okay, Pa. Molly's been very nice about the whole thing."

Pa pulled us down off Molly's back.

"Cliff, you take the horse back to the barn. The two of you get in the car. You're in trouble!"

And I was. Colleen was merely an accessory to the crime and got off with a scolding; I received a hard switching for the horseback adventure. My grandfather administered the punishment, but my grandmother ordered it. Pa was inclined to be easy going on a punishment, but she was a stern disciplinarian with a cruel streak of which I was often the recipient. Perhaps she resented being burdened with a small child after having raised four children of her own. But even as I nursed the burning marks on my bottom, I was becoming more defiant and in conflict with my grandmother.

***

Before Bobo came along, my best friends on the farm were the chickens and the cats. I was friends with Jack the German Shepherd, but he saw his mission as the grand protector of the farm, instead of a cuddly pal for a lonesome six-year-old girl.

I delighted in raising the baby chicks Pa brought home from the feed store in Sioux Falls. I fed them and herded them around the yard, protecting them from hostile roosters and the ever-present hawks. I named each one and got to know them as they grew.

For as long as I can remember, I have had a sense of nonverbal communication with animals. In my childhood days, I took for granted that I could understand what nonhumans were thinking and feeling. It was one of the things that led to conflicts with my grandmother—and to her feeling that I was a witch. There were times when I blurted out something that I could not have possibly known, which later turned out to be true.

"Dah," I said on one occasion, standing at the front door, "there's a big storm coming."

She came to the door and looked outside. "There's not a cloud in the sky. That's silly."

"Well, anyway, Pa'd better put the animals in the barn."

Dah shook her head and went back to kneading bread dough. But an hour later, a terrible thunderstorm blew up with rain, strong winds, and orange-sized hail stones. The window in Pa and Cliff's bedroom blew out and rain poured through it. Pa and Cliff nailed rugs over the opening to keep out the worst of the wind and rain.

When the storm was over, I overheard Dah telling Myrna and Norma about it.

"How on Earth could she have known that?" Myrna asked.

Dah shook her head. "She just *knows* things."

Then two events happened that sent me into a tailspin. One Sunday morning, I checked on my chickens, and one of my favorite hens was missing. Her name was Betty. I went to Pa and asked if he had seen Betty. He shook his head. I went inside to ask Dah, but before I could speak, she said, "Wash up, Joanie. It's time for Sunday dinner."

I washed my hands and went to the table. Pa said grace, and everyone began passing the food around. When the main dish came to me, I froze.

It was chicken. I looked around the table, and everyone stared at their plates. I looked at my grandmother.

"We had to take one of your chickens, Joanie," she said mildly.

I slammed the serving plate on the table. "Betty! You killed Betty!"

"Serve your plate, Joanie," Dah ordered.

"No!" I bolted from the table and ran upstairs, Bobo following. I cried into my pillow, clutching the dog to me.

And there was the fox I discovered in the garage. Cliff had caught him raiding the hen house and locked him up awaiting execution. I had been told to stay away, that he was vicious and might bite me. But when I opened the door, all I saw was two frightened little eyes staring out from a furry red body. I felt something from the eyes. A message of fear and a wish to live.

"Hi, fox," I said softly. "Don't be afraid of me."

I looked around. No one was in sight. "Get out while you can," I whispered. "I'll leave the door open."

I left the door ajar and walked away. Later, Cliff came into the kitchen and leaned his rifle next to the kitchen door.

"I went out to kill the fox," he said in astonishment, "but he was gone."

Dah eyed me suspiciously. I turned away and smiled to myself.

***

The Bennett farm had been homesteaded in the 1800s by Pa Bennett's parents, my mother's grandparents. It had a small farmhouse with no electricity or running water, a few cows, a horse or two, and acres of tillable land. The Olander farm a few miles away was homesteaded by my father's grandparents, who had also come to America from Sweden in the 1800s, lured by the prospect of farmland that could be had for free if you built a house and planted crops on it.

Despite the similarities in their origins, the two families could not have been more different. The Olanders were aristocratic and well-to-do. They had been successful farmers and businesspeople in Sweden and brought their money and business acumen with them. The Olanders built the Beaver Valley Lutheran Church, the first church in Brandon. They were regarded as the pillars of Minnehaha County. They stood at the church house door with the minister after Sunday services, greeting the parishioners as they left the service with a sort of noblesse oblige attitude.

On my mother's side were the Bennetts and the Carlsons. They were a hard scrabble bunch who still managed to found Rowena, lay out the blueprint for the town, and establish the post office, the general store, a one-room school, and a volunteer fire department. My great uncle owned the general store. When I went in to buy a penny candy, he accepted my penny without looking at me, handed over my candy, and pretended I didn't exist.

I was considered a bastard. Well, maybe not quite. Perhaps just the issue of a shotgun wedding. But the Olanders did not approve of my father's choice of a wife, and they most certainly didn't approve of my mother's pregnancy with me.

When Warner Olander met Lucille Bennett on the steps of the Beaver Valley Lutheran Church, he was the most eligible bachelor in town, a twenty-year-old, tall, dark-haired Swede who fancied Indian motorcycles. My mother was drop-dead gorgeous, a hazel-eyed wild child of sixteen, who knew a good catch when she saw one. They chatted each other up on the church steps for a while. And when no one was looking, they climbed onto the Indian and drove off.

The story, as my father later told it, was that they went to his house, an elegant, white clapboard farmhouse on their sprawling farm, where they immediately consummated their relationship in his parent's bed. According to family mythology, that is where I was conceived.

Lucky Ole hit the bullseye with the first shot.

***

It was a cold spring morning in the year I turned eight when I was riding into town with my Aunt Myrna and Uncle Cliff. We were going to see a movie, I was told, and have a chocolate malt afterward. We neared the outskirts of Rowena, and the ugly hulk of the orphanage loomed ahead. I was always afraid whenever we passed the terrible place. To my horror, Cliff slowed and turned in the driveway.

"What's going on?" I demanded of Cliff.

Myrna spoke up. "This is where you're going to be staying, Joanie."

"No! No, I am not!" I looked frantically from one to the other. "Why are you doing this? Is this Dah's doing?"

"It'll be for the best, Joanie, really. Mom's not able to take care of you anymore. Someone your age is just too much for her. You'll be happier here."

She reached out to take my arm, and I slapped her hand away. "No! I won't stay here. I want my dog, and I want to go back to the farm."

"Joanie, listen, we—"

I jerked open the door and jumped out of the still moving car. I stumbled and fell into the dirt. There was a roaring in my ears, and I was sweating and shaking in terror. I bolted up the driveway toward the road. I stumbled and fell again, screaming and crying. When I tried to get to my feet, I felt rough hands grabbing hold of me. I blacked out.

I woke in a large room filled with children sleeping in small beds. Late afternoon sun was slanting through the high windows. I was away from the rest, standing in a large crib with tall sides, holding the bars like a prisoner, sobbing uncontrollably. I started screaming, "Myrna! Dah! Please take me home! Help! Mother! Daddy! I want Bobo! Please help!"

A nurse came in and scolded me. "You must be quiet. The other children can't sleep."

"I want to go home!" I cried.

She turned away and left.

I was shivering with cold and fear. My throat was raw from crying and screaming. There was a desolate, empty ache in my heart. I pulled myself up the side of the crib, got a leg over the top, and swung myself over. I lost my handhold and fell to the floor on the other side with a loud thump. I ran to the door and opened it. The nurse confronted me.

"Where do you think you're going, young lady?"

"Home," I said.

"No, you're not. Get back where you belong and go to sleep like the rest of the children." She lifted me back into the crib and shook her finger at me.

I stood holding the bars of the crib all night, staring at the door, praying for someone to rescue me. When the nurses brought me food, I refused to eat it. I do not remember much else, only the gnawing agony of abandonment.

In late morning the next day, the door opened and Myrna walked in.

"Oh, Myrna," I cried, bursting into tears. "Please take me home."

"Okay, Joanie." She lifted me out of the crib and carried me out of the room.

The nurse said, "She never slept or ate. She just stood there staring at the door."

Cliff was waiting with the car. Myrna put me on the ground, but I was too exhausted to walk. She loaded me into the back seat and they drove me back to the farm. Bobo was waiting in front of the farmhouse. He jumped into the back seat as soon as the door was opened and covered my face with kisses. It was the best welcome I could hope for. Despite what I had been through, everything seemed strangely normal.

Dah looked up from kneading bread and said, "Hi, Joanie."

"Hi, Dah," I answered.

"They said she never slept or ate the whole time, only stared at the door." Myrna reported. "She climbed out of her bed and tried to escape once."

Dah nodded. "Better get into bed and get some rest, Joanie."

I trudged up the stairs to our bedroom and crawled into my bed. It felt heavenly compared to where I had been. Bobo jumped onto my bed. Ignoring Dah's rules, I tucked him under the covers next to me and fell asleep.

Over the next few days, I tried to understand why I was sent to the orphanage. I knew my grandmother was *why*, but I couldn't untangle the reason that I was such a burden to her. I didn't realize at that early age that she had raised five children to adulthood on a primitive farm on the harsh South Dakota prairie. My mother had stupidly gotten pregnant and then dumped me in my grandmother's lap. Dah was angry and couldn't find it in her heart to give love to a little girl who had no say in the matter.

***

After the orphanage, my relationship with my grandmother was never the same. Both of my aunts, Myrna and Norma, and my Uncle Cliff were complicit in my mind in sending me to the orphanage. I stopped speaking to all of them. Pa was the only one I would talk to. It was lonely in an already lonely time for me.

Bobo had the run of the farm during the day. Around dinnertime every day, he would show up at the kitchen door. When he didn't show up one night, I became anxious. I couldn't eat dinner but wandered outside calling his name.

Dah called through the door, "Joanie get back to the table and eat your dinner."

I ignored her and kept searching for Bobo. He did not come home that night, nor the next. I was so distraught that Pa and Cliff went searching for him. They came back empty-handed; the only good news was that they did not find his dead body.

The ache and the emptiness became nearly unbearable. The calamities of being banished to the orphanage coupled with the loss of my only friend, Bobo, were tearing me apart. There was no comfort in sight. Pa tried his best to console me, but I was consumed by grief. It felt like the end of my young life, and because of my anguish, I could not see past the source of my pain.

Pa took me aside and said, "Joanie, I don't think Bobo's coming back."

I nodded tearfully. "Yes, Pa."

"He might have been taken by a coyote. We've got a few of them around here. Or he might have jumped in a car with someone. If he was out by the road and someone stopped and opened the car door, he would've jumped in. You know how he loved to ride in cars."

I smiled wistfully. "I know. I hope that's what happened. And I pray he was picked up by someone who'll love him like I did."

I dissolved into tears again.

Over the next few days, I noticed my grandparents whispering with my aunts. I couldn't hear what they said, but I knew instinctively the subject was me. As I climbed the stairs to my bed, I was haunted by the phantom of Bobo bounding up the steps beside me. I dragged my old cardboard suitcase from under my bed. I looked at the spot on the bed where Bobo used to lie beside me.

"I guess it'll be the orphanage for me again, Bobo," I said with resignation. "I don't care anymore. Nothing could be worse than living here."

I packed the few clothes I had and shoved the suitcase back under the bed. When they came for me, I would be ready.

The next morning, I heard my parents' voices downstairs. It wasn't the weekend, so something must be up for them to be here. I tiptoed downstairs and heard them talking with Dah and Pa in the kitchen.

"I can't take care of her anymore," Dah was saying.

"Losing her dog has just about done her in," Pa added sympathetically.

Dah went on, "I spoke to the orphanage, and they don't really want her because she's too old. People want to adopt infants or toddlers. But they'll take her if you don't. I really have no other choice."

I held my breath, my eyes filling with tears.

My father spoke up. "We'll take her. No orphanage. We're not in that rooming house in Sioux City anymore. We've rented a nicer place. She'll have her own room."

I sobbed loudly, and everyone turned to see me standing in the door. I jumped into my father's arms.

"Pack your things, Jo. You're going to Sioux City—permanently."

I dashed up the stairs two at a time. "I'll be back in a minute, Daddy. I'm already packed."

I only said goodbye to Pa and Jack the German Shepherd. Dah, Myrna, Norma, and Cliff stood silently watching us go. I clutched Bobo's red leash and collar to my chest as we drove away. I didn't look back.

My parents were silent as we drove the ninety-or-so miles to Sioux City. I knew they didn't want to take me, but apparently some small grain of parental instinct had awakened in them. Rather than see me cast adrift in an orphanage, they brought me home with them. I knew how undependable and occasionally volatile they could be, but anything was better than where I was.

The little walk-up in Sioux City was cramped for the three of us, but I had my own tiny room, indoor plumbing—no spider-infested privy, a bathtub I could bathe in every night, and electricity. Compared to the Bennett farm, it was paradise. And for better or worse, I was living with the two people in the world I loved the most.

Best of all, the school I would be attending—Smith School—was across the street. Smith School had been built in 1872 as a private residence. In 1899, the Sioux City School Board purchased it and turned it into an elementary school. When I attended there in 1939, it had been recently remodeled and looked brand new. After the one-room country school I had attended in Rowena, the pink quartzite Smith School building, styled like a medieval castle with turrets and parapets, looked like something out of a movie. It housed grades one through six, and I couldn't wait to get started.

As a seven-year-old, I would have normally been in the third grade, but because my grandmother wanted me out of the house, I had started first grade early, when I was barely four. Rather than repeat the third grade, I was enrolled in fourth grade, putting me a grade ahead of children my own age. It made me appear to be a bit unusual—the smart girl from the sticks who was a grade ahead of everybody. Being younger than my classmates wasn't a big deal then, but it would be something that would make my life difficult later on.

Most of the other students came from well-to-do families. I had very few clothes to wear when I started classes, and I must have looked a little shabby. My Aunt Doris, my mother's older sister, was the fashion coordinator for Fantles Department Store and sent me a gorgeous blue snow suit. It was the warmest and most beautiful piece of clothing I'd ever had. In cold weather, I wore it to school every day and hated to take it off because of my well-worn clothes underneath. As time went on, my parents were able to gradually upgrade my wardrobe.

Attending Smith School and living with my parents was an important turning point in my life.

Shortly after I enrolled, the school nurse gave me a physical exam and called my mother in for a conference. While I was on a par or even ahead of the other students academically, my teachers were sharp-eyed enough to see that my physical condition was not good, and they alerted the school nurse. I was underweight for my age and unable to keep up with the other students in activities that required strength, running, or jumping. The nurse strongly recommended to my mother that I see a doctor.

My father was furious.

"Where are we going to get the money to take her to a doctor?" he growled.

If they had skipped a weekend's drinking at the Tap, it would have covered the doctor's visit. They didn't consider that, but they took me anyway.

After the doctor gave me a going over, he called my parents into the treatment room. "This child has malnutrition," he began sternly. "She weighs forty-five pounds and has little energy for physical activities at school." He eyed them both gravely. "Why don't you give her a better diet? When I asked her about what she eats, she was very vague about her meals."

My mother said, "Well, she's a finicky eater."

"And times are tough," my father added.

"Well, you two look well-fed. I think you could pass an extra plate to your young daughter. I'm prescribing a multiple vitamin pill to build her up." The doctor wagged his finger at them, and I smiled inwardly. "You make sure she gets a proper diet: protein, vegetables, and fruits—three times a day. The school will monitor her progress, and I want to see her again in a month, so make sure you do this. For God's sake, do it for her."

I knew they would blame me for having to spend the money on a doctor and the vitamins, but I didn't care. It was worth it to hear the doctor scold them.

I took my vitamins religiously, even though the pills were the size of something you might give to a horse. Before my next doctor's appointment, I began feeling better. I put on weight and got stronger. I was able to keep up with the other children in my physical education class.

At the same time, I discovered chocolate-malted milks. There was a small drugstore a short distance from home where I could get a chocolate malt for a dime and, when I could afford a little extra, a sandwich. And best of all, the store owner was kind enough to allow me to spend hours sitting cross-legged on the floor by the magazine racks, reading comic books.

As a fourth grader, my taste ran toward adventure comics. In 1938, I bought the first Superman comic. The Man of Steel stole my heart for a time, and I religiously read and re-read each issue until the next one hit the stands. Then, in 1939, my heart was stolen away by Batman. I bought the first Batman comic too and waited impatiently for the next one to arrive at the drug store.

My parents managed to find a little extra money to get me some new clothes for school. I tossed out everything I had worn on the farm. I no longer looked like I was straight out of the cornfields. I became more confident and took part in school activities. I wanted to become a baton twirler, so my dad brought home a baton for me, and I started taking lessons.

As my health and self-image improved, I came into more conflict with my parents. My father was a strict disciplinarian who believed if you spared the rod, you would spoil the child. I got frequent spankings if I neglected my chores or if I got a little too sassy. The spankings turned into whippings with a belt if my father had been drinking. On one occasion, he thought I was getting too independent and became so enraged that he whipped me with a length of rubber hose. My mother watched it happen and didn't attempt to stop him. The beating left bleeding welts on my butt, and I was unable to sit down or even sleep on my back. At school the next day, I was visibly uncomfortable, shifting from side to side at my desk. When the bell for recess rang, my teacher asked what was wrong. I explained my father's beating, and she nodded sadly.

"Don't go outside for recess," she said kindly. "Put your head on your desk and take a nap." I gratefully did what she said.

When class was over, she took me aside. "Stay home for a couple of days, Joanie. Let yourself heal."

In those days, beating children and wives was looked upon as the right of a father and husband. I asked my father near the end of his life why he had treated me so badly with so many beatings.

"That's how I was raised," he said with a shrug. "I thought that was what you were supposed to do to raise a child."

I recovered from the beating in a few weeks. When the welts on my butt healed and I could move again without pain, I went back to practicing my baton twirling. I was getting pretty good at it, except that once in a while the baton would bump my right wrist. If I practiced too hard, it hit my wrist more often. Before long, my wrist was swollen and discolored, constantly throbbing with pain.

I needed to see a doctor. My father was again furious over spending money on some ailment of mine. Over the next few days, the pain got worse, and I couldn't go to school. My mother wrapped the wrist in hot compresses, but it only got worse.

She finally convinced my father, and he drove us to the doctor's office. They waited outside while the doctor examined me. As he probed and prodded my wrist, now swollen the size of an orange, I winced from the pain. The doctor's brow furrowed, and his jaw clenched. He patted my arm and smiled.

"I'll be right back," he said. He walked into the other room where my parents were waiting and shut the door.

"Why didn't you bring her in sooner?" I heard the anger in his voice through the closed door. "She has a severe injury to her wrist. She needs to be in the hospital immediately. This condition could require surgery."

I felt a knot in my stomach. My parents followed the doctor back into the room. I could see the upset on their faces. I was suddenly scared.

"I'm going to call ahead so that the hospital's expecting her. You've already lost valuable time."

"What's going on, Mother?" I asked, trembling.

"The doctor says you need to go to the hospital to get your arm fixed."

"Oh, no." I began to cry. I climbed down from the examination table, and my mother took my hand.

The doctor gave me a hug as we walked out. "It'll be okay, Joanie."

When we got to our car, I threw myself face down into the back seat and sobbed into my folded arms.

My father started the car, and we pulled away. "I don't see how in hell we can afford this," he groused. "Every time you go to that doctor, it costs a fortune."

"So should we just ignore the doctor and let her infection get worse?"

"When I was her age, I never went to a doctor."

They reluctantly checked me into the hospital. I was put in a room with another girl around my age who had a similar problem with one of her legs. My arm was packed in hot compresses overnight and the next day, but when they unwrapped it, the swelling was worse. My skin was an ugly greenish color, and it smelled bad. The nurse shook her head and brought in the doctor. He looked at it and motioned my parents out into the hall. When they came back in, their faces were solemn.

"Jo," my mother began, "your arm's not getting better. The doctor is going to give you a new drug." She looked at the doctor for the name.

"Sulfa. It's a new drug that's just been developed," the doctor explained. "It's never been used in a case like this, but I think it's worth a try. You have tendonitis, Joanie. Sometimes it can lead to an infection of the bone called osteomyelitis, which is very serious. If the Sulfa doesn't reduce the inflammation, we may have to use surgery."

I was becoming more alarmed by the minute. "What does he mean, Mother? Daddy?"

My father was almost in tears himself. "If it doesn't work...." He looked away, then back. "They might have to amputate your arm."

"Cut off my arm?" I shrieked. "No! No!"

"They might have to do it to save your life," my mother said, trying to calm me.

I became hysterical with fear. The doctor ordered the nurse to give me a sedative. As I began getting drowsy, my mom and dad left. They both wore expressions of concern I'd never seen before as they said good-bye. The doctor and nurse came in and injected me with the red liquid that was supposed to help me. They were kind and gentle. They finished and left quietly.

Sometime in the night, the girl in the other bed began making gasping sounds. The nurse and doctor came in and spoke softly. Moments later, an orderly wheeled her out.

I was desolate. I turned to the wall and prayed to God to spare my arm. I wiggled my fingers and clenched my fist. It was painful, but it still worked. I could not imagine losing my arm. It felt like the end of my life. There would certainly not be a one-armed glamorous movie star like Harlow. That dream was dashed. I thought it would be better if I snuck out of the hospital tonight and ran away. If I died because of my arm, it would be for the best. At least I would die in one piece. I finally drifted into a nightmare-plagued sleep.

When I woke at daybreak, the first thing I noticed was that my roommate's bed was missing. When I asked the nurse where she was, she told me the girl passed away during the night. But I had no tears left for her. I had spent them all crying for myself.

My mom and dad arrived early. The doctor and nurse followed them into the room. The doctor gently took my arm and unwrapped the compress. It smelled terrible, but he smiled.

"It's working," he said to me. "The swelling has definitely gone down. There won't be any need for surgery."

"Thank God!" my mother exclaimed. My father laughed with tears in his eyes and clasped my shoulder.

Joyful tears came to my eyes too. "Thank you, doctor," I said.

"Don't thank me," he said. "You and Sulfa did all the work." He turned to the nurse. "Leave the compresses off, and let her skin get back to normal. Let's give her another dose of Sulfa right now, and a second one tonight."

I spent another two days in the hospital while my arm healed. There was almost no swelling by the time they discharged me. My father couldn't get off work to take me home, so my mother had to pick me up in a taxi cab. It was hellishly expensive, but there was no other way for me to get home.

The compassion my parents had shown me the night we thought I would lose my arm evaporated. It angered my mother that I could barely walk to the taxi. She reminded me that the cost of the taxi on top of my hospital bill was a huge burden on our family. I laid across the back seat, exhausted. When we arrived home, I couldn't climb the stairs to our apartment.

"Why can't you get up the stairs?" she snapped.

I could only murmur that I was sorry. She finally relented and half carried me up to our apartment. I got into a hot bath and soaked for a long time. I dried off and crawled into my bed and slept for twelve hours.

***

I had settled in on the floor amid the comic book racks with my chocolate malt when the cover of a movie magazine caught my eye. The face of Jean Harlow covered nearly the entire page. Jean Harlow would have been thirty years old a few days ago on March 3, 1941. I put the new Captain Marvel comic book aside and settled in to read about my idol.

Harlow's life was summarized in the article: her beginnings with Mama Jean, her over-protective and demanding mother; her abusive stepfather; her rise to stardom; and her tragic death.

I skipped my sandwich and bought the magazine. I read and re-read the article and wore out the pages looking at her pictures. I resolved to somehow get to Hollywood, though I hadn't figured out how. From where I sat in a small town in the middle of a mid-western prairie, still cold and damp in March, it seemed like an impossible goal.

It seemed even farther away that Thanksgiving. We had a Thanksgiving dinner of wild pheasant on the farm with Pa, Dah, Cliff, Myrna, and Norma. I endured the visit back to the farm as best I could. It snowed early, and the fields were already dotted with patches of white. Pa worried that the bitter winter would arrive before he could get the crops in. Dah bossed Pa and everyone else constantly. I ignored anything she said to me. I spoke when I was spoken to. It was a great relief to return to Sioux City.

In early December, I woke with an itchy spot on my left shoulder. It was a little blister that I scratched until it hurt and fluid oozed out. I noticed more little blisters on my breasts and stomach. When I showed my mother, she said, "Dammit, Jo, you've got chickenpox."

The health department quarantined our house and me in it with a big red sign on our front door. I had a sore throat and fever, so I stayed in my bedroom listening to the radio. It was not an auspicious start to the holiday season of 1941.

On the first Sunday morning in December, a news bulletin broke into the music program I was listening to. The Japanese had attacked Pearl Harbor. I ran into the kitchen and told my parents.

"What's Pearl Harbor?" I asked.

"It's a city in Hawaii," my father answered. "There's a big Naval base there. It's our Pacific fleet's homeport."

He went into the living room and turned on the big radio. Reports of the destruction kept coming in—battleships sunk, hundreds of casualties—it was more than my ten-year-old mind could wrap itself around. But judging from the voices on the radio and the reaction of my mom and dad, it was very bad. My instinct was that my world, and the whole world with it, was about to be turned upside down.

The War Department ordered able bodied men to report to their draft boards immediately. My father left early the next morning, while my mother and I waited.

"I don't know what we'll do if he has to go," my mother said, half to herself.

I didn't know what to say. The day's bad news added to my feverish, sick chickenpox feeling, so I wandered off to my bedroom and fell asleep. After a while, I woke to the sound of my father and mother talking in the living room. I sat on the floor and listened.

"Well," my father was saying, "I'm too old by just a few months to enlist, but the recruiter said they need men my age in defense plants back east and out west in California."

The three of us looked at each other.

"I talked with four other men at work who are all too old to sign up. We all think it's an opportunity to make some good money. But we'll have to leave here."

"Move somewhere else?" my mother asked anxiously.

"We'll have to go where the jobs are. What do you think?"

"It's a big risk."

"It's wartime," my father said. He turned to me. "How about you, Jo?"

"Where would we go, Daddy?"

I didn't get an answer to that question that first Sunday of WWII. I was praying for California because that's where Hollywood was. But there were fears that the West Coast was vulnerable if the Japanese decided to follow up on the Pearl Harbor attack with an invasion of the mainland. The East Coast was perhaps safer, and there was probably more industry there anyway. However, for a ten-year-old, still star-struck, still mad about Jean Harlow, and still fantasizing about being the next platinum blonde, the West Coast—and nothing but California—was the only choice.

Before the week was over, my father and his four buddies, all of whom were mechanics at the same garage, sat in his new 1939 Ford about to flip a coin.

"Okay," my father said, "heads we go east, and tails we go west." He flipped the coin that all of our futures were tied to. However it landed would determine nothing less than the course of our lives.

It was tails. Hollywood, here I come.

***

But first there was the war.

With my father in California, my mother and I were left alone and with no money. He promised to send money as soon as he had a job, but until then, it was touch and go. We had to leave the apartment and move to a rented room across from a skating rink. My mother clerked in a hat shop to earn enough for rent and very small meals. We lived on White Castle hamburgers.

My father and his buddies went to San Diego first and found jobs quickly. I was disappointed when I heard that. I looked up San Diego in the Smith School's library atlas and discovered it was nowhere near Los Angeles. After a few weeks, however, my father became disillusioned with San Diego and decided to try his luck Los Angeles. He found work there too, but the pay was low. The Great Depression wasn't yet over. The prosperity that a wartime economy would eventually bring was still just over the horizon.

Mom and I struggled along in Sioux City through January, February, March, and April. Then, in May, my father wired the money he had saved up—just enough for train fare to Los Angeles for the two of us. We would take the train from Omaha to Los Angeles, but first we had to take a bus the ninety-some miles from Sioux City to Omaha. I sold my bicycle, and we sold everything else we could to have enough money for bus fare and food on the trip.

The Sioux City bus station was several miles away—too far to walk carrying everything we owned. We had no money for a taxi and no way to get there. A friend of my mother's came to our rescue and drove us to the bus station at 5:00 a.m.

The cavernous train station in Omaha was crowded with service men and women of all kinds. Mobilization for the war effort was fully underway. Troops from all parts of the country passed through the center of the country. After the long bus ride to Omaha, we waited for hours for our train to depart. Rail schedules were geared to moving troops. Civilian travel had to wait.

The train ride from Omaha was impossibly long, boring, exhausting, and hungry. The journey should have taken two days, but several times a day our train was shunted off to a siding for hours while troop trains raced past. Mom and I slept in our seats as best we could, but there was little room. Our train was also crowded with soldiers and sailors. Many of them slept in the aisles, and you had to step over them just to get to the toilet.

Our money quickly ran out, and we couldn't afford to buy food. The servicemen shared an occasional sandwich and coke; and the black porters sneaked food to us from the dining car.

It took five days for the rolling prairies to change to the rugged sierras. I had never seen anything like it. I craned my neck to see the mountain peaks as we plunged into the dark tunnels through them.

I was sleeping fitfully next to a window when I opened my eyes. What I saw made me sit upright and let out a little squeal of joy. It could have been a vision, a part of a dream I'd been dreaming for a long time, but it was real: a palm tree.

We disembarked at the Los Angeles Union Station amid the bustle of crowds of soldiers, sailors, and marines. Everyone seemed to be going in a different direction. Whichever way we turned, my mother and I were buffeted by a tide of uniforms. We finally worked our way to some empty seats and tried to get our bearings. Over there was the entrance, up the broad flight of stairs to the huge art deco doors. We glued our eyes to it, searching for my father coming to pick us up. Streams of people poured through the entrance, but our hearts sank as the minutes passed.

"Where could he be?" my mother fretted. "He knew when we were arriving." She put her head in her hands. "What will we do if he doesn't come for us?"

I felt my own fear rising—stranded in a strange city, broke, knowing no one—it was terrifying. I was eleven years old, and my mother was dissolving into tears of despair. All of a sudden, I had to be the adult for her.

"I'm sure he'll be here, Mother." But I wasn't sure he would be either.

My father was a hard worker. He had carried quarry rocks for fifty cents a day; he had worked as a garage mechanic during the day and as a watchman at night to provide for us. But there was a side to him that was unpredictable, wild. It meant that he might do anything. It was part of what my mother loved about him, even in spite of his sometimes-abusive nature.

"C'mon, Mother," I said, taking her hand, "let's get some fresh air."

We gathered up our bags and worked our way through the crowd and up the stairs to the entrance. Outside it was warm and sunny. The giant American flag in front of the building flowed in a light breeze. My hair ruffled around my face, and I inhaled the unique smell of Los Angeles: part auto exhaust and part distant desert sage. To me it was exotic, the incense of a magical place. Though I was as alarmed as my mother that my father was nowhere to be seen, in my heart of hearts, I felt an excitement at being *here.*

"Lucille! Jo!" a familiar voice shouted. Mother and I turned toward the sound, and there was my father shoving his way through the crowd. His black hair was longer than when I'd last seen him, and he was tanned from being outdoors in the California sun. We both threw ourselves into his arms.

"Where have you been?" Mother scolded.

"I couldn't get off work. I got here as soon as I could."

He picked up our luggage, and we loaded ourselves into his once-new 1939 Ford.

"I've been living in a one-room apartment in a small court. They don't allow children, Jo, so we'll have to sneak you in the back way until we can get a better place."

"Okay, Daddy," I said. For the three of us to be safely back together, I would've slept in the backseat of the car.

I watched bug-eyed as we drove. Street cars sped past, automobiles dodged in and out of the street-car tracks. People crowded the sidewalks.

"Look," I said, pointing at them. "Everyone's wearing dark glasses. Why?"

"Maybe because it's sunny," Mother said.

"Everybody wears them," my father said.

"They all look like movie stars."

"We've got to get some dark glasses," my mother said.

We turned a corner, and the hillsides came into view. I'd never seen houses like these, perched on hillsides, precariously anchored with posts into the rock. The whole city was built on hills and cliffs that looked like they couldn't possibly support a house.

Then I saw *it* and let out a yelp. I excitedly pointed out the front windshield.

"Look at that!"

High on the hillside in front of us, the sign read: Hollywoodland. My eyes filled with tears. I had no idea there would be this kind of welcome, especially for me. Jean Harlow had seen it when she came to Hollywood. The five women who drove away from the rooming house in Sioux City that morning saw it too. I had made it this far. I had no idea what I would do next to become a movie star. And I certainly had no idea what would be required of me to make my dream come true. But whatever the price, at age eleven, in Los Angeles for just a matter of hours, I was willing to pay it.

Coda

Not all dreams come true, even in Hollywoodland, the land of dreams. Peg Entwistle was an actress in New York. One of her stage roles was seen by Bette Davis, and, it is said, it led Bette into acting. Peg came to Hollywood in the early 1930s, dreaming of getting into movies. But she was not lucky. Only a few disappointing uncredited bit parts came her way. She finally received screen credit in her last role, but it was not enough to sustain her. On September 16, 1932, she took her dreams and her despair and climbed to the top of the "H" in Hollywoodland and jumped to her death.

Eventually, the "land" in "Hollywoodland" would slip down the hillside, be dismantled, and tossed away—it was a 1923 promotion for a subdivision anyway. Only a vague, persistent promise would remain attached to the word "Hollywood."

Peg was a prime example of Hollywood's power to deny promise and crush hope. But even those whose dreams appear to have come true are likely to discover that success was only momentary. The dreams of Marilyn Monroe, Dorothy Stratten, Sharon Tate, and Frances Farmer, to name only a few, were swept away and turned into nightmares. That, boys and girls, is Hollywood.

I wake every day to a new obituary. I have been blessed with a long life. When you reach this point in the hill climb, it's only natural to see one's contemporaries fall by the wayside. Father Time doesn't miss. But I keep dodging.

Karma appears to be on my side, and that's lucky, because I've got some really good stories for you. Some are fun. Some are not. And like Ishmael, orphaned by Moby Dick, floating in a restless and hungry sea, I'll dare to quote the Book of Job, King James version,1:15.

And I only am escaped alone to tell thee.

Chapter Two

The Black Dahlia

"Tragedy is not glamorous…tragedy is ugly and tangled, stupid and confusing."

—E. LOCKHART

One spring morning in LA, the wind from the open streetcar window blew my very blonde hair as I rode uptown. My handmade white suit with a green flowered pattern—the skirt daringly short, the jacket snug around me—was making heads turn.

Since I could remember, I had been obsessed with *looking good.* Though my family had no money to spare, I saved up pennies and lunch money and tips from an occasional waitress job to buy yardage. Even though everyone said the war was winding down, rationing was still in place, and it was difficult to find really beautiful yard goods. But once in a while I could find something really lovely, like the smooth Guatemala cotton my suit was made of. I had made friends with a talented seamstress named May Ching, who could whip up a fantastic outfit, fit for cocktails or high tea, out of next to nothing, for very little money. My suit this morning was one of her finest.

I pulled the cord for the conductor to stop and swung down onto the safety island. I crossed the street and boarded the Vine Street bus. It was a short ride to the storied corner of Hollywood and Vine. From there It was only a few steps to the Osco drugstore, my destination this morning.

Why there?

I was fourteen years old, dolled up to disguise my baby face to look, maybe, twenty-one, acting out the grand Hollywood fable of discovery. Lana Turner, the legend told, had been discovered sitting at the lunch counter in Schwab's Pharmacy on Sunset Boulevard. (Many years later we would learn that Lana had actually been discovered at the Top Hat Malt Shop, two miles east of Schwab's.) I truly believed in that legend, but Schwab's was too crowded for my taste these days, and I wanted my own legend. *Besides*, I thought, *if you're looking for lightning to strike, you don't go to the place it has already struck.*

So, I sashayed up Vine in my sexy little suit, my mother's green high heels clicking on the concrete. It was early for the Osco lunch crowd, and I found a stool with plenty of empty seats around it, giving me room to show off my legs. I ordered a chocolate malt, paid my nickel when it came, posed, and went to work on it. (Thanks to the chocolate malts I drank back in Sioux City while reading comic books, I was obsessed by that finest achievement of the soda jerk's art. To this day, I cannot resist a chocolate malt.)

I was so concentrated on my malt that I didn't notice a tall man wearing a suit and tie sitting two stools away, staring at me. When I looked up, he smiled and pushed a business card down the counter to me.

"Hi, I'm NTG."

I giggled. "What's that?"

"My name: Nils Thor Granlund." He pushed the card closer to me. "Read my card."

The card read: *Nils Thor Granlund, Producer/Director.* There was an address and a phone number.

My eyes lit up. "Nice to meet you, Mr. Granlund."

"And you, Miss—?"

"Olander. Joanie Olander."

"You're a Swede, aren't you, Joanie?"

"My grandmother's from Gothenburg."

"Ah, yes, Joanie. Well, I'm producing a number of live shows in LA, one of which will be at the Florentine Gardens. Would that be something you're interested in?"

I felt a rush of excitement. The Florentine Gardens! It was a popular restaurant that featured live music and dancing, as well as floor shows with risqué nightclub acts and gorgeous Las Vegas-style showgirls.

When service men hit town, the Florentine Gardens was one of the first places they wanted to visit. Getting to be in a show there would be fantastic.

Geez, I thought. *Maybe this drugstore counter thing really works.*

"Yes, Mr. Granlund, I would be interested. But I will need to ask my mother."

"Call me NTG. Everyone does." He got off the stool and turned toward the door. "Speak to your mother, Joanie. Have her call me any time at that number and let me know your decision."

"Okay, Mr., er, NTG, I will."

I rushed home and showed my mother NTG's card. She was impressed, but her brow furrowed when I mentioned the Florentine Gardens.

"That's a place where they do girlie shows, Jo. What on Earth would you do? You're only fourteen."

"I don't know, Mother. Why don't you call NTG right now and ask him? I really want to do this."

She picked up the phone and dialed the number on the card. NTG answered, and they spoke for several minutes. Then she said, "Oh, that's very nice of you, NTG. Yes, I'm sure Joanie would like to see it too. Okay, we'll see you this afternoon."

"What'd he say, Mother?" I was jumping out of my skin.

"He wants us to visit him at the Florentine Gardens this afternoon. He'll show us around and tell us what he has in mind for you."

I threw my arms around her neck. "Thanks, Mother!"

"You're welcome. I'd better get dressed."

NTG greeted us at the ornate entrance of the Florentine Gardens beneath a giant banner that read: *NTG Victory Girl Revue*. Inside there was bustling activity everywhere. Showgirls were rehearsing a dance routine, tables and chairs were being arranged around the dance floor, and electricians on ladders were working on stage lights. Giant pictures of showgirls hung on every wall, statuesque, scantily clad girls with large plumes on their heads. When I saw them, my jaw dropped. I instantly wanted to be one of them, even though I was far too young.

NTG proudly walked us through the show room, the backstage and dressing rooms, and the kitchen. We ended the tour in his office just off the backstage area.

"Here's what I've got in mind, Joanie, Mrs. Olander. Joanie, you're a little young yet to be part of the revue. However, I will be producing a television show in front of a live audience here in the show room, interviewing movie stars and celebrities. It'll be broadcast live on the new television station, KTLA Channel 5. Joanie, I want you to be Little Joanie the Flower Girl. You'll be the centerpiece that introduces every broadcast. You'll walk through the room, welcome the audience, and give a flower to each person. You'll have a pretty dress, befitting Hollywood's first Little Flower Girl. I'm sure you'll be a big hit." He looked from my mother to me. "What do you think?"

"I think it sounds fine," I said. "Mother?"

"How much will she be paid?"

NTG rubbed his chin. "Five dollars an episode. What do you say, Joanie?"

I didn't hesitate. "Okay!"

"Then it's settled," NTG said, rubbing his hands together. "You're now part of our family."

At that moment, a well-dressed man with graying hair walked into NTG's office. "And right on cue." NTG went on, "Here's the owner of the Florentine Gardens, Mark Hansen. Mark, this is Joanie Olander, our newest cast member. And this is her mother, Lucille. Joanie'll be the Little Flower Girl on our new KTLA show. She'll begin each show by welcoming the audience members with a flower. And by the way, Joanie and her mom are Swedes too. Mark here is from Denmark."

Hansen extended his hand. "Mrs. Olander, it's a pleasure to meet you. And Joanie, you are adorable. I know you're going to be a big asset to our show. I'm really looking forward to it."

I flushed at the compliment and shook his hand. "Thank you, Mr. Hansen. I can't wait."

"I'm guessing that you're interested in getting into movies, right?"

"Oh, yes," I said.

"Well, you should stick close to NTG here. He's got an eye for talent and has given lots of stars their starts. He discovered Yvonne De Carlo right here at the Florentine Gardens."

"I can tell this one's got what it takes," NTG put in, nodding at me.

"I think you're right," Hansen agreed. "Why don't you two stay for dinner and the show on me? We'll have to tuck you away in the back of the house because Joanie's underage, but the food's good, and I know you'll enjoy the show."

"That's very nice of you, Mr. Hansen," Mother said. "I'll have to call my husband and let him know he's on his own for dinner."

Hansen pointed to the telephone on NTG's desk. "You can use that one. And call me Mark."

Mom and I waited in NTG's office while the Florentine Gardens was readied for the night's show. By the time the stage lights were set and the waitresses were at their stations, we were hungry.

A pretty dark-haired waitress showed us to a small table in the back of the room. When we were seated, we got a good look at her and my jaw dropped. It was like looking at a copy of my mother. They both had hair piled on their heads in a high pompadour, set off with a white flower, and both wore bright red lipstick. Mom's hair was dyed coal black. The waitress' hair was a dark brown, and she was blessed with flawless, snowy white skin and eyes of ultramarine blue.

"My, God," mom exclaimed, "it's like looking at myself." We all laughed.

"I'm Lucille Olander, and this is my daughter, Joanie. She's going to be in the cast of NTG's new television show."

"Oh, that's wonderful," the dark-haired girl answered. "My name's Elizabeth Short." She placed menus in front of us. "The food's really good here."

My mom asked, "What's your favorite, Elizabeth?"

"I think you can't beat the spaghetti and meatballs."

"Okay!" I said, "I'm starving."

"That's what we'll have," mom said. "And I'll have a glass of red wine."

Elizabeth smiled and jotted down our order. "Back with the wine in a moment."

"She looks enough like you to be your sister," I said when she was out of earshot.

Mom shook her head. "My own sisters don't look that much like me."

Elizabeth returned with mom's glass of wine and a baguette of bread. "Your food'll be out in just a few minutes."

"Are you from around here, Elizabeth?" I asked.

Elizabeth glanced over her shoulder. The room was quickly filling up with customers. "I'm from Boston originally, but that's a long story. Gotta go take care of my other tables. Bye for now."

She hurried away to her other guests. I took a sip of mom's wine. The house lights dimmed, and lights along the walls illuminated the showgirl pictures. We ate some bread. The orchestra started to play and a few couples got up to dance. I took another sip of mom's wine. Elizabeth brought our dinners—two enormous plates of spaghetti and meatballs.

Mom eyed the plates in front of us. "That's enough food for thrashers."

Elizabeth said, "Mark told me there was to be no check for your table. And he told me to give you anything you wanted and to make sure you were enjoying it." She smiled. "So, enjoy. You can always take the leftovers home. I'll bring you some more wine."

We stuffed ourselves. Between the two of us we drank three glasses of wine.

By the time we finished dinner, the tables were crowded with uniformed servicemen and a scattering of civilians. The orchestra stopped. The house lights went dark. A single spotlight lit NTG on stage at a microphone.

"Ladies and gentlemen, welcome to the Florentine Gardens! I'm your host, Nils Thor Granlund, but you can call me NTG. We have a fantastic show in store for you tonight, featuring the most beautiful girls in Hollywood. And as you men in uniform know by now, Hollywood is the right place to find beautiful girls."

The soldiers and sailors stamped their feet and whistled and cheered.

When the cheering subsided, NTG went on, "Excellent! Everybody knows that there's fighting going on, but we've got the Krauts and Japs on the run." More applause and cheers. "Tonight's show is entitled, *NTG's Victory Girl Revue*. I'd be damned worried if I was our enemies. They won't have a chance because once you guys get a gander at the beauties in our show, you'll have no doubts about what you're fighting for! Ladies and gentlemen, please welcome, *NTG's Victory Girls*!"

The stage went black and the orchestra struck up a military march. The lights came up on a chorus of the tallest, most scantily costumed, most gorgeous girls I'd ever seen. They strutted off the stage and into the audience, to the delight of the servicemen.

The show lasted for an hour with singers and comics and more dancing girls. I was so awestruck I barely moved during the entire show.

When it was over and the hooting and whistling from the servicemen had subsided, everyone headed for the exits. Elizabeth brought two packages with spaghetti and meat balls to our table.

"This'll feed you and Mr. Olander for a while," she said. "I gave you a few extra things."

Mom took a dollar out of her purse and gave it to Elizabeth.

"No," Elizabeth protested, "that's not necessary."

"Yes it is," Mom replied. "You earned this, and Joanie and I want you to have it."

Elizabeth pressed my mom's hand in hers. "Thank you so much."

"I hope we'll see you again," Mom said.

"Me too," said Elizabeth.

Mom and I sought out Mark Hansen to thank him for his hospitality. He smiled and clapped his hands. "My pleasure. So, you liked the show?"

"Oh, yes!" I said. "Very much!" mom added. "And the dinner was excellent."

Hansen gestured to our take-home packages. "And I see you've got plenty to feed Mr. Olander. That's excellent."

Mom and I started for the door. "Thank you again, Mark."

"Hey, Mrs. Olander, why don't you and Joanie join me and some friends for dinner on Tuesday at my house? It'll be a few friends and some of the people from the club. Nothing fancy. I have a house just around the corner on Harold Way. Come around five o'clock."

"Yes, we'd love to."

I chattered excitedly all the way home. I'd never seen a show like it before. I was thrilled to be starting work on a new television show.

Over the next few months, Mom and I had lunch or dinner on several occasions at Mark's house on Harold Way. They were family-style dinners, mostly with waitresses and staff from the Florentine Gardens. Mark seemed to relish being a father figure among the employees of the Gardens.

Elizabeth Short was often part of the group at Mark's, and she and my mom became friends. Mom was a few years older than Elizabeth. Elizabeth even changed her hair color from dark brown to coal black like my mother's. Elizabeth confided in her that she was trying to get into movies, but it was difficult to get noticed by an agent without new clothes. And getting new clothes was impossible without enough money. Her wages and tips from the Florentine Gardens were barely enough to keep her afloat. Mark allowed her to work extra shifts and let her stay free of charge in one of the bedrooms in his Harold Way house to help her get by.

Mark particularly doted on Elizabeth. He was clearly fond of her as more than just an employee. On one occasion, I noticed that Elizabeth was not part of the dinner party. When I asked Mark where she was, he said, "I don't know exactly. She asked for a two-week advance on her salary—I gave it to her—but she left without saying where she was going. She has friends in San Diego, so she's probably visiting with them. And I understand she also has family in San Francisco. Could be she's up there."

I was busy every week as Little Joanie the Flower Girl on NTG's TV show. I had May Ching make a blue dress with white polka dots for my first show (it cost me a whole dollar!), and I wore my mother's green high heels. I was late for my call the first day. The crew hustled me into the backstage dressing room and quickly applied the grotesque make-up required for early television: a pale foundation and brown lipstick. The cast all looked like cadavers. The stage manager pushed me onto the nightclub floor with a basket of flowers, and I began handing out flowers to the audience. I was too nervous to notice one of the giant tv cameras following me from table to table. But with all the attention lavished on Little Joanie, I felt like Lana Turner.

Occasionally, NTG would ask me to have lunch with him at the Brown Derby restaurant. After lunch one day, NTG and I were walking down Vine Street when he pointed to two men coming toward us. One was older and quite small, walking with an elegant cane; the other was average height, clearly solicitous of the older man.

"That's Cole Porter," NTG whispered.

NTG extended his hand as they got near us. "Cole, how've you been, you old darling?"

"Older but not wiser," Porter said, his voice soft and reedy. "We were on our way to have a late lunch." He gestured toward the young man. "This is Michael."

NTG shook his hand. "And this is young Joanie, the flower girl on my new celebrity interview TV show." Porter smiled and shook my hand in a perfunctorily way. "By the way, Cole," NTG continued, "why don't you come by and be a guest on the show? People would love to hear from the great Cole Porter, who wrote 'Night and Day' and 'Begin the Beguine.'"

"Perhaps I could do that, Nils. Maybe next week. I'm just getting over a cold."

NTG handed him a business card. "Call me soon, Cole. You'll be a great interview."

Porter and his friend continued up Vine Street, while NTG and I watched them go. Porter was leaning heavily on his cane.

"It's a shame," NTG said shaking his head. "He's in constant pain."

"Why? What happened to him?"

"A horseback-riding accident in England. Almost ten years ago. But he never stopped writing songs."

During the summer months while I was playing Little Joanie the Flower Girl, I saw NTG regularly. I took seriously that he had discovered Yvonne DeCarlo and other stars. If there was a way for some of that lucky dust to rub off on me, I was all for it. My mom and dad trusted him because he was a fellow Swede, and I always trusted him too. He was always a gentleman to me, until one summer afternoon.

NTG lived near the Florentine Gardens, and it was commonplace for me to drop into his house just to say hello. On one occasion, NTG said he was about to take a nap.

"Why don't you join me, Joanie?" He reached into his closet and took out a filmy lady's nightgown. "Put this on and lie down on my bed."

It was very unexpected. And creepy. All my alarms went off. But it was NTG who had always been nice, and who had given me a job. Still, I didn't like it. I'm sure he could tell from the mix of puzzlement and fear on my face.

"It'll be all right, Joanie. I'm not going to touch you. Just lie down next to me while I sleep."

"Well, okay," I said reluctantly. I stripped down to my underwear, slipped the gown on, and laid on the edge of the bed as far from NTG as I could get. After a few minutes, he began snoring softly. I eased off the bed, got dressed, and tiptoed out.

The incident with NTG left me very troubled. I was suddenly disillusioned about someone who I thought was a trusted friend but who had revealed himself to be a freak. It also left me in a quandary about whether I would tell my mother. If she knew about it, that would be the end of my career as Little Joanie, and I didn't want that—at least not yet. I didn't think of Little Joanie as a career, but thanks to the show, people around town were beginning to recognize me. Who knows, maybe eventually, the right person would see me, and I might get a movie contract. My first impulse had been to shun NTG and never speak to him again, but I thought better of it. I damn sure wouldn't be alone with NTG again, but I would keep up appearances. And I wouldn't tell my mother.

***

A week later, Nils Thor Granlund said to me conspiratorially, "Joanie, I know a very important Hollywood director who wants to meet you."

My ears perked up immediately. "Really? Who?"

"He directed Gloria Swanson and Rudolph Valentino." He told me the director's name and several of the movies he did. I'll call him "Henry." "He's seen you on the show and thinks you're wonderful. He told me he may have a part for you in a new movie he's making. He wants to take you to dinner so you can get acquainted."

"Wow, that sounds interesting. I'd like to go, but I'll have to ask my mom," I said.

"Of course. Tell your mom I said that Henry is a really nice guy."

That evening I told my mother about the invitation. "I've heard of Henry," she said. "But you're pretty young to go on a solo date with someone his age. NTG said he was on the up-and-up?"

"Yeah. He said this guy's nice. I want to go, Mother. It could be a break for me."

"I know, Jo. As long as NTG said he's okay, go ahead."

***

I drove my dad's Ford to NTG's house to meet Henry for our date. It was a chilly late afternoon, and I was wearing a plaid tailored suit with a tight skirt and a beige sweater under the jacket. My mother's green high heels completed the outfit.

Henry was a tall, slim man in his fifties, a pipe clenched in his teeth, graying hair, wearing an expensive suit and a monogramed shirt. He drove an enormous maroon Lincoln Continental convertible.

We went to dinner in a small, dark place on restaurant row on Sunset. It was a place where an older man like Henry could bring a young girl, and people would pretend to believe that she was actually his "niece."

Henry made small talk over dinner about the movie stars he'd worked with. The food was excellent. Most memorable was the desert: tiramisu, which I'd never had before. It was still daylight when we got back into Henry's Continental.

"Why don't we drive to the beach and watch the sunset?" he suggested.

I'd always loved the beach—I practically lived there in the summertime—so I said, "Why not?"

Henry drove down Sunset Boulevard to the intersection at Pacific Coast Highway. There was a brightly lit gas station on one corner of the intersection. A short distance away was a small wooded area, secluded from the road, with a postcard-worthy view of the Pacific and the setting sun. Henry parked there, and we took in the view in silence.

After a few minutes, Henry reached across the seat and took my hand and placed it in his lap. Suddenly, I realized that something felt very strange. I looked over and saw that he had unzipped his pants, taken out his cock, and placed my hand on it.

"Ewww! What the—" I snatched my hand away like I'd touched a hot stove. "What are you doing?" I jerked the car door open and jumped out. I slammed the door and bent down to hide behind it.

"Joanie, Joanie," Henry whined, "please get back in the car. It's okay."

"No!" I stayed hidden behind the door. "I want to go home! Now!"

"Look, I'm sorry I startled you. I didn't mean any harm. I just want you to help me out a little."

"I'm not going to help you do anything. Take me home."

There was a pause. "I'll take you home if you want, Joanie. Just get in the car and let's talk."

"No."

"I'm not going to hurt you. But I'll give you thirty-five dollars if you'll, um, give me a hand."

I peeked over the door, and he was holding a twenty, a ten, and a five in his hand. I opened the door and eased into the seat as far from him as possible.

"All you have to do is put your hand over here and"—he made a massaging motion with his hand—"and just help me out."

Boys had tried to talk me into hand jobs before, and I had said no. But this man, who seemed ancient to me, was outside my experience—too gross, too creepy. I stayed in my seat and didn't say anything.

"It's not such a terrible thing," he chuckled. "Other girls have done it and survived." He fumbled in his pocket a moment and produced a fifty-dollar bill. "Look, I'll make it fifty, okay? How about that?"

I got out of the car again. "Take me home, or I'm going to walk to the gas station on the corner and find someone to take home. And when I get there, I'm going to tell NTG what a slimy creep you are."

He chuckled again. "Joanie, it was NTG who told me you might be interested in a little offer like this."

I was stunned. NTG, whom I had trusted like family, had set me up with this vile clown, knowing what he would try to do. And this after the disturbing nightgown scene at his house. I could feel my temper rising.

"First you had thirty-five, then you had fifty. Make it a hundred."

Henry's jaw dropped. "Well, no, no, that's just not—I don't have that much on me."

"Then I'm going home anyway I can get there."

"Okay, okay, wait." He fumbled in his wallet and came up with another fifty dollars. "Here, I've got it. Now please get back in the car."

I held my hand through the open car window. "Give it all to me. Now."

He sighed and put the one hundred dollars in my hand. I stuffed it in my bra and got in the car. "What do I have to do?"

"Just give me your hand, and I'll put it on my—my thing, and then I'll move it with my hand. You really don't have to do a thing."

I was seething with anger and humiliation. This was a nightmare not of my own making. I turned my head away and thrust out my left arm like I was signaling for a left turn. It hit Henry squarely in the chest and he went, "Oof!" He took my hand and lowered it on to his cock, his breath coming in gasps. I had caught a glimpse of it, tiny and white, and it had a sweaty, sickening, fleshy feel. He was whimpering and panting as he began to move my hand. After a few strokes, his body stiffened and he let out a loud grunt. I felt something hot and sticky on my hand.

"Arrgh! What the fuck is that?" I drew my hand away covered with his semen. "You sick son of a bitch!' I slapped at his face and smeared it on his cheek. I wiped my hand on his suit coat and shirt, on his car seat, and on whatever else I could find. "Let me out of here!" I jerked the door open and started running down the beach in the direction of the gas station.

Henry jumped out of the car and ran after me. But his pants were still unzipped and down around his ankles. After a few steps, he stumbled and fell into the sand. He struggled to his feet, trying to wipe away the sand stuck to the semen on his face and clothes.

"Don't try to follow me," I screamed back at him, "or I'll call the cops."

There was a young guy manning the gas station by himself when I stumbled in, barefoot, disheveled, and clearly upset. I was carrying my green high heels, sweating after my sprint from Henry's car.

"Hi," the young guy said. "Are you alright?"

"Yeah, I'm okay. Just had a date that went bad. I need to get back to Hollywood to pick up my car. Is there someone who could give me a ride? I'll pay for the gas."

"I close the station in an hour. I don't have a car, only my motorcycle. But if you don't mind waiting an hour and riding on the back, I can take you there."

"A motorcycle!" I said, perking up. I loved motorcycles. I had ridden many miles on the back of my dad's Indian, and I'd even ridden it by myself a lot. "That sounds like fun. I'll wait. What's your name?"

"Jake."

"Nice meeting you, Jake. I'm Joanie. Do you happen to have a place I could wash my hands?"

I was coming out of the washroom when Henry's Continental lumbered out of the beach turn off and roared through the intersection. He was close enough for me to see that his hair was disheveled, and he was still covered with sand. He had a death grip on the steering wheel, and his teeth were clenched as he gunned the big car up Sunset.

Jake came from inside the station and handed me a bottle of soda. "You look like you could use this." He motioned toward the maroon Continental disappearing up Sunset. "Was that your lousy date?"

I took a drink of the soda and grimaced. "Uh-huh."

"Nice car though," Jake said appreciatively.

"With an asshole driving it."

Jake locked the gas pumps and turned out the station lights, kick-started the motorcycle's engine to life, and straddled the seat. He reached back and handed me his jacket. "You'd better wear this, Joanie. It's gonna be cold."

I put my arms through the sleeves. It was still warm inside and smelled of gasoline and sweat. "Thanks." I hiked my skirt up to my thighs and threw a leg over the passenger seat. Luckily, I still wore panties in those days. I made sure my green high heels were secure on the foot pegs, opened Jake's jacket and my suit jacket, and wrapped both around myself and Jake. His back felt warm against my breasts. Jake stomped the bike into gear, and we shot off up Sunset.

I guided him to NTG's house. We stopped next to my dad's Ford and I climbed off the bike. My legs and feet felt frozen solid. I climbed off the motorcycle and handed Jake's jacket back. "Thanks for letting me wear it, Jake."

He grinned sheepishly. "Thanks for keeping my back warm."

"Don't mention it." I unlocked my dad's car, reached under my sweater, and pulled a dollar bill from the roll of cash Henry had given me. "Here, Jake, this for some gas."

"No, no, I don't want that. I'm just glad to help—"

"Don't be silly. Put some gas in that thing and enjoy yourself." Gasoline was eight or ten cents a gallon back then. You could get a whole dinner for two people at Charlie's Boxcar Diner for fifty cents. Jake carefully folded the dollar and slipped it in the pocket of his jeans.

"Uh, Joanie, could I call you some time?" he asked with a grin.

I kissed Jake on the cheek. "Give me your number, and I'll call you."

I started my dad's car and turned toward home. Jake had been so sweet, I'd almost gotten over my anger at what I'd just been through with Henry. Now it came surging back, and I was furious.

I turned on to a side street and pulled to the curb. I shut off the engine and took a deep breath. I sat for a long time grappling with my rage at NTG. For him to betray me in such a disgraceful way, when my whole family had trusted him so implicitly, actually pimping me out to some scumbag on the pretense of a role in a movie was unforgivable. Then there was my shame. I had Henry's hundred dollars in my pocket that I had earned with a disgusting act.

Tears began to flow. I felt I couldn't tell my mother what had happened with NTG and the nightgown, and I couldn't tell her about tonight's humiliating experience with Henry. Her disapproval and certain disappointment in me was more than I could deal with. It was my own fault that for the first time in my life, I was forced to deal with serious life problems on my own, without the support of my mother.

***

Summer came and went while I handed out flowers at the Florentine Gardens. The show seemed popular, at least from my point of view. People on the street said, "Hi, Little Joanie!" A girl younger than me approached me on the streetcar and said, "I want to be a flower girl like you, Joanie." I was flattered and a little baffled about the recognition. Did movie stars feel that sort of sweet guilt? Did they worry, as I did, that someone would pull back the curtain to reveal that I'm making it up as I go along?

As Thanksgiving approached, Mark Hansen began planning a lavish dinner at his house for the Florentine Gardens family. His restaurant would provide a couple turkeys and a ham and a few bottles of wine, while the rest of us would bring a covered dish. My mom's contribution was her signature sweet potato-marshmallow pudding.

When the big day came, the small kitchen in Mark's house was crowded with cooks, each trying to get their pet dish ready to be served. Wine was flowing and voices were getting louder. By the time we sat down and began passing the food, everyone was laughing and chattering and eating. I sat on one side of Elizabeth, and mom sat on the other. They were engrossed in conversation throughout the meal, often giggling guiltily behind their hands at some dirty joke.

After the pumpkin pie and coffee, we were all glassy-eyed from overeating. Some of the women finally began clearing away the dishes. More people pitched in. Elizabeth volunteered to wash, and I volunteered to dry. It was a pretty big job that required some care—the dishes belonged to Mark personally.

Elizabeth was up to her elbows in hot, soapy water, scrubbing plates and flatware, when she suddenly screamed.

"What's wrong, Elizabeth?" I immediately asked.

Elizabeth held up her left hand. "I lost my ring!" she sobbed. "My ring's gone! It must have gone down the drain." She wailed hysterically. "Oh, my God! Oh, my God!" Others stuck their heads into the kitchen to see what was wrong.

I immediately plunged my hands into the soapy water and began feeling around the bottom of the sink. My fingers found it, and I held it out to Elizabeth. "It's not lost, Elizabeth. Look, it's right here."

She took the ring with trembling hands. "Oh, Joanie, you're a lifesaver. I'd die if I lost that. It's my engagement ring." She embraced me with a crushing hug.

"I didn't know you were engaged," I said. "Who's the lucky guy? Where is he?"

Elizabeth burst into hysterical tears again. Mom and another woman took over the dishwashing. Mom said to me, "Why don't you take her into the other room until she calms down?"

I ushered Elizabeth into a quiet corner of Mark's living room and handed her a tissue. She blew her nose hard and gradually got hold of herself.

"I'm sorry to cause such a fuss," she sniffled. "The ring is all I've got left of Matthew."

"Your fiancé?"

She brushed back more tears and nodded. "He was an Army major. God, he was wonderful! It's such a long story...." Her voice trailed off into tears again.

"Don't talk about it if you don't want to Elizabeth."

"Call me Beth, Joanie. I want to talk about it."

I scooted my chair closer to hers.

"Matthew. Matthew Gordon. Matthew Gordon. He was a major in the Army Air Corps." She repeated it softly as if the invocation of his name could make him appear. A shudder ran through her body. "A fighter pilot. Silver Star. On his last mission, killed in action."

I grasped her hands. "Oh, my God, Beth! What a terrible thing." Suddenly I was crying too.

"Joanie, we both can't cry," she said tenderly. "There's only grief enough for one."

She was right. It was her tragedy deal with. It was my job to bear witness. I wiped my eyes. "Tell me about Matthew."

"We met in Florida. Vero Beach. You know where that is, Joanie?" I shook my head. "On the Florida east coast. It's beautiful there. Matthew lived in Vero Beach. I was down in Florida getting warm. I'm originally from Boston, and it was the dead of winter there—cold and damp. And full of Bostonians too—also cold and damp, come to think of it. Anyway, a couple of my friends were as fed up with Bean Town as I was—and unemployed—and they were going to drive their old car to Florida in hopes of finding jobs. I had a little money saved up so I could pay my share of the gas, and I tagged along."

Elizabeth softly touched the ring as she spoke, rotating it gently on her finger, looking at it, making sure it was still there.

"When we got to Vero Beach, my friends wanted to go on to Miami, but I wanted to stay in Vero Beach—I don't know why. It was kinda scary. No job and running low on money. But I decided to stay there by myself. So, when Matthew and I met—"

Mark Hansen appeared by her side and put a hand on her shoulder. "Everything all right, Elizabeth? They told me out in the kitchen that you were upset."

She smiled. "I'm okay now, Mark, thanks to Joanie here. I thought I lost my engagement ring in the dishwater, but Joanie fished it out. I guess I made a real fool of myself."

"Don't give it a thought. Joanie to the rescue." He patted my shoulder, then hers again. "See you later."

"'Bye. Thanks for asking."

"Mark's a very nice man," I said. "He cares a lot about you."

"Oh, yes. We're just friends," Elizabeth replied. "Now, where was I?"

"You were telling me how you met Matthew."

"Right. My sister wired me some money. I was coming out of the Western Union office stuffing the cash in my purse when I stumbled over this handsome guy in a uniform. *Really* stumbled. We both sprawled on the sidewalk in a heap."

"'Oh, geez, I'm so sorry!' he said. He quickly jumped to his feet and helped me up. 'Are you all right?'

"'I'm fine. It was my fault for not looking where I was going.'

"'No, I should have seen you. You sure you're not hurt, miss?'

"'There was no harm done,' I told him. I had a little scrape on my knee and his crisp uniform was wrinkled where he hit the ground. We stood stammering and brushing ourselves off for a couple of minutes. He finally said, 'How about we have a coffee at that diner across the street?'

"Joanie, he had the bluest eyes and the sweetest smile I'd ever seen. We didn't even know each other's names, but I said, 'Yes.'"

Elizabeth calmed down and went deeper into the story. They were barely out of each other's sight after that chance first meeting. Matthew was on two weeks' leave in Vero Beach. He was a fighter pilot—a good one—a member of the Flying Tigers, which nearly everyone had heard of by this time in the war, fighting the Japanese in India-Burma-China. He'd shot down enough Japanese planes to qualify as an "Ace." And he had been decorated with the Silver Star and the Flying Cross.

They both loved Glenn Miller's "String of Pearls," and The Andrews Sisters' "Rum and Coca Cola," and they both loved to drink it as well.

Their love affair blossomed in that two weeks in Vero Beach. They began talking about marriage right away, but Matthew put on the brakes. He was about to deploy again to India, and he wanted to postpone their marriage until they could have a proper honeymoon together. Elizabeth agreed that they should wait until he returned.

"But I didn't know what I would do in the meantime," she told me. "I only knew I didn't much want to stay in Vero Beach."

Elizabeth suggested to Matthew that she had always wanted to go to Hollywood and see if she could get in movies.

"Most men would've said, 'No way!' Too many opportunities to meet someone else. But Matthew said, 'Yeah, why don't you give it a try? I'll pay for your train fare to get there.' How's that for a great guy, Joanie?"

I shook my head in awe. "Amazing."

"So that's how I got here. I found a couple of shitty jobs waiting tables—the owners always want to get in your pants for the privilege of having a job. But then I ran into Mark Hansen and got this job at the Florentine Gardens. He's been a peach. I wrote Matthew at his military post office box and gave him this address. I wrote him every day, and he answered as often as he could."

She paused and looked sadly into the distance.

"That's the good part of the story. There were several weeks that I didn't get any letters back. Naturally I started to worry that something had happened to him, then after a month I got an envelope in his handwriting, and, boy, did I breathe a sigh of relief. In the letter, he told me he was in the hospital. He couldn't go into much detail, but his plane had been hit by enemy fire. He made it back to his home field but crash landed. He had been hospitalized, but he was healing fast. At the end, he said he was coming to the end of his hitch and wanted us to be officially engaged. Soon as he got home, we were going to be married." She held up her finger with the engagement ring on it. "This was in the envelope."

Her eyes filled with tears; she held them back as best she could. "We exchanged more letters. I still have them tied up in a red ribbon. When he got out of the hospital, he went right back to flying missions. His last letter said he was about to fly his final mission. It was." She burst into tears. "His sister called me a week later and said he had been killed." She raised her hand to her lips and kissed the ring. She whispered, "Matthew. Major Matthew Gordon." She looked at me with red eyes full of pain. "He was my one true love."

I was quiet as my mother and I drove home. It is either my curse or my blessing that I involuntarily ingest others' emotions like they were viruses. I see things through others' eyes and experience their moods, feelings, pleasures, depressions, anger, and vulnerabilities as if they were mine.

Beth's joyful discovery of happiness in love, and then of grief through the tragedy of Matthew's death had infected me with an inexplicable sense of dread. And guilt.

My mother broke the silence. "Are you thinking of Beth?"

"Yes. Why must people experience such terrible things?"

"I don't know, Jo. Life throws things at you. You either dodge them, run from them, or fight them head on. Sometimes you can choose.

Sometimes you can't. You can only keep moving or die. And try to be brave."

I thought guiltily about my secret of the hundred-dollar hand job at the beach. My shame was compounded by my cowardice over telling my mother. It was so strong that I thought I might tell her now.

"Are you brave, Mother?"

"No."

"Me either."

She looked at me. "I don't know about that."

But I didn't tell her.

***

Two weeks before Christmas, we were told that the NTG show was closing. There would be one more show on the Florentine Gardens set before the holiday. I had already realized that I had taken being the little flower girl about as far as it would go.

I was looking at myself in a dressing room mirror, removing my makeup. I was glad to get the horrible stuff off my face. And I was happy to know that I would only have to wear it for one more show.

I looked up in the mirror, and there was the reflection of Elizabeth standing next to me, white porcelain skin, black pompadour, flower in her hair, and icy blue eyes.

"Beth!"

"Hi, Joanie."

"I'm so glad to see you, Beth. It's been since Thanksgiving."

"And bending your ear with my big boo-hoo fest."

"You didn't bend my ear. You needed somebody to talk to. I'm glad it was me. Have you been busy?"

"Busier than three people. I'm working double shifts. The tips are huge this time of year. So, I'm saving every penny. I'm going to make some changes. What've you been up to?"

I sighed. "Little Joanie the Flower Girl once a week. School and studying. I—I guess I'm doing okay."

Elizabeth frowned. "'I guess' means you're not doing okay. Want to tell me what's going on?"

I really needed someone to talk to. I looked around to make sure no one was listening.

"I'm feeling really guilty about something, Beth. I did something bad that I shouldn't have done. Promise you won't tell anyone."

We huddled in a corner while I explained the blind date that NTG had set up for me with Henry. She shook her head in disbelief until I got to the part where Henry offered me money for a hand job. She started giggling when I told her the details of negotiating the payment from thirty-five to one hundred dollars. The giggling got louder when I told her about wiping his own semen on his face and running away up the beach. And about how he ran after me with his pants tangled around his ankles, how he stumbled in the sand and fell, and the hilarious sight of him driving away covered with sand and semen. By the time I finished my story, Elizabeth was doubled over laughing out loud.

I felt a little bit miffed that she found the whole humiliating scene so funny.

"Oh, Joanie, don't be mad. I'm not laughing at you. You did good! You talked this creep up to one hundred dollars! He deserved everything he got—and a good ass kicking to boot."

"I've been afraid to tell my mom. I'm so ashamed."

Elizabeth patted my hand. "Don't be. You couldn't know what a creep-ass freak like that would do when you put up a fight. You kept yourself safe. That's the main thing. But don't tell your mother, at least not yet. It'll serve no purpose for her to know. I'm certain you won't do that again. And don't worry, your secret's safe with me."

She crossed her heart.

"Oh, Beth, thank you." I wiped the tears from my eyes and gave her a hug.

"Don't mention it, Joanie. Now, I've got a secret I'm dying to tell, and I need you to keep it. Can you do that?"

"Cross my heart."

"I'm saving all my money to go to Hawaii."

"Wow! How wonderful! I hear it's beautiful there."

"Shhh. Yes. I've finally decided to be realistic about becoming a movie star." She laughed. "It ain't gonna happen for me."

"Hey, Beth, don't give up so soon. You're so beautiful, someone is bound to give you a chance."

"Thanks for saying so, Joanie, but it's not 'so soon' for me. It's later than you think. All the ones that want to give me a chance also want to get fucked in return. Hollywood's full of skunks like the one NTG fixed you up with." She laughed out loud again. "You—I can't get over it—you handled that so perfectly. Anyone who can turn a losing situation like that around the way you did—you're going to be just fine in Hollywood, Joanie. You're smart and you can think on your feet. But me? I've played enough poker to know when it's time to fold my cards and walk away from the table. I wouldn't have had the presence of mind to do what you did."

She looked over her shoulder to make sure no one was nearby. "And I've got my reasons for going to the islands. Matthew is buried in Hawaii at a big military cemetery. His sister told me about it in a letter. I've decided to pull up stakes and make Hawaii my home. That was what Matthew and I planned to do when he got out of the service. Matthew had friends in Honolulu who were starting businesses. I'm going to take all the money I've earned here over the holidays—it's pretty substantial—and start a new life."

There was an earnestness in her eyes when she said it. I asked, "When are you going?"

"Right after the first of the year. I could take a cargo steamer delivering to the islands, but it's too slow. I found out you can buy a seat on a cargo plane going to Honolulu, so that's what I'm going to do. It's more money than a boat, but I don't want to waste any time. As soon as I get there, I'm going find Matthew's grave and spend the night there, if I can."

Her determined look faded. "I don't know what else to do, Joanie. I only know that Matthew was my one true love. With him gone, I need to fill the emptiness. Every bit of my life here reminds me of him. I'm going to make a new start."

"I understand," I said, embracing her. "You need to do what you need to do. My heart's with you, even though I'm sorry to be losing a friend."

"We'll always be friends, Joanie. We'll write letters. And I'll come back to visit. And when you get to be a big movie star, you'll come visit me, and we'll paint the town. Okay?"

"Okay, Beth." I rummaged in my purse and took out the wad of bills that Handjob Hank had given me. I pushed them into Beth's hands. "Here, you take this money to help."

"No, no, Joanie, I can't take your money."

"Yes, you can. This'll help us both. You'll have some extra dough to fall back on, and I'll get relief for my conscience. We both win!"

She folded up the money and put it in her purse. "I'll never forget this, Joanie. And I'll pay you back, so help me, as soon as I get a job over there."

We embraced again. "Don't worry about it. I'm giving to a good cause."

"I heard your show's been canceled," she said.

"Yeah. I can't say I'll miss wearing makeup that makes you look like Marley's Ghost. I may not see you before you leave, Beth, so please, please take care of yourself."

"I will, Joanie. I promise." She crossed her heart again.

***

I heard the loud *FLOP!* as the *Los Angeles Daily News* hit our front doorstep. It was a cold morning, January 15, 1947. I wrapped myself in my housecoat and took the paper into the kitchen. I poured a cup of coffee and unfolded the newspaper. The headline screamed: "Young LA Girl Slain; Body Slashed in Two." The photo on the front page showed police cars lined up next to a vacant lot on Coliseum Street, a group of detectives staring at something on the ground, and an arrow pointing to an indistinct white figure lying in the grass that might have been a department store mannequin.

The area was known as Leimert Park, a sparsely populated residential area, mostly vacant lots, notorious as a lover's lane. The police concluded that the girl had been murdered at a different location and the body had been dumped there. Police described it as a "sex fiend butcher murder [the] worst in the history of Los Angeles."

"Mother, look at this." I spread the front page on the kitchen table.

"Oh, my God," she muttered, "what a horrible thing."

My stomach churned as I read the description of the crime scene. The pretty, dark-haired girl had been found near 39th Street and Norton Avenue. Her body had been severed at the waist, the mutilated torso several feet from the lower body. Her mouth had been cut from ear to ear, one breast had been cut off, and the other severely mutilated. The lower body had also been mutilated and was lying spread eagled on the ground.

"Who would do such a thing?" Mom asked.

I shook my head. "Someone who really hated her. I wonder who she is."

The whole city was reeling. The murder was the only subject of conversation in barber shops and beauty salons, in diners and bars. The grisly details were the stuff of nightmares. I couldn't get them out of my mind.

The next morning, I felt a sense of dread when the paper arrived, knowing that the murder would still be front page news. But when I unfolded the paper, I wasn't prepared for what I read. The coroner's office had identified the victim. Her name was in the headline and there was a picture: dark hair, icy blue eyes, a flower tucked into her pompadour. She was smiling at the camera. Elizabeth Short.

At first, I couldn't make sense of it. I wadded up the paper and threw it on the floor. I screamed, "No! *No*!"

Mother came running from the kitchen. "Jo! What is it? What's wrong?"

By then I couldn't talk. I could only scream. "Elizabeth! Elizabeth was murdered! That picture of the girl cut in pieces—it was Elizabeth!" I collapsed on the floor sobbing uncontrollably.

Somehow my mother got me into my bed. I was thrashing and crying, and I couldn't stop. Mother was trying to sooth me, but I was so deeply in hysterics, I couldn't hear her voice.

Mother called our family doctor and explained the situation. He prescribed a sedative, but he was too busy to make a house call. She would have to pick it up at his office. She called my dad at work and told him it was an emergency and that he needed to pick up the drug at the doctor's office. He brought the sedative home, but when he tried to give it to me, I recoiled in terror. I was so blinded by fear that I didn't recognize my own father.

I was babbling over and over, "What if the killer saw me with her? What if he's coming after me too? I need to hide. Where can I hide?"

Finally, my mother cajoled me into taking the pill. Gradually my hysterics subsided enough that they could get me into their bed. Weeping softly, I drifted into a troubled sleep peopled by knife-wielding fiends.

When I woke, my mother was lying next to me, her eyes red from crying. I realized that it must have been difficult for her. Elizabeth was her friend too. And, like me, she was afraid for her own life. If the killer was someone we knew, he could very well have us in his sights now.

The Los Angeles papers went into a feeding frenzy over what they began calling "The Black Dahlia Case." Speculation ran wild about Elizabeth's private life—she was a prostitute, she had been killed by a jealous lover, she had been killed by a mob hit. I read those things about Elizabeth in disbelief. It was not the Elizabeth I knew.

After a few days, there was a new shocker: Mark Hansen, owner of the Florentine Gardens, was listed as a prime suspect by the LAPD. Some of Elizabeth's belongings were sent to the *Herald Examiner*'s offices by the killer, along with a note with letters cut from newspapers. Among her belongings was an address book with Mark Hansen's name embossed on the cover. The papers made much of the address book and of information that Elizabeth had stayed in one of Hansen's houses. Again, the innuendo of the newspaper articles was that Elizabeth had been a tramp, and because of that, she somehow got what she deserved. All of it infuriated me. Mark Hansen had been a good friend to my mother and me. We had many dinners at his house, and he had treated us like family. The shock that he might have been involved in Elizabeth's murder was unbelievable.

And yet....

The idea that Mark might have had something to do with it took hold of my mother and me. If it was true that Mark had murdered Elizabeth, then he could be stalking us as well. I refused to leave the house.

The case dragged on and on unsolved. The local newspapers all vied for readership by rewriting every morsel of evidence—no matter how far-fetched—speculating on who might be responsible for the murder.

Elizabeth's mother was cruelly tricked by reporters who told her that her daughter had won a beauty contest. Only after they had pumped her for personal details about Elizabeth did they reveal that she had been brutally murdered. The *LA Examiner* paid to bring her mother to LA to identify the body and to give the *Examiner* an exclusive on the story. It was not the LA press's finest hour.

When I finally ventured outside my house, I started going to Beverly Hills instead of Hollywood. I wouldn't go near the Florentine Gardens for fear of somehow attracting the attention of the murderer.

"Jo," my mother admonished, "keep your mouth shut about all this. Don't mention to anyone that Elizabeth was your friend or that you even knew her. Someone might mention it to the police. They'd call you in for questioning, then maybe me, and the next thing you know our faces will be plastered all over the front pages. We'll be targets. Say nothing to anyone."

I promised that I wouldn't. And for the next seventy-plus years I did not. My mother went to her grave without ever mentioning that she knew Elizabeth Short, Mark Hansen, NTG, or anyone else involved in the Florentine Gardens. If I mentioned it to her, she would only put her finger to her lips and say, "Shhhh!"

Coda

I married the band leader, Ray Anthony, in 1955, and we honeymooned in Honolulu, Hawaii. Ray had served there during the war and had always wanted to return. When we got married, he suggested we go there on our honeymoon. We took the big Pan Am flight—propeller then—with bunk beds in first class, where you could drink champagne and have gourmet food for the whole twelve-hour flight.

Honolulu and Waikiki were enchanted for me, another world, beautiful, fragrant, exotic, and romantic. Ray and I made full use of that romantic atmosphere, enjoying each other's warm embraces in a lovely suite at the Royal Hawaiian Hotel, with sliding glass doors that opened up to the warm tropical breezes just a few yards from the beach.

One afternoon, we were shopping in the international marketplace, wandering in and out of the stalls, tasting street food and buying nick-nacks. We turned a corner, and I stopped in my tracks. A girl was selling shrimp kabobs out of a stall, jet black hair teased up in a pompadour, a pink flower in her hair, bright red lipstick, and dreamy azure eyes.

The blood drained out of my face.

"My, God," I said under my breath.

"What is it?" Ray asked. "You're pale as a sheet. You look like you've seen a ghost."

That was exactly what I thought. I struggled to get control of myself. I was staring so hard, the girl looked up at me. She smiled. Then she looked less like Elizabeth.

"It's nothing," I said to Ray, "I just felt dizzy for a moment. I probably need some lunch."

He bought a couple of shrimp kabobs from the dark-haired girl, but I couldn't look at her anymore.

That night the image of Elizabeth wouldn't leave me—Elizabeth as she had been in life, and Elizabeth as she had been in death. I felt restless and haunted. After Ray went to sleep, I slipped out the sliding glass doors and walked down to the water's edge, still wearing the flower lei from the marketplace that afternoon. I sat on the sand, giving in to memory and melancholy.

Had Elizabeth lived to fulfill her dreams, she would be living here, perhaps sitting with me on the sand tonight. In her alternate future, she might have married one of the many successful American entrepreneurs who, rather than give up paradise, stayed behind to open hotels and restaurants and prosper in the inevitable tide of tourism to the islands. She would have found Matthew's grave and prayed there. Perhaps she could have put his memory to rest. But that future didn't happen for Elizabeth. The unspeakable had happened to her instead.

And so, I sat alone, smelling salt air and hearing the drumbeat of the surf, shedding a tear. I dried my eyes, remembering Elizabeth, my mother, and me huddled around a small table at the Florentine Gardens, gossiping and giggling, the two of them tipsy on wine, and me getting a contact high on milk.

I stood and walked into the surf, allowing it to tug gently at my feet. I took the lei from around my neck and pressed it to my lips, inhaling the fragrance of the ginger flowers. I tossed the lei into the surf and watched it drift on the tide in the moonlight. A warm breeze caressed my face, and I knew that Elizabeth's spirit had seen and was smiling.

Chapter Three

Vic Damone

I took a couple more practice strokes with my backhand. It made a twinge in my right wrist, the one that had been so seriously bruised just a few years ago from baton twirling that I had to be hospitalized. I still babied the wrist a little, and it affected my backhand. But it was only my first official lesson.

"That's enough for today, Joanie," said Frank Feltrop, the Beverly Wilshire's tennis pro.

Feltrop had spotted me in the early morning a couple of days ago on the Beverly Wilshire's courts trying to teach myself tennis. When he approached me that morning, I thought he would tell me the courts were for guests only and run me off. Instead, he gave me a once-over, smiled, and offered to give me lessons. Fan magazines were always showing movie stars playing tennis. As one who aspired in her every waking moment to be a movie star, learning the game seemed to my teenage mind like a good career move. So far, Frank Feltrop's only requirement had been that I allow him to put his arms around me from behind while he guided my backhand and forehand.

"You're a fast learner, Joanie—doing good! Come see me tomorrow."

"Okay!" I clapped my hands. "Thanks, Frank. I'm going to get a sandwich. I'm starved!"

I found a table by the pool and ordered a ham sandwich and a chocolate malt.

It was 1947, the war had been over for a couple of years, and LA was booming. Wartime restrictions were being lifted, veterans were coming home, and movies were being made. I was a few months shy of my sixteenth birthday. After the rationing and anxiety of being at war, LA felt newly alive with an air of possibilities. My determination to get into movies was alive and growing too.

I hungrily took a bite of my ham sandwich, and a shadow fell across my table. A man's voice said, "That backhand of yours looks good."

It was a youngish baritone, softly modulated, inviting.

I wondered momentarily if he meant my back*hand* or my back*side*. Squinting into the afternoon sun with a mouthful of sandwich, I said, "Thanks." I could barely make out his face silhouetted against the bright sun. "It's only my first lesson."

"If you're having lunch alone, would it be all right if I joined you? What's your name?"

"I'm Joanie…." I shielded my eyes, and I could see that he was really handsome. And I knew that face. "And it's very all right." He pulled up a chair and sat. I said, "I've seen you before. Are you who I think you are?"

He shrugged. "Yeah, I confess. I'm Jack Benny."

I laughed. "Oh, stop it! Not him! Seriously, who are—no, wait a second, you're Vic Damone, aren't you?"

"Bullseye, Joanie."

"I've got your records. You have a wonderful voice. My favorite's 'Begin the Beguine.'"

"Thank you. That's one of my favorites too." The waiter came and took Vic's order. "So, are you a guest at the hotel, Joanie?"

Vic was just a few years older than me, younger-looking than his pictures on the record sleeves. He was dressed in a dapper blazer and slacks, his shirt open at the neck. He smiled easily and was very charming. I was feeling a little swoony.

"No, I'm just here for my tennis lesson. And a dip in the pool after lunch. My bathing suit's underneath my tennis clothes."

"You know, Joanie, if you're not in movies, you should be. You're a very beautiful girl, if you don't mind my saying so."

Score one for the guy in the blazer. "I don't mind at all." I digested the compliment for a moment along with my ham sandwich. "Do you live in Los Angeles, Vic?"

"I live here now. I grew up in Brooklyn. When I signed my recording contract with Mercury Records, they thought it would be a good idea for me to live in LA to be close to the opportunities in the movie business. My favorite singer is Frank Sinatra, and the movies worked out pretty well for him."

"Oh, I want to be singer too. My idol is Lena Horne. I try to do everything like her."

"Are you from LA, Joanie?"

"South Dakota. We came out here when the war started. I'm glad to be far away from there. Terrible winters! Do you live here at the Wilshire?"

"No, no, I have an apartment over near the Sunset Towers. I come here because it's a pleasant place to have lunch."

We finished our lunches, and Vic picked up my check. "I'd better let you get your swim. I'd really like to see you again, Joanie. Could I have your number?"

"Sure." I wrote it on a napkin and pushed it across the table. "Don't lose it, Vic."

I was so excited, I skipped my swim. I hopped in my dad's old Ford—which I kept hidden discretely around the corner from the Beverly Wilshire—and hurried home.

I burst through the front door of our rented flat on Harvard Boulevard. "Mother! Mother! Guess what happened?"

She hurried out of the kitchen. "What's going on, Jo?"

My mom was a stunner. She never allowed me to call her "mom," only "mother." She was always seductively dressed for my dad when he got home from work. Today's outfit was a tight red sweater over black-and-white checked slacks and tall wedges. Her dyed black hair was swept up in a huge pompadour, some of it cascading over her shoulders. She wore bright red lipstick, accented by sharply drawn Joan Crawford eyebrows and dangling earrings. Mother fancied herself a glamorous leading lady. She worshiped Hedy Lamarr, Joan Bennett, and, most of all, Joan Crawford. She even named me "Joan" after Crawford. Mom never allowed herself to be seen outside the house without full makeup and a perfect hairdo.

She always told me, "Be dressed up and sexy, and have dinner on the table when your husband comes home." She would waggle her finger at me and add, "That's how you keep a man." I would always nod in agreement, but the truth was I had no interest in even getting a husband, much less keeping one. Being married and settling down to have babies and raise a family was nowhere on my horizon. Becoming a movie star was my only goal.

"Well," I went on excitedly, "I was having lunch at the Beverly Wilshire after my tennis lesson, and who came over to my table and asked me to join him? Vic Damone."

"Really? Vic Damone? That's amazing." She turned and headed back to the kitchen. "Come tell me all about it while I finish your daddy's dinner."

The aroma of a roast in the oven was wafting out of the kitchen, spinach was steaming on the stovetop, and a lime Jell-O fruit salad in dessert dishes was waiting on the counter. My father would be home from his job as a mechanic in a little while, and he'd be hungry and ready for a drink and supper. I gave her the details about my meeting with Vic while she prepared dinner.

"So, he's going to call you?" she asked. There was a hint of skepticism in her voice.

"Well, he said he would," I answered defensively. Mother took the roast out of the oven and gave me a doubtful look.

When two days passed and Vic had still not called me, I began to think my mother's skepticism was justified. She was unsophisticated in many ways, but her intuitive understanding of men and their motives was on target more times than I liked to admit.

And then the phone rang. Mother answered it and handed the receiver to me smiling. She mouthed the words, "It's Vic."

I took the phone and tried not to sound too eager. "Hi, Vic."

"Hi, Joanie, how've you been? Would you like to have dinner tomorrow night?"

"Yes, sure. Tomorrow night's great."

"It's a date then. But I don't know where you live." I gave him my address. "Got it! Pick you up at 7:00?"

"Okay! See you."

I was so excited that I barely slept that night. I spent the next day trying on my mother's sexy dresses until I found a black one that had the right combination of sexy and sophistication. My favorite green high heels and a flower in my hair completed the outfit. I was dressed, lipsticked, and perfumed when Vic arrived promptly at 7:00 in a new pale-yellow Buick convertible. I met him at the front door and introduced him to my mother. As we walked out, she said, "Have a good time, you two."

Vic held the car door for me and asked if I wanted the top up. It was a warm evening just after sunset. "No," I said, "it's a beautiful night."

"Yes, it is," Vic said, "and so are you."

Vic left the top down, and we pulled away from the curb. "I made a reservation for us at Sugie's Tropics in Beverly Hills. Have you been there?"

"No, but I've always wanted to go."

"You're going to love it."

Sugie's Tropics was one of the granddaddies of LA's Polynesian restaurants. The Seven Seas, Don the Beachcomber, and The Tonga Hut, along with Sugie's Tropics, all inspired the post-war Tiki craze. Tiki-themed restaurants and bars would eventually spring up all over the country.

The Tropics was created and owned by an Englishman named Harry Sugarman. "Sugie," as he liked to be known, was also the manager of Grauman's Chinese Theatre. He enticed his many contacts in the movie industry to visit his restaurant with on-the-house dinners and drinks. It became an LA hotspot where you might catch Cary Grant or Joan Crawford sipping cocktails with little umbrellas in them. He named exotic rum drinks after movie stars to entice the public to come in and rub shoulders with the stars. It was a place I definitely wanted to visit.

A sarong-clad hostess ushered us through the curtained dining room entrance. It was darkly romantic, the air redolent of incense, flowers, and rum drinks. Fountains gurgled in the background, and Hawaiian music played softly. Tropical plants and flowers created a jungle mood beneath twinkling lights in a starry nighttime sky. Several times a night tropical rains accompanied by thunder sound effects pattered on a faux roof near the dance floor.

The tables and chairs were bamboo and wicker. Vic and I sat at a table enclosed by a large, circular bamboo canopy, creating an intimate feeling of seclusion, as though dinner was being served in our own private jungle hut.

We studied the menu of celebrity-named drinks for a couple of minutes.

"Who's your favorite star, Joanie?"

I ordered a Dorothy Lamour Sarong. The waitress wrote it down, unconcerned that I was obviously under drinking age. Vic ordered an Ava Gardner for himself and a *pu pu* appetizer platter. When the platter arrived, I realized I was really hungry. I dug into the fried wontons and egg rolls while we sipped our drinks. Vic did most of the talking. Pretty soon we agreed that the *pu pu* platter required another round of drinks.

Vic ordered the house special, curried chicken, and I ordered a rare New York steak. Our dinners came, and we chatted about our favorite movie stars and their movies while we ate. I tried a bite of Vic's curry and a forkful of the fruity relish.

"Hey, what's that?" I asked as I chewed.

Vic grinned. "Chutney. Never had it before?"

"No. Never had curry either. Yum!"

The curry and the chutney and the steak combined with the effects of my second Dorothy Lamour Sarong to make me warm and comfortable. It was a night of discovery—not just curry and chutney and potent rum drinks—but the Hollywood of fan magazines and gossip columnists that had always seemed just out of my reach. Tonight, it was all around me.

As we were finishing our dinners, the hostess came to the table and delivered a written note to Vic. He read it and smiled. "It's from Joe Pasternak at MGM. Joe and some of the other MGM bigwigs and stars are having a dinner party in the Chinese Buddha private dining room. He must have seen us come in. He invited us to come say hello. Are you game?"

"You bet!"

The rum from those two Sarongs hit me when I got out of my seat. I wavered a little and Vic steadied me. "Wooowee! I'm feeling those drinks."

"Yeah," Vic said with a chuckle. "They've got some authority. I'll give you a hand."

Vic guided me through the tropical shrubbery and flickering tiki torches. He held open the bamboo Chinese Buddha Room door and whispered, "Everybody who is anybody at MGM is in here."

The room was thick with a blue haze of cigarette smoke. The walls and ceiling were covered with bamboo mats. An intricate bamboo chandelier hung over a long rectangular table crowded with chattering people.

I looked down the table and my eyes got wide. My brain started doing somersaults. My thoughts were racing: *Holy shit, that's Ava Gardner and Lana Turner. And there's Esther Williams and Van Johnson.*

Everyone was talking at once, and you could barely make out the conversations. Louis B. Mayer was holding court at the head of the table, complaining to one of the executives about the sex scenes in *The Postman Always Rings Twice*. "The Hayes office was on the set for every goddamn scene with Lana and Garfield. And it didn't help that the two of them couldn't keep their hands off each other. Every time you turned around, they were sneaking off to go fuck."

Joe Pasternak was seated next to him in animated conversation with Esther Williams. "I'm telling you, Esther, we've got a beautiful set with your pool and gorgeous choreographed numbers planned. This next one could be your greatest movie." I knew from the fan magazines that Pasternak had recently produced Esther Williams's most successful movie, *Thrill of a Romance,* that costarred Van Johnson.

Vic was introducing me around the table as people greeted him. Van Johnson and Walter Pidgeon looked up from their conversation to say hello to me. Pidgeon raised an appraising eyebrow when he shook my hand.

What do I say to Van Johnson? Geez, I wish I could clear the cobwebs from those rum drinks.

I recognized Kathryn Grayson leaning close while Peter Lawford whispered an off-color joke in her ear. She burst into delighted laughter at the punchline, covered her mouth, and blushed.

Lana Turner and Ava Gardner were bantering back and forth, trading gossip, sipping whiskey, and smoking cigarettes. They stopped long enough to acknowledge me with handshakes.

"Aren't you a pretty one?" Lana said, smiling. Ava winked slyly. "You'll have no trouble getting noticed in this town, darling."

Joe Pasternak rose from his chair and took Vic by the arm. "Ladies and gentlemen, if you haven't met Vic Damone, it's high time you did. This young man possesses a superb singing voice and budding acting talent. You might be saying hello to MGM's next musical star."

The group applauded and cheered. A few gathered around and shook Vic's hand. Others waved and blew kisses from their seats. Ava Gardner paid particular attention to Vic. She tapped Lana Turner on the arm and whispered something to her. Lana smiled and nodded.

I could have stayed all night basking happily in the attention of so many big-screen faces. There must have been gossip being made as some wondered about the identity of this very young blonde on Vic's arm.

We stayed for perhaps fifteen minutes before Vic made our excuses. We slipped out the door to a chorus of well-wishing.

We returned to our table and ordered Kahlua and coffee.

"Whew! Was that an experience?" Vic said.

"Oh my God, you're not kidding." My head was still spinning from the rum and the heady atmosphere of smoke and movie stars within arm's reach. "I've never seen so many stars—and they were so nice. It was fun! And you! He said you were in line for an MGM musical. That's really something!"

"Yeah, Pasternak has had his eye on me for a musical. He's the chief architect of all those MGM hit musicals."

"Oh, you'd be fantastic in one!"

Vic grinned. "Let's hope Joe keeps seeing it that way."

We finished our coffees, and Vic paid the check. "Why don't we get out of here, Joanie? Would you like to see my new apartment?"

The night had turned chilly. We got into Vic's convertible, and I asked him to put the top up. After a minute or two, it was cozy and warm inside. I slid across the seat, and Vic put his arm around me.

"What do you want to do with your life, Joanie?" he asked as he drove.

I didn't hesitate. "I want to be a singer and an actress."

Vic smiled. "Let me hear you sing something."

I launched into a couple of lines of "That Old Feeling."

"Not bad at all," Vic said kindly. "Listen, let me show you how you might do it."

Vic sang "That Old Feeling" as I'd never heard it. His seemingly effortless baritone mined every nuance, coaxed every feeling from the lyrics. It sounded like a different song from the one I sang.

"Beautiful," I said, a bit chagrined. "I've got a lot to learn."

"It takes time and practice. Either you sing the song, or the song sings you. But I've got a feeling you're going to learn it real fast."

I snuggled closer to him. I had never felt this way. I was still tipsy from the drinks, but most of all I was high on everything I'd seen and heard tonight. My desire to become a movie star had never been stronger. Moreover, the desire I was feeling for this man next to me was new in my experience. If a meteor struck and ended the world right then, I would have perished at the happiest moment of my life.

When we reached Vic's apartment, I was still loopy and in love. Vic gently took my arm and steadied me as we walked into the foyer. The apartment had been decorated by someone with taste and a sense of what the home of a rising musical star ought to look like. It also echoed an appreciation of the right ambiance for a successful bachelor's pad. Vic ushered me through the living room into a well-equipped kitchen. "I like to cook," he said. "I'll make dinner for you sometime. C'mon, I want to show you something else."

He guided me down a hallway past a cozy den and into his bedroom. It was large enough to accommodate a king-sized bed with room to spare. An enormous closet dominated an entire wall. Vic opened the sliding doors to reveal neat rows of color coordinated suits, matching shirts and ties, and an orderly queue of shoes—dress, sport, and casual—shined and waiting their turn. Vic grinned. "I like nice suits."

There was a hint of childish delight in his voice. I understood. He had grown up with next to nothing in his Brooklyn childhood. I remembered my grandparents' South Dakota farm with an outhouse and a wood-fired kitchen stove. And I remembered my parents' struggles to keep food on the table when I went to live with them in Sioux City, Iowa, and later in World War II Los Angeles. I was more familiar than I liked to admit with what growing up with nothing felt like. That closet full of tailored suits and custom shirts was more than just having an outfit for every occasion—it was a symbol of having made it out of the old neighborhood.

He motioned to the bedroom door. "Let's go sit in the den and talk."

I admit to a flash of disappointment at leaving that big bed behind. Some women will tell you that they make the decision of whether or not to go to bed with a man long before they walk out the door on a date. I'd never really considered it. I had approached dates with boys close to my own age with a certain uneasiness, knowing that I would spend most of the night grappling with inquisitive hands on my breasts and a barrage of lipstick smearing kisses. I damn sure wasn't anxious to expand their mauling into having sex. Well, usually. But no matter how hot and heavy the situation became, I never gave in. But tonight, in the afterglow of a romantic dinner and the excitement of meeting so many stars at the MGM party, I felt so relaxed and cared for with Vic—this was different.

The den was decorated in warm colors and softly lit. In my mellow state, it felt wonderfully inviting. A long sofa and two easy chairs faced the mirrored wet bar and record player. In one corner near the bar was a shiny baby grand piano and a conga drum, snare drum, and hi-hat cymbal.

Vic dimmed the lights and put on soft music. We sat close to each other on the sofa. As Vic slipped his arm around me and kissed me tenderly on the mouth, there was a loud knock at the front door. We both jumped.

"Vic? Hey, Vic!" said a loud voice. "Lemme in, Vic, it's me!"

"Damn!" Vic exclaimed, getting off the sofa. "That sounds like Mickey."

Vic went to the door. I sat up straight on the couch and smoothed my clothing. Vic opened the door and Mickey Rooney bounded into the hallway and made a beeline for the den. "C'mon, man, we gotta play some music. I just came from the Club Oasis, and I heard some hot stuff. Serious bebop! Dizzy and Charlie Parker jamming like crazy—Oh, sorry, I didn't know you had company."

Vic covered a look of consternation and smiled at Mickey. "It's okay, Mik. Meet Joanie Olander. Joanie, this is my neighbor, Mickey Rooney." Mickey extended his hand, and I shook it. "Pleased to meet you, Joanie."

I probably had a dumbfounded look on my face. After tonight's MGM party, suddenly meeting Mickey Rooney, one of MGM's highest-paid stars, seemed like some sort of cosmic fluke. The gods of Hollywood were smiling down on me tonight. "Pleasure to meet you, Mr. Rooney," I blurted out.

"Call me Mickey, please. I'm not that old!"

He strode across the room to the drums and cymbal. "Get on the piano, Vic. Gimme a solid boogie beat. Lotsa left-hand action, you know?"

Vic went to the piano and struck up a lively boogie beat. "Like that?"

"Yeah!" Mickey pounded out the rhythm on the conga. It was infectious. Vic picked out a melody with his right hand. I couldn't help tapping my feet. "Whaddya think, Joanie?" Mickey yelled across the room.

"I like it! I love it!"

I was transported. There was nothing in my memory that compared with this impromptu jam session. A man that I was sure I was in love with was at the piano improvising a melody, and a legendary movie star I had just met was banging out a pulsing beat on a conga drum nearly as big as he was. The whole scene was surreal. I don't know how long they kept playing, but when the music stopped, the silence was beyond belief.

Mickey stood up and gave Vic a sheepish grin. "Hey, I'd better be going. Thanks for the jam." Under his breath he said, "Sorry to interrupt."

"You bet, Mik," Vic said. "Good night."

Mickey waved in my direction as he closed the door behind him. "Nice meeting you, Joanie!"

Vic sat next to me on the sofa again and smiled apologetically. "Mickey sometimes comes over when he's having problems with his wife."

"That's okay. He seems very nice."

"He is. Some say he's a genius actor. Others say he's a pain in the ass. The fact is, he's dynamite at the box office." He slipped his arm around me. "Now, where were we?"

Vic leaned in and kissed me on the lips again. I responded and kissed him back. I felt spellbound. He pulled me closer, and we kissed more passionately. He slipped his tongue into my mouth, and I received it hungrily. My body felt like it was melting and trying to flood every pore of Vic's body. My breath was coming harder as he removed my blouse and bra and ran his hands over my breasts. He squeezed my nipples and sucked one. The sensation shot through my body like a lightning bolt, and I let out a surprised squeal. Suddenly, the moment was rushing headlong toward the outcome I had been fantasizing about all evening. I was losing control, but I didn't care. I eased onto my back, and Vic removed my dress and panties. My breath was coming in gasps as he removed his clothes and got on top of me. His cock was very hard, and I spread my legs so he could enter me. I winced when he tried. He stopped.

"Joanie, are you a—"

"A virgin. Yes."

Vic started to sit up. "Hey, I don't know. Are you sure you want to do this?"

This was a magical night, a night for breaking rules. It was a night ripe for abandoning good judgement. It was a night for testing the fire, for stepping off into space, for diving into deep waters. My mother's warnings echoed in my head. Briefly.

I pulled Vic down on top of me and kissed him. "Yes, I'm sure. I want you to be the first one. Just go slowly. Be gentle."

He hesitated a moment. "I will."

Vic carefully worked his way into me, unhurried but ardent. Deep in me, he moved in subtle ways to avoid pain for me, small movements triggering exquisite sensations. I was inexperienced but learning fast. Together we explored the expanding horizons of our desire, our bodies moving in unison. Our breathing became more rapid, matching in tempo and intensity. I could feel Vic's swollen cock pulsing inside me.

"I can't hold off much longer," he rasped.

I was teetering on the edge of my own orgasm—a deep, volcanic surge was rising to meet Vic's own climax.

"Please not inside me. I don't want to get pregnant."

"Mmm. Okay."

My orgasm broke over me like a giant wave. My emotions spilled over—love, ecstasy, passion, joy, warmth—scattering like fireflies in the dark.

Vic pulled out and ejaculated on my stomach. We collapsed in each other's arms in a languorous, sweaty heap. I slipped into a light slumber, half aware of Vic and the sofa, chasing after the fading ecstasy of our love making.

Vic got wash cloth and towel for me to clean up. He bent down and kissed me earnestly.

"You are truly amazing," he whispered.

***

I sat huddled near the passenger-side window as Vic drove me home. I was thinking clearly now, wondering how much I was going to tell my mother about tonight. I seldom kept secrets from her, but I was certain she would be angry once she heard the details of tonight with Vic. She had always been adamant about saving my virginity for my husband. Now it was more than just academic. I'd given myself to a man before marriage. But as I thought back on the night—the drinks and dinner, the MGM party, Mickey Rooney and Vic jamming, and our blissful interlude on Vic's sofa—it had ended the way I wanted it to. If there was any shame to be felt, it was washed away by my glorious orgasm.

"Hey, Joanie," Vic roused me from my reverie. "Come sit over here." I slid across the seat and nestled into his outstretched arm. "Are you warm enough?"

I felt comfortable, wanted, and secure. "I feel perfect."

When we arrived at my house, Vic walked me to the door. I could see a light on inside, so I knew my mother was waiting up for me.

"I can't tell you what a wonderful time I had, Vic. Everything was heavenly. Everything." Vic took me in his arms, and we kissed passionately under the porch light.

"I thought so too, Joanie. Good night." Vic turned and walked to his car. I opened the front door and went inside.

My mother came out of the back hallway. "How'd it go, Jo?"

"I had a great time, Mother. It was the best date I ever had."

She followed me into my bedroom, and I started undressing. I told her about our drinks and dinner at The Tropics and the surprise invitation to the MGM party. I ticked off the names of the stars I was introduced to and what they said that I could remember. Mom was impressed.

"Really? Lana Turner and Ava Gardner?"

"Lana said I was a 'pretty one,' and Ava said I'd have no trouble getting noticed in Hollywood."

I took off my panties and bra and put my pajamas on. I told mom about visiting Vic's apartment and the jam session with Mickey Rooney. When I mentioned going to Vic's apartment, I saw a shadow of concern pass over her face. The time had come to tell her the truth or let it slide past.

"You might as well know, Mother, I lost my virginity tonight to Vic."

There was a long silence. She retrieved my panties from the clothes hamper and looked at the tiny red dot of blood in them. "Yes, you did." She tossed the panties back in the hamper. "Jo, I've told you so many times not—"

"I know, Mother, I know. But it was so beautiful. It—"

"It always is beautiful… Well, not always… But it always seems like a good idea at the time."

"I just felt like—ready. He didn't let go inside me. He pulled out before he did."

"Well, at least that's good. Dammit, Jo, you could have gotten pregnant if he didn't."

I sat on the edge of my bed and started to cry. "Oh, Mother." I felt ashamed now. "He was such a gentleman—so considerate, so caring."

She sat on the bed next to me and handed me a tissue. "I'm sure he was, Jo. But he's a man—and men are not always what they pretend to be." Mom thought for a moment. "Jo, you can't see him again if you're going to do this. It'll only be a matter of time until you get pregnant. Then what happens to your dreams about getting in movies? You can forget those dreams when you're tied down to a child. No, when you see Vic again—if you see him again, you'll have to tell him no more sex."

"I really want to see him again."

"Then those are the terms: no more hanky-panky."

I moped around all the next day hoping Vic would call again. The phone rang twice and I dashed to answer it, but both were calls from friends of my parents. I went to bed that night sad and disappointed, feeling that I had been used.

Early the next morning, there was a knock on our front door. A florist was standing there with an enormous bouquet of two dozen red roses. "Mother!" I shouted as I brought them into the living room.

She gasped at the roses. "My God, Jo, what beautiful flowers. Who—"

"They're from Vic!" I exclaimed. I read the attached card aloud. "Dearest Joanie, thank you for a magical evening. I would love to take you out again. How about dinner tomorrow night at 7:00? I'll call you." I turned to my mother. "Can I go?"

"Tell Vic what I told you, and if he agrees, you can go."

Vic called me later that day. I explained my mother's reservations about my going out with him. I put it to him straight. "I can't see you anymore if that's what you expect from me."

"No, no, I don't expect that, Joanie. I want to see you because I really like you, okay?"

I nodded at my mother, and she nodded back.

"Okay. See you tomorrow night."

I went out with Vic the next night and several more times after that. I kept my promise to my mother, and we didn't have sex. We necked heavily, but we didn't have sex.

Coda

As Vic grew in popularity, his career took him to New York, London, Vegas, and everywhere in between. I got my contract at Universal, and my career took off too. We went our separate ways in pursuit of our professions, though we remained fond of each other through various marriages and long stretches of time when we didn't see each other. If our paths crossed and we were unencumbered by husbands or wives, we cheerfully broke my promise to my mother. Our reunions were always followed up by a huge bouquet of two dozen red roses.

The last time I saw Vic was in Chicago. I was appearing in a play at the Drury Lane Theatre, and Vic was playing at the posh Palmer House. When Vic called and invited me to see his show on my night off, I felt—as always—a tingle of anticipation.

When I arrived at the Palmer House, I discovered that my table was set on the stage. Vic played the whole show to me, while I watched with rapt attention. His velvety voice and flawless phrasing were as perfect as always. After singing his last song, he introduced me to the audience.

We embraced, and I kissed him warmly. The audience gave us a standing ovation.

We went to his suite later for cocktails and a late dinner. And then, with the passion and familiar delight that long-time lovers enjoy, we broke my promise to my mother one last time.

Vic continued his tour when his Palmer House gig ended. And after I closed at the Drury Lane, I went on to Vietnam.

Vic died at age eighty-nine in Miami, Florida. He will always have a special place in my heart. If there is a heaven where we can meet those we have cherished in life, the first one I'll look up is Vic Damone.

Peace, Vic. Until we meet again.

Chapter Four

Howard Hughes

"Play off everyone against each other so that you have more avenues of action open to you."
"Every man has his price, or a guy like me couldn't exist."
"I'm not a paranoid deranged millionaire. Goddammit, I'm a billionaire!"

—HOWARD HUGHES

FADE IN:

The Garden of Allah at night, an ancient-looking Spanish-style hotel set back off Sunset Boulevard, crouches behind tall trees and overgrown shrubbery as though it has something to hide. It does. The windows are dark but for an occasional flicker of a candle or a shaded night-light. Listening closely, you may hear past echoes of ecstasy, hilarity, gleeful intoxication, and, on occasion, delirium. On certain nights, this charming old ruin hosted the antics of the most debauched, decadent, and altogether depraved citizens of Hollywood.

Originally built in 1913 as a private residence by real estate magnate, William H. Hay, it was purchased by Russian-born silent movie star, Alla Nazimova, in 1919. Nazimova, who was openly and flamboyantly bisexual, gave lavish parties at the Garden of Allah, attended by all the Hollywood elite of the day. However, the advent of "talkies" ended Nazimova's film career, thanks to her impenetrable Russian accent. No longer able to command extravagant salaries (as much as $13,000 a week in the 1920s—before income taxes!), she could not afford the sprawling estate. She converted it into a hotel in the late 1920s, with the addition of twenty-five secluded villas. She lived in Villa 24 until her death in 1945. In the flashy tradition of Nazimova, the Garden of Allah remained party central for Hollywood's in crowd.

Though it is quiet on this night, that does not mean there isn't a party going on. The swimming pool is shaped like the Black Sea, and if you look closely, there is a shapely young girl of sixteen in a skimpy bathing suit standing next to it.

The Black Sea looked dark and cold, and I shivered in the night air. It occurred to me that this was the wrong occasion to wear this daring new style of swimsuit called a "bikini." Maybe it was the newest thing in swimwear from Paris, but I might as well have been bare-assed in the evening chill. I cursed myself for not bringing a robe, or at least a towel. In fact, I cursed myself for being here at all tonight.

I had told my mother that I was working in a night shoot at the studios at RKO. As far as she knew, I was in a scene in which extras would get wet, and that it might go late into the night.

The pool lights snapped on, and I jumped.

"Okay, Joan," Howard Hughes said, "you can go in the water now. You know, this used to be the largest swimming pool in Los Angeles."

"The water looks dirty," I said between chattering teeth, "and it's cold."

"Get in the water and start swimming," he said with a hint of impatience, "and stop thinking about being cold."

I recalled the tradition of my South Dakota Swedish relatives, who took delight in a blistering hot sauna, before running outdoors and jumping into a snowbank. So, I probably wasn't *that* cold. I walked down the steps into the water. Brrrr.

There was a scraping sound as Hughes pulled a chair closer to the edge of the pool.

"Make sure you get your hair wet, Joan."

***

My history with Howard Hughes went back a few years. When I was fourteen years old, some older friends took me with them to El Mocambo, the hottest night spot in LA. (The world was much more *laissez-faire* then. In wartime LA, there was little enforcement of underage drinking laws. Even though I was as baby-faced as they come, I was seldom asked my age in bars or nightclubs. On this night, El Mocambo's *maître d'* looked the other way.)

El Mocambo was one of *the* places in Hollywood to rub shoulders with celebrities. Scattered around the elegant room that night were Lauren Bacall and Humphrey Bogart, Errol Flynn and Olivia de Havilland, George Raft, and Doris Duke. Doris was there for a specific reason: the piano player, Joe Castro.

Doris Duke had a long-running affair with Joe Castro. In addition to having swoon-worthy leading-man good looks—which, of course, Doris liked—Castro had another requirement of hers—an enormous penis. Doris was a size queen, for sure. Her second husband, Porfirio Rubirosa, was also said to be extravagantly hung. Doris showed up at El Mocambo on most nights, just to make sure Castro was behaving himself. It was said they had terrible fights because Joe had a habit of leaning back on the piano bench while playing, just to ensure that ladies ringside could see the bulge in his trousers.

My friends and I were sitting at a table near the front close to the musicians and got full benefit of Castro's personal floor show. My friends pointed out Doris at her VIP table along the side wall. She was steadily glaring in my direction.

A waiter approached our table and slid a folded, handwritten note in front of me. It read: *Howard Hughes would love to meet you. Write your phone number on this note.* It was signed, *Johnny Meyer.*

The waiter motioned to where the VIPs were sitting along the side wall. "From the gentleman in the striped tie."

My friends were impressed. Johnny Meyer, they told me, was Howard Hughes's right-hand man and number one flunky. He was known around town by the nickname, "Johnny-pick-up-the-check-Meyer." Because Hughes famously never carried any money, Meyer was the one who paid the tabs when Hughes went out. He was always on the lookout for new young girls for Hughes. Though I didn't realize it then, Johnny Meyer was also Hughes's pimp. I scribbled my number on the note and sent it back.

Early the next morning, Johnny Meyer called and said, "Howard Hughes would like for you to join him for breakfast. A car will pick you up in ten minutes."

As I wrote in *Playing the Field*, I met Hughes at the Paul Hesse photo studio that morning. We chatted for a while and then went next door to The Players restaurant and had breakfast. I met with Hughes several more times in the same circumstances. Eventually, he quit calling me, I think because I was just too young, even for an experienced pedophile like Hughes.

***

My mother had forbidden me to see Howard Hughes a few months before tonight's session at the Garden of Allah swimming pool. Three years after the El Mocambo night, Hughes spotted me when I won the Miss Palm Springs beauty contest and ordered the RKO casting director to get in touch with me. I met with Howard a couple of times once again at his unofficial office in the Paul Hesse photo studio. He hinted at movie roles in upcoming pictures. I was mad to get into movies. Naturally, I was interested.

When told him I was attending a Palm Springs Chamber of Commerce luncheon as part of my Miss Palm Springs duties, Howard offered to have his chauffeur drive my mother and me there. He would be staying at the Palm Springs Racquet Club at the same time and wanted to see me there.

My mother and I were staying at the Montecito Hotel that had sponsored me in the Miss Palm Springs contest. Because they were my sponsor, Mom and I got to stay for free. Soon after we arrived at the Montecito, Howard called and insisted that I come see him right away at the Racquet Club. My mother balked at letting me break my promise to appear at the Chamber of Commerce luncheon. Howard was furious and threatened to never see me again if I didn't do as he said. My mother stayed steadfast that I fulfill my obligation to the Chamber of Commerce instead of meeting Hughes. Hughes was so incensed that he refused to let us use the chauffeured car that brought us to Palm Springs. We were stranded and forced to take a bus back home to Los Angeles. Mother had no use for Howard Hughes after that.

"I don't want to get my head underwater. I never like to get my hair wet."

"It's important that I see you with your hair wet."

"Why?"

Howard Hughes was not accustomed to cheeky backtalk from the likes of me. There was a pause before he replied.

"I have something in mind for you, Joan. An important role if you look good when you're wet—especially with wet hair."

And as in nearly every encounter between unequals in the wonderland of Hollywood, it was all always about the movie role you *might* get, if you just do what you're told.

I ducked my head under the water and paddled around the pool. Howard watched from his chair, face concentrated, his lips compressed into a thin line. My arms and legs looked white and vulnerable in the pale glow. He never took his eyes off me. I couldn't hear him breathing, but he cleared his throat nervously several times.

"Can you swim on your back?"

I obliged by back-stroking across the pool. My breasts were very visible on the surface.

From the far side of the pool I said, "I'm cold. I want to get out now."

"Just a minute more. Swim across the pool again."

I swam across the narrow corner of the Black Sea and back to the poolside nearest Hughes. I lifted myself out of the water. He extended a hand and helped me out. There was no towel to dry myself. I shivered, staring at Howard, wondering what was next. He stared back, taking in my body in the tiny bikini. I shook the water out of my hair. Some of it sprayed Howard.

"I'm too fucking cold!" I turned and took off running back to his bungalow.

"Don't use that kind of language," I heard him say as I ran up the tree-lined path.

Inside the bungalow, I went straight for the shower, turned the water on blazing hot, scrubbed my body and washed my hair. I couldn't get over the idea that the pool water was dirty. When I finally got warm through and through, I shut off the water and toweled myself dry.

I stepped out of the bathroom in a cloud of steam, wrapped in a towel.

Hughes was lying in bed under the sheet, his arms and shoulders bare. He was naked.

"Why don't you lie down here, Joan?" He patted the sheet and smiled. "You are beautiful when your hair's wet."

I might have been young, but I recognized that this was the moment of truth. The thought flashed through my mind that Jean Harlow had most likely faced this same moment of truth with Howard Hughes. In all the talk about dreaming of Hollywood and becoming a movie star, this part always gets left out. Nobody tells you, "Go ahead, kid and follow that dream. Just remember, the day or night will come when you'll have to put out." When you get a little older, it's easier to say, "No, I won't do it." But when you're sixteen and on the outside looking in, and there are hundreds of girls lined up outside the studio gates wanting the same thing you want, and all you can think of everyday is being a star up there on that big screen—you'd be smart to realize it might be your only chance.

I hesitated a moment, wondering if Hughes and Jean had done it in this very bungalow. *No matter*, I thought, *if Jean could do it, so can I.*

"Howard, I think you should wear a rubber."

In answer, he lifted the sheet to show his erection sheathed in a condom.

I could clearly see that Howard had a number of burn scars on his body. There were scars on his face as well, which he covered with a scraggly beard. Not long before, Howard had been in a near fatal plane crash while testing a prototype military aircraft. The plane developed mechanical difficulties during the test flight and began losing altitude. Hughes was unable to return to his private airport in Culver City, and he made a crash landing in Beverly Hills. He was unconscious and trapped in the burning wreckage. He only survived because a marine home on leave managed to free him.

I had only experienced one penis before tonight, when I lost my virginity to Vic Damone. In my naivete, I had assumed that a man's physical size was related to the size of his penis. Hughes, however, was a tall man with a small penis.

I unwrapped the towel and exposed my breasts. Howard's eyes widened and he smiled.

"Sit next to me on the bed, Joan."

He caressed my breasts admiringly, then leaned toward me and suckled my nipples. My breathing quickened, and I got under the sheet. Howard rolled on top of me and entered gently. It had been eighteen months or so since I lost my virginity with Vic Damone, and I hadn't had sex with anyone. It was a tight fit, slightly painful. Howard was considerate that I was comfortable in our love-making, handling me carefully. I began to get into the mood. I moaned slightly, moving my hips. Howard answered my movement with gentle thrusting that soon became more ardent. Through raspy breathing he suddenly let out a loud groan. When I opened my eyes, his face was twisted into a passionate grimace. The reserved and controlling Howard Hughes usually seen by the world at large disappeared into a trancelike mask. A moment later he grunted, "Oh, yes! Yes!" he sighed heavily and had an orgasm. Sweating and breathing hard, he rolled onto his back.

I felt like a secret door had opened, and I had caught a glimpse of an unseen Howard Hughes. I was a little embarrassed and intrigued.

"Are you all right, Joan?" he asked. "I didn't hurt you?"

"Oh, no," I said, getting out of bed and putting on one of the hotel's bathrobes. "It was wonderful, Howard." I had not had an orgasm myself, but for his sake, I thought a white lie was in order.

He nodded and got out of bed and began getting dressed.

"I'm hungry," Howard said. "How about you?"

"I'm starved," I said honestly. "I worked up an appetite swimming in that pool."

"Good! Then tell me what you'd like, and I'll order it from the hotel's kitchen. They have just about anything you want."

I thought about what the most expensive dish on the menu might be. "Lobster?"

"Lobster it is. Drawn butter? Baked potato?"

"Umm, yes. Sour cream for the potato too and extra lemons for the lobster and iced tea."

"Very good. I'll have a steak and a baked potato."

Howard buttoned his shirt and tied the laces on his tennis shoes. He motioned me toward the living room and sat on the couch.

"Come sit, Joan." He patted the cushion next to him and I sat down. I made an effort to cover my frustration from not having an orgasm.

"You—are you a virgin? I noticed that you were quite, um, tight. I was concerned that I might hurt you."

"It was fine. A little bit of pain in the beginning, but it went away. I had sex only one time before tonight—about a year and a half ago, and none since."

"Who was it?"

"I'd rather not say."

"But only that one time?"

"Yes. I've gone out with quite a few guys, Howard, but I don't jump into bed with just anyone."

"That's good," he said. "And why aren't you in school?"

"I have home schooling."

"Really? Why home schooling? I would think it'd be more fun to go to classes with people your own age?"

I hesitated. The answer was a deep wound in my young life, one that I didn't want to open now. I had never told anyone outside of my mother and father. I took a deep breath.

In spite of myself, I said, "There was an…incident."

"Go ahead. What kind of incident?"

"I was thirteen when I started tenth grade at LA High School. Back in South Dakota, I started first grade at age four. It was a little country school, all the grades in the same room. The teacher was a cousin of my grandmother. I was living with my grandparents on their farm, and I guess they wanted me out from under foot as soon as possible, so they put me in school. I was pretty smart and my grades were good. I kept getting promoted to the next grade. When the war began and I came to Los Angeles with my parents, I started school two grades above my age."

"Thirteen's pretty young for a tenth grader," Howard put in.

"Yes, it made me kind of a loner. I had only one girlfriend. Anyway, one day I was having lunch by myself on the lawn when a group of boys came walking in my direction. They were seniors, eighteen or nineteen years old, maybe six or eight of them. I thought they would just pass me by, but they stopped and formed a circle around me. They picked me up and carried me to the other side of the lawn. I struggled to get free, but they held me tighter. When I started screaming 'Put me down! Put me down!' they laughed and tossed me up in the air. The louder I screamed, the harder they laughed. They tossed me into the air again and again like a rag doll. They handled me roughly, and it hurt my arms and legs when they caught me. My whole life I've never liked wearing underpants… and I didn't wear any on that day. They smirked and whistled when my skirt flew up, and they saw my privates. I wasn't wearing a bra either. My breasts are larger than most of the girls my age, and they catcalled and squeezed them when they caught me. I don't really know how many times they threw me into the air. They finally stopped when the bell rang to end lunch period. They left me lying on the lawn, crying. When I looked around, there was not a soul in sight. It had all been in full view of other students and teachers outside at lunch time. No one came to my aid."

I was sobbing now. Howard handed me a clean, folded handkerchief. I dried my tears and blew my nose. I handed it back to him, but he grimaced and said, "Keep it."

"I was so bruised and sore, I could barely walk back to where I left my books. I made my way to the school nurse's office. I was crying so hard, I could hardly tell her what had happened. She called my mother at home. Mom called my dad, who left work and picked me up. He was furious and wanted to see the principal, but the nurse told him I needed to see a doctor right away. We drove to the only doctor we knew, who also knew we couldn't afford to pay him. He was flabbergasted when he examined me. I had bruises and lacerations on my arms, legs, butt, breasts—all over."

I stopped and began to cry again. Howard put his arm around me and patted my shoulder.

"You went through a terrible ordeal, Joan. I've never heard of such a thing. Did they punish the boys who did it?"

I shook my head. "Nothing. The school claimed they investigated but couldn't identify them. It was bullshit. LA High is full of rich kids. Their parents probably pulled the right strings to keep them out of trouble."

Howard nodded. "No doubt. So, the school did nothing for you?"

"I didn't go back to school because I was terribly bruised and sore. The doctor said I should have bed rest for a week or so to make sure I had no internal injuries. My mother called the school and read the riot act to the principal. They sent a nurse and someone from the principal's office to make sure I wasn't lying. When my mother brought them into my bedroom, their jaws dropped at how bad I looked. My mother said she was forbidding me to go back to school."

"Of course," Howard said, "for your own safety. Since these hoodlums got away with it once, what's to prevent them from doing it again?"

"So, the school administration provided a tutor to come to my home once a week and give me assignments. I think they felt like they got off lucky."

"They could have had a huge lawsuit over what happened to you, Joan."

"Yeah, but my folks didn't have the money to hire a lawyer. And the school knew it. They were more afraid of the rich parents of the boys who did it than they were of mine."

Howard growled, "I'd like to call that damn school and find out why nothing was ever done."

"Thanks for saying that, Howard, but too much time's past. Those guys are probably long gone, drafted, and sent off to fight. Besides, I really like school at home. It gives me time during the week to try to get into movies."

There was a knock at the door and room service brought in our food. I ate as much as I could to be polite, but I had lost my appetite. Recounting the story and reliving it all left my stomach churning. I felt as if it had just happened.

"It's late. I think I'd like to go home," I said when we finished dinner.

Howard showed me to the door and we embraced. We kissed in an offhanded way. "I'll be in touch," Howard said.

I threaded my way down the darkened path of the Garden of Allah. I got into my dad's Ford and leaned my forehead on the steering wheel. I wanted to cry, but I had spent my tears on my lunchtime disaster at LA High. Now I felt drained and exposed. And worst of all, used. I was now part of that multitude of stories about the casting couch.

So, how do you become a star in Hollywood? Get under a good producer and work your way up.

I felt guilty for going to bed with Howard, for going against my mother's wishes and violating her trust in me. How many more lies would I have to tell before I got what I wanted? As I drove home, I asked myself if this was the way I wanted to become a movie star. Tonight, the answer had clearly been that I would fuck for it. But there was a cold, sick knot in the pit of my stomach, signaling that my conscience was weighing in.

So, did I want to continue this? *Well, I'm in it now*, I told myself. *Let's not waste tonight's fuck. Let's see what the next move will be.*

I was learning a hard lesson about Hollywood's promise and threat: You may be allowed to reach the heights, but at the same time, you may be cursed to feel powerless and unprotected—and slightly sullied.

***

It was perhaps a week later that a call came from RKO's casting department. I was to show up at oh-dark-thirty and bring some sort of "cute" outfit for a costume. I had a part in a small movie called *Footlight Varieties*. I never actually knew what it was about, but, like thousands of actresses just starting out, if there was a paycheck, I was all in. Of course, I knew that this was payback for my night with Howard at the Garden of Allah, but I was on my way to, well, somewhere in the movies.

My scene was pretty simple: to sit in the back row of a movie theater necking with a young man. It was memorable only for the names of the people I was working with. I was making out with a young actor named Jack Paar. He was probably only in his twenties, but as we positioned ourselves in the movie seats, I couldn't help noticing the obvious line of his toupee. It was one of those things that, once you've seen it, you can't take your eyes off it. The director was an older man who hovered over us whispering encouragement. "Closer, closer. Make it sexy."

The director's name was D. W. Griffith, who had directed such greats as Gloria Swanson, Rudolph Valentino, Mary Pickford, and Douglas Fairbanks. Griffith had become a household name after directing the notorious *Birth of a Nation*, which celebrated the rebirth of the Ku Klux Klan. Directing shorts for RKO and Howard Hughes had to have been a comedown for a director with Griffith's pedigree, but it was likely that he needed the money, and Hughes gave him the job to help make ends meet. I did the best I could, but I'd never acted on camera before. We spent the entire afternoon on the scene.

I made other trips to the Garden of Allah at Howard's whim. Howard was a man ruled by his impulses and obsessions. We met a couple of times at the Paul Hesse photo studio, where I had met with him the first time. He kept an apartment hideaway for trysts with young girls at the Hesse studio. The format of our meetings was basically the same, minus the swim in the pool.

When Howard decided that I needed some new dresses, he sent me to a small dressmaker in Hollywood. She measured me, and I selected some materials. I love clothes, so an opportunity to have some custom-made frocks was very appealing. While I was there, the seamstress told me that she made dresses for all of Howard's girls.

"How many?" I asked.

She laughed, "Jesus, I have no idea. I wonder if Howard even knows. Quite a few."

She told me that Howard kept a bungalow at the Beverly Hills Hotel, as well as the Garden of Allah and the Paul Hesse photo studio. On the way home, I had to laugh. I guess the Beverly Hills Hotel was for girls who were of legal age. Underage girls like me had to be met at the Garden of Allah, or the Hesse studio, or secreted away in houses around town that Howard owned.

After one of our meetings, Howard said, "I've got a part for you in a movie I'm filming in Las Vegas. It's called *Jet Pilot.* I'm flying up there day after tomorrow, and you can go with me. You'll be playing a female Russian soldier, and you'll have a couple of lines."

I flew to Vegas with Howard in one of his airplanes. He had a copilot, and I sat in the back. By now my attitude toward Howard was very different. I cringed being in the same room with him. It was a relief to not have to talk. One of his old Chevy limos took us from the airport to the Last Frontier Hotel. Howard went his own way, and I went to my room. I never saw him again for the two days I was there.

Jet Pilot starred John Wayne and Janet Leigh. I was, of course, just a lowly extra. In those days, extras were the lowest life-form in movies. Because there was no transportation for any of the cast from the hotel to the location, I hitched a ride with Janet Leigh in her limo. Janet could not have been less happy to have a mere extra in her limo. Other than a cursory nod, there was no acknowledgement from her that I existed. She had the only star trailer at the airfield where we were shooting, and she was unmotivated to share it. I spent the day taking refuge from the dust and heat in the back of the limo.

Jet Pilot was directed by another Hollywood legend, Josef von Sternberg, whose many credits included directing Marlene Dietrich in *The Blue Angel.* He was credited with creating the glamorous, femme fatal image of Dietrich that Dietrich herself loved. Unfortunately, von Sternberg was unlikely to create a similar image with me. He treated me, and every other actor he came near, like dirt. My big moment in the movie is standing on a tower as airplanes fly past at low altitude, pointing and shouting, "Look!" He had me do multiple takes.

I flew back the following morning on a TWA plane with some of the other cast, including Janet Leigh, who studiously avoided contact with any of us.

I did a few small roles in other RKO movies, but the one I learned the most from was *His Kind of Woman,* starring Jane Russell and Robert Mitchum. The director was John Farrow, Mia Farrow's father. It really began my education in movie-making.

Much of the movie takes place in a nightclub in Mexico. We shot for almost two months on an enormous set that required three soundstages. As in all movies, there were long hours waiting for the next shot. I carefully observed the stars, especially Jane Russell and Robert Mitchum, as they worked in front of the camera. I learned what it meant to find your key light and to hit your marks. The profession of acting in movies is as much craft as it is art. The ones capable of combining both in harmony are the ones who create magic on the screen.

I nosed around the set whenever I could, peeking into everyone's job. Crews on movies are some of the hardest working people in the world. Much of what they do is exhausting donkey work. I always made it a point to talk to the grips and gaffers and Best Boys, scene carpenters and painters. They're the ones who can tell you what's what and who's doing who.

When my stint on *His Kind of Woman* ended, I had made a nice little pile of money. I was living rent free with my parents, and I saved enough to buy a car—the righthand drive Magic MG. I bought it from Humphrey Bogart.

I realized that my Howard Hughes relationship had gone as far as it could go. There was never going to be a starring role for me at RKO. Howard liked his girls to be young, dumb, obedient, and docile. I was too smart-assed, and I didn't take orders well. (I still don't!) So, when the call came one day with orders from Howard to show up that evening at the Garden of Allah, I said no. When the threat came from Howard's spokesman,

"Joan, if you don't show up, Howard will never see you again."

I said, "Okay, bye."

It was a relief to walk away from Howard Hughes. I learned a lot by just being around him, even if it was what not to do. His handling of people around him was often abrupt and unfeeling. His chief loyalty was only to himself. All the rest of us in his world were expendable.

But he had told me once that I needed to take acting classes, and I realized he was right. After I bought the Magic MG, I still had money left over for drama lessons. I signed up with a drama coach. It was time to get to work.

Coda

Not too many years later, the drama lessons paid off. Some lucky breaks went my way, and I got a contract at Universal Studios and a new name. I made my first movie, *The All American*, starring opposite Tony Curtis. *Look* magazine devoted a large part of an issue to the introduction of Mamie Van Doren. There were many photos of me at home, in my car—by then a Jaguar—and at the studio. Coincidentally, Howard Hughes appeared on the cover. The featured article in that issue was a profile of Howard.

One day the studio told me that Howard Hughes had called and wanted to see me. He was interested in a loan-out to have me appear in a picture he was making.

I dolled up in a striped sweater and a tight, white skirt. I admit I wanted to gloat a little. Our meeting was at the familiar Paul Hesse photo studio. I was shocked by the way Howard looked. He appeared to be unwell, thinner, and pale; his beard was longer, and his hair was grayer and in need of a trim. He sat in a chair the entire time.

His attitude toward me was very different from the days and nights at the Garden of Allah. He was very respectful and deferential—a kind of unspoken acknowledgement of how far I had come. The movie he had in mind for me was a romantic comedy titled *Susan Slept Here.* I wrote about our meeting in *Playing the Field*, but sufficient to say that I wasn't right for the role. The wayward husband, played by Dick Powell, was infatuated by my character, Susan, but ultimately returned to his wife, played by Anne Francis.

"But why would he go back to her, if he was in love with you?"

The bottom line: I wouldn't fit in the role that Debbie Reynolds ultimately played.

After that meeting, I never saw Howard again. He sold RKO and 20th Century Studios soon after, and he turned his attention to Las Vegas. He began buying hotels and changed Las Vegas from a mobster town to a family destination.

In the end, karma caught up with Howard Hughes. His wealth and influence allowed him to become a recluse. But addiction to drugs and declining health coupled with his increasingly debilitating obsessive-compulsive disorder brought him down. We'll probably never know the details of his final years or his death, but it seems certain that they were not peaceful.

When I drive to Los Angeles on the 405 Freeway, I pass under the Howard Hughes Freeway. I still cringe. And I roll down my window and shout,

"Fuck you, Howard!"

Chapter Five

John Dillinger—Lawrence Tierney

I was tingling all over as I walked out of the theater. I looked back at the marque that read simply: *Dillinger*. Beneath the title were the names of the stars: *Edmund Lowe* and *Anne Jeffreys*. Below them it read: *Introducing Lawrence Tierney as John Dillinger.*

My teenage hormones were working overtime. I already knew who Lawrence Tierney was. His name was often in the papers, getting into scrapes with the police for bar fights or being drunk and disorderly. But when I saw him on the screen as Dillinger, it was all over for me. I was in love, or, at the very least, in lust.

I mean, he was John-fucking-Dillinger! Growing up on the prairies of South Dakota, Dillinger had been in my life as a name—a bank robber in the headlines, a bogeyman in campfire stories, and a dashing Robin Hood figure who had out-foxed the cops, the G-men, and J. Edgar Hoover himself. Like Bonnie and Clyde, Dillinger's bank robberies were the stuff of legend—car chases, blazing Tommy guns, hideouts in remote farmhouses. On my grandparent's farm, we were always on the lookout for crooks on the lam. There were a couple of shotguns near the farmhouse door in case of trouble, though even as a youngster, I couldn't imagine they'd be very effective against a Thompson sub-machine gun.

I remembered that the real John Dillinger had visited our farm when I was three. I should have begged him to take me with him. A life on the run kidnapped by Robin Hood would have been preferable to the cold, dreary life of an unwanted grandchild on a South Dakota farm in the 1930s.

I took a happy little skip-step as I got to my car, the Magic MG.

I wonder, I thought, *if I could ever meet Lawrence Tierney.* I made up my mind as I started the car and drove away: *Lawrence Tierney had to meet me.*

So, I formulated a plan.

The next day, I drove over to Saks Fifth Avenue and used some of my savings to buy a gorgeous blue knit two-piece outfit. The skirt snuggly showed off my butt, and the top was tight, tight, tight, presenting my breasts to best advantage.

I hurried home and took a quick shower, put on my makeup, combed out my hair, and applied my favorite Apple Red lipstick. Very kissable. My mother's green shoes completed the ensemble. At first, the shoes were shocking with the blue knit, but the more I looked, the more I liked them. I gave the whole picture one last glance in the floor mirror by the front door.

Perfect.

I had done a lot of movie magazine research on Lawrence Tierney. He was a drinker, for sure. Story after story detailed his bar fights and rowdy behavior around Hollywood. A couple of magazines mentioned that he was known to hang out at the Tail o' the Cock, an upscale restaurant and bar on La Cienega Boulevard in Restaurant Row. That was all I needed to know.

I put the key in the ignition and pushed the starter button. The Magic MG came to life and purred. I slipped it in gear and took off. I had one more stop to make before my pursuit of John Dillinger could begin…eyelashes.

Everyone turned around when I dashed into the beauty salon. My favorite beautician looked up from her customer and said, "Hi, Joanie, I'll be done in a minute."

"Hurry, Dolly," I said, slipping into an empty chair. "I've got a heavy date and I'm running late."

"Gotcha!"

Fifteen minutes later, I emerged with the longest, darkest, most Jezebel-ish eyelashes you would ever want to see. I was loaded for bear… or at least for John Dillinger.

When I pulled up in front of the Tail o' the Cock, the parking attendant waved me into a space next to the front door. "Just leave it there, miss. I ain't drivin' one of them right handers."

"That's good. Thanks."

It was dark and chilly inside, all walnut paneling and red leather booths. Off to one side was the cocktail lounge and bar. It was well after the lunchtime drinking hours, and there were two men sitting at opposite ends of the bar. I put on my most mature face and attempted to look twenty-one. I perched on a stool at the middle of the bar. The bartender was a middle-aged man wearing a crisp white shirt and black vest.

"I can't serve you," he said before I could speak. "You're too young."

Dammit! I thought. *It's hard to disguise a baby face.*

"Right," I said. "Can I get an orange juice? Have you got any fresh ones you could squeeze?" I gave him my most innocent smile.

He smiled back. "Sure."

The customer at the left end of the bar got up and left. The one to my right was thoroughly engrossed in a glass of Scotch. The bartender brought my orange juice, and I took a sip. The man at the end of the bar turned in my direction and lit a cigarette. I froze. My hand started shaking, and I spilled my orange juice.

"Oh, shit! I'm sorry," I apologized to the bartender.

"Don't worry, miss. I'll get you another." He quickly wiped up the spilled juice.

I looked toward the man again. *Holy shit! It's John Dillinger.*

He grinned and said, "Hi there."

Hoping I had regained my composure, I gave him a vague, "Hi," and turned back to my orange juice. This is the way you play it: act disinterested. I stared at my reflection in the mirror behind the bar. He paid attention to his smoke and his Scotch. When he looked up again, he caught me staring at him in the mirror.

"Hey, why don't you come sit down here?"

I sipped my juice again.

"C'mon, slide down here next to me."

I got up and sat on the stool next to Lawrence Tierney. How many hunters bag their quarry on the first try?

"What's your name?"

"Joanie."

"I'm Larry. Pleased to meet you, Joanie. How old are you?"

"Twenty-two."

He guffawed. "Honey, if you're twenty-two, my ass is a typewriter."

I giggled. "Okay, seventeen."

Larry nodded and sipped his Scotch. "Well, at least we're getting closer." He peered closely at my face. "Are those your eyelashes?"

"Of course they are. I bought them and the beautician put them on me."

"Well, you sure got enough of 'em."

Just for good measure, I batted my lashes a couple times. "The movie magazines said you like to hang out here. Nice place."

"So that's how you found me? From a fucking movie mag? Jesus!

There's no such thing as privacy anymore, is there, Joanie?"

I nodded. "You're right."

Larry drained his glass and banged it on the bar. "You got a car, Joanie?"

"Yeah, I do."

"Then let's get outta here." He threw some money on the bar and made a beeline for the entrance. I jumped off the stool and followed. Outside he looked around. "Where's your car?"

I pointed to the Magic MG by the door. "Right there."

Larry looked at the car and back to me. "That's your car? Well, ain't that the cat's ass?"

"Get in," I said. He looked skeptically at the steering wheel and the left hand passenger seat. "Direct from merry old England, eh?" He walked around to the left side and opened the door.

"You can slide the seat back, Larry."

He worked the seat back as far as it would go, then carefully folded himself in. I got in when he was settled.

"You can actually drive this thing, right Baby Joanie?"

I pushed the starter button and the MG's little engine growled. I slipped it into first gear and roared away from the Tail o' the Cock.

"Damn right, Mr. Dillinger."

"Where are we going?" he asked over the wind noise.

"Why don't we go to the beach?"

"Sold!"

It was already late afternoon and the air was getting chilly. "I'm going to stop by my house and get a jacket and scarf. It'll be cold at the beach."

A few minutes later, I pulled up in front of our house. "Wait here, Larry, I'll just be a minute."

He nodded and reached for a cigarette. I hurried up the walk and through the front door. Mom stuck her head out of the kitchen.

"Hi, Jo."

"Hi, Mother. I just stopped to pick up a jacket. We're going to the beach and it's a little cold."

She peered out the front window. "Who's that in your car?"

"John Dillinger."

"Oh, c'mon, Jo, John Dillinger's been dead for years."

"Not *the* John Dillinger. He played Dillinger in the movie. It's Lawrence Tierney."

"Tierney? God, he's always getting into fights. I read about him in the papers all the time. How on Earth did you find him?"

"I ran into him in a restaurant. He's a really nice guy. We're just going for a drive, maybe down to the beach." I put on my jacket and slipped a scarf over my hair. I touched up my lips with Apple Red. "How do I look?"

My mom shook her head. "I'm not happy about this, Jo. And if your father knew, he wouldn't like it either. You can't just pick up with strangers."

"I just want to have some fun. You know how I am, Mother. He isn't really a stranger. He's a movie star. Everybody knows who he is. Nothing bad's going to happen."

Her voice sharpened. "Jo, remember what happened to Elizabeth Short."

My eyes suddenly filled with tears. "Oh, why did you bring that up?" I sobbed. The memory of the "Black Dahlia Murder" was still fresh.

"I'm sorry, Jo, I shouldn't have said it. But I worry about you every minute when you're out. I don't sleep until you get home." She put her hand on my shoulder. "It's okay. Dry your eyes and go have fun. For God's sake, just be careful."

I made some quick repairs to my eye makeup and new lashes.

"I will, Mother. Hey, it's just fun. You'd do the same thing." Our eyes locked for a moment, and we both began to giggle.

Of course she would.

"Get outta here, Jo. You can't keep John Dillinger waiting."

I dashed out the door and down the walk. Mom stood on the front stoop and watched. I got in and started the car. Larry looked at my mom and asked, "Who's that?"

"That's my mom."

"Damn! It runs in your family."

"What's that?"

"She's beautiful too." He waved at her. "Hi, Mom!"

I put the car in gear and pulled away.

We drove down Sunset Boulevard toward the beach. It was around twelve miles as the crow flies from my house to the beach, but it might be twenty miles if you take Sunset. Sunset Boulevard meanders across the brow of LA through canyons and bluffs, Beverly Hills, Holmby Hills, Westwood, UCLA, Brentwood, and Bel Air, sidesteps Pacific Palisades, and swoops down to the beach.

The sun was sinking fast now, and I wanted to see the glow. My body was tingling like it did the day I walked out of the Dillinger movie. It was a teenage itch that I needed to scratch. And thanks to my encounter with Hank the Yank, I knew just the place to do it. The special spot frequented by lovers at the junction of Sunset Boulevard and Pacific Coast Highway was secluded and shielded from Pacific Coast Highway by trees. I turned off PCH onto the short dirt track. I stopped near the trees and killed the engine.

"Here we are," I chirped.

Larry looked around. "Nice. You come here often?"

It was a pointed question. I shuddered at the memory of my first horrible experience here. "Not often."

"Sure is romantic," Larry admitted.

The sun was dipping into the ocean. The light morphed from brassy afternoon to soft evening shadows.

I fidgeted as we sat in silence. My tingle was growing by the minute. My itch was not getting scratched, and I was getting pissed.

Finally, I blurted out, "Aren't you even going to kiss me?"

Larry looked at me and sighed. "Look, Baby Joanie, you are young—very young and I'm not. If I get involved with you, and anyone finds out, I could get into serious trouble—doing time in a federal prison, serious trouble. My reputation in Hollywood is already on pretty shaky ground. Messing around with an underage girl could be a disaster."

I turned toward him. "But you don't have to worry. I would never tell anyone, not even my parents."

"Especially not even your parents."

"And right now I can't get pregnant. I just had my period."

"Oh, shit," Larry growled under his breath. He leaned over and kissed me hard on the lips.

"Now that's more like it!" I squealed. I kissed him back deeply. His breath smelled of scotch, but I was beyond caring.

I kicked my leg over the gearshift and straddled his lap. I hiked up my skirt and began grinding my hips. (*Nota bene*: I have never worn panties in my entire life, and if I could avoid it, then or now, I never wear a bra. That's as true today as it was that night.)

"What are you doing, you crazy little shit? I just told you—"

I kissed him big and deep again.

"You're going to make me explode in my pants!"

I pulled up my knit top to expose my breasts and reached down and unbuckled his belt. "We can't have that." He unzipped his pants, and his penis slipped out.

Holy shit, there's a big *similarity between John Dillinger and the actor who played him.*

It slid into my vagina effortlessly. And then we were out of control, headlong into what Larry had been protesting about, and what I had been scheming for. We fucked really hard for I don't know how long. It was probably only a few minutes, but it felt like a lifetime. As he neared an orgasm, his penis began to swell inside me. I moaned from the pain. Larry made grunting noises. We were gasping for breath as we climaxed.

We were both sweating, and I hung limply on Larry's neck. I wondered idly if anyone in the cars parked around the trees heard us.

"Dammit," Larry said ruefully, "that was not supposed to happen."

"But it did," I breathed in his ear.

"Hmm. Mind you, I'm not complaining."

We remained coupled for a few minutes, kissing, reluctant to separate. When I climbed off his lap and we tidied up, the night air off the ocean made me shiver. Larry helped me put up the MG's top and snap the side curtains into place. We got in, and I started the engine to warm up the heater. We wrapped ourselves in the blanket I kept behind the seats until it got warm in the car. We stared silently out over the ocean at the distant lights of ships, lost in thought, sharing the afterglow of our love making.

"Where do you think they're going, the ships?" I asked.

"Everywhere," Larry mused. "Servicemen coming home. Cargo arriving. The whole world is passing by out there on the horizon."

"I'd love to be going someplace exotic on one of those ships. Would you?"

Larry patted my thigh. "With you, sure."

We kissed again, and I pulled back giggling. "I don't want to be a killjoy, Larry, but you're covered in my Apple Red lipstick."

He swiveled the rearview mirror and peered at his reflection. "Oh, fuck, what a mess," he said, wiping lipstick off his face. "I look like I've been in a knife fight."

"It's getting late," I said reluctantly, "I'd better drop you off and get home."

I didn't want to go home ever. I wanted to sit on this beach in the dark, making love with Larry, listening to the surf and watching ships on their way to my fantasies.

I put the MG in gear and threaded up the dirt track to Pacific Coast Highway. I turned onto Sunset Boulevard and drove us back. We spoke only occasionally on the drive to Larry's house. It had been a long, eventful, even bizarre day. It had ended in exactly the way I had fantasized it, but I was still coming to grips with it.

I stopped in front of Larry's house. He leaned over and kissed me deeply.

"This has really been something," he whispered.

"Sure has," I answered.

Larry shook his head. "I can't believe it, but I'm really crazy about you."

"Me too, about you."

Larry kissed me again and got out of the car. "I'll call you. 'Night."

"Good night, Mr. Dillinger."

"Aw, fuck John Dillinger, kid."

"I just did."

He chuckled, and I drove away.

The stardust began to wear off as I drove home. My vagina was aching from being stretched by Larry's sizable penis. We hadn't bothered to slow our passion and allow my near-virginal vaginal muscles to slowly stretch. Instead, our hunger for each other pushed all caution to the side. We dove in without second thoughts. But all that hormone-fueled joy was not without a cost. I was paying up.

My mom and dad were in bed when I got home. I ducked into the bathroom, took a hot shower and washed my hair, then filled the bathtub and soaked my sore and throbbing parts. The pain subsided, only to be replaced with misgivings.

Larry had said he would call me. I wondered if he actually would. There were plenty of reasons for an affair like this to quickly lose its momentum, not the least of which was the dangerous fact that I was underage. When he mentioned it, I dismissed his concerns. And judging from the outcome, so did he, at least temporarily. Next was the test of his courage or foolhardiness. And mine.

The phone rang the next day just before noon. The gruff voice on the other end was softly anxious.

"How're you feeing, Baby Joanie?"

"Sore." I quickly checked over my shoulder to make sure my mom was out of ear shot. "I'm really feeling the effects…down there, Larry."

"I'm sorry," Larry said, meaning it. "I'll be more careful. I promise. How about a burger and some Susie Qs at Dolores Drive-In tonight?"

"I'd love to, but if you're expecting another night like last night, the answer is no." I got what I wanted last night, but the aftermath was more painful than I had bargained for. Even my hormone-fueled teen brain was willing to concede that a grown man built like Larry might take more of a physical toll on my body. So, if Larry felt like he was entitled to a fuck every time we went out, then I would need to lay down some rules.

I lowered my voice to a whisper, "I enjoy doing it with you, Larry, but I can't walk around nursing sore privates. It looks kinda obvious."

"I understand, Joanie. I don't expect anything. I just like you a lot and want to see you again. Whaddaya say?"

On the set of The All American *in Jimmy Sears' arms, while Frank Gifford looks on. Tony Curtis was waiting on the bench. Summer 1953.*

On the set of my documentary, being made up by Katy McClintock, my dear friend, makeup artist, and wardrobe guru. June 2025.

On the beach with Lilimae. Spring 2018.

Decca Records anniversary party. L-R - Myrna Hansen; Piper Laurie; Milton Rachmil, owner of Decca and Universal Studios; me; unknown Miss Universe contestant. 1954.

Glamour shot by Alan Mercer. 2015.

Classic Mamie. 1957.

Vietnam. Posing with a helicopter pilot. These brave guys had my life in their hands on a daily basis. April-July 1971.

Glamour with a peppermint glove. 1956.

Photo contact sheet. Personal collection. 1966.

My mother, Lucille, with her giant pompadour, circa 1940s. She looked enough like Elizabeth Short (the tragic Black Dahlia) to be her sister. 1943.

Perry, age four, and me. 1960.

Makeup test. 1957.

Graham Hill, Formula 1 superstar. 1960s.

Ray Anthony playing while I sing. 1955.

In a boyfriend's Studebaker, adjusting my shoe. He took the picture without me knowing. 1946.

On camera with Julie Strain. A dear friend taken too soon. 2000.

Taking my bows onstage in Vietnam. April-July 1971.

On the farm in Rowena. My maternal grandmother holding me while my grandfather looks on. 1931.

At age six, still on my grandparents' farm, but excited to be wearing my new yellow party dress. I still have it in my closet. 1937.

Age eight and living with my parents in Sioux City, Iowa. 1939.

The Beaver Valley Lutheran Church, Brandon, South Dakota. Built by the Olander side of my family in 1837. My parents met on the church steps one Sunday morning in 1930.

Here I'm at twelve-years old on the lawn of our Harvard Blvd flat in LA. I was eleven when WWII started and we came to LA, my father looking for a better job, and me dreaming of being a movie star.

In front of the Harvard Blvd house, posing with my favorite tree, age thirteen. I grew from a girl of eleven to a woman of twenty-two while living there. 1944.

Another photo shoot with Julie Strain. Early 2000s.

A picture of mom and me in the backyard taken by my dad. We were often mistaken for sisters. 1970.

Me, mom, and cousin, Jean Shirley, taken by my dad. 1942.

The end of my joyride with cousin, Colleen, on Molly the plow horse. My grandfather and grandmother were very angry. Colleen got a scolding, but I got a switching for being an instigator.

With Perry at age six. 1962.

Toasting with Perry at the Beverly Hills Hotel Polo Lounge. 1960.

Three generations: Mom, me, Perry, and Ray. 1957.

Perry meeting me at the LA International Airport. 1957.

Buzz Aldrin and me at an Oscar party in the Crystal Room of the Beverly Hills Hotel. Early 2000s.

My mother would've had a fit if she'd heard our conversation. But, well….

"Pick you up at seven in the Magic MG?"

Larry chuckled. "I'll bring a jacket."

Dolores Drive-In quickly became an LA sensation after the war. It looked like a flying saucer parked on the corner of Wilshire and La Cienega. You could order hamburgers, Suzie Qs curly fries, a coke, a cherry-lime rickey, or a chocolate malt and eat in your car. Just pull into a parking spot and a waiter came to your car and took your order. A few minutes later, they brought your dinner on a tray.

I wheeled the MG off Wilshire and parked next to the building. A waiter in a white shirt and captain's cap hustled over and jotted our orders on his notepad. He disappeared inside, and Larry slipped a small flask out of his jacket pocket and held it out to me.

"Drink? Dewar's Scotch."

I wrinkled my nose and shook my head. "Tastes like medicine."

Larry nodded. "Against the cold night air." He took a quick swig and smacked his lips, then leaned over and gave me a Scotchy kiss.

We necked briefly, and I began to get that tingle. I pulled away. "Don't get me started. If I straddled you here at Dolores in front of God and everybody, people might spill their milkshakes."

"Fair enough. Why don't we go see a movie?"

We saw Larry's favorite actor, Humphrey Bogart, in *Casablanca*. I dropped Larry off at his apartment, we kissed goodnight, and I went home. Frustrated.

Larry and I saw each other frequently over the next six months. Our dating settled into a pattern of dinners, movies, occasional drinks at favorite bars, sundowns at the beach, and sex. I chose to ignore the sameness of our relationship. We were highly attuned to each other sexually, despite the difference in our ages—or perhaps because of it. And we loved being in each other's company. We had fun.

The only real flaw in my relationship with Larry was his drinking. My parents were fond of bar hopping on weekends, so being around inebriated people was not unknown to me. But I had never met anyone like Larry, who spent the day sipping at a flask of scotch to maintain a certain level of high. Most of the time it wasn't a problem, but on the ever-increasing occasions when Larry got blitzed, his temper would flare, and he'd become jealous if another man came near me.

One night, we were at a bustling little Mexican restaurant that had live music and good food. I did a couple of tequila shots, and the band got into a groove. I got on the tiny dance floor and began gyrating to the music. Pretty soon a good-looking young guy from the other end of the bar got up and began dancing with me. It's not my nature to flirt with a stranger when I'm with someone else, so I did my best to ignore him. But when I glanced over at Larry, he had his John Dillinger face on, glowering in my direction. Larry got out of his seat and headed toward the young man dancing with me.

"What the fuck do you think you're doing?" It was directed to the young man and me.

"What'd you say, pops?" the young guy taunted.

I didn't wait for an answer. I grabbed Larry by the arm and pulled him toward the door.

"What're you doing with that young punk? Lemme go, Joanie. I gonna beat the shit out of him."

"You do and you'll never see me again, Larry. I'm leaving."

I walked out the door and went to my MG in the parking lot. After a moment or two, Larry stormed out and made a beeline for me.

"I don't like it when you pay attention to somebody else," he barked.

"I couldn't help it that he came over and danced next to me. I didn't invite him."

"Well, you were damn sure dancing real sexy with him. That pisses me off."

"Get in the car, Larry. I'm taking you home to sleep it off."

"I'm not drunk."

"If you're not drunk, my ass is a typewriter."

He blinked at me boozily and grinned. "Nice one. You learn fast, Baby Joanie."

Larry immediately fell asleep in the passenger seat and dozed all the way to his apartment. While I drove, I kept turning over in my mind the things I was learning about him. Over the months we'd been dating, his behavior became more predictable. Like tonight, we were having a great time—we were consuming more than a few drinks, to be sure, and laughing at each other's jokes. Larry was gossiping about people in movies with me egging him on. But when a guy down the bar noticed me and decided to intrude on the good time we were having, trouble was unavoidable. I had barely managed to avert a brawl by convincing Larry it was time to go, but it could easily have gone the other way.

Most of Larry's altercations had occurred when I wasn't with him. Sometimes a guy recognized him as John Dillinger from the movie. If the guy was drunk enough, he'd want to prove he was tougher than the pseudo Dillinger. And if Larry was too oiled up to ignore him, he would take a swing and deck him. Occasionally, Larry would be obnoxiously drunk and pick a fight on his own. Even in spite of my teenage crush, I realized that if a drunken donnybrook erupted and the cops were called, I'd be involved too. Just the kind of publicity I didn't need if a movie studio was to be interested in me.

When we arrived, I tried to get him out of the passenger seat, but he was passed out and too heavy. Larry shared his apartment with his two brothers, Scott Brady, the actor; his younger brother, Edward; and his ailing mother. I rang the bell and Scott answered. He put Larry's arm over his shoulder and hauled him out of the MG and into the house. He lowered Larry onto the sofa.

"Thanks for bringing him home, Joanie."

"He nearly got in a fight over me. I managed to get him out before he worked up a full head of steam."

"He's lucky that you did. LAPD's lost their sense of humor about his fighting. One of these days they'll lock him up, or somebody'll kill him." He shook his head at Larry sprawled forlornly on the sofa. "I'll get him to bed. You go on home."

Driving back to Harvard Boulevard, I felt like it was time to face the facts about this romance. At that moment, I could've made a wise decision about my Dillingeresque affair with Larry. It would've certainly made my mother happy. She had been after me for months to stop seeing him.

"Mark my words, Jo," she said, wagging a finger, "he's trouble—maybe seriously nutty—and you could get pulled into a bad situation."

I only set my jaw and shrugged. I don't like to be told what to do. And I thought I could handle whatever might come along. So, instead of ringing up Larry and calling it quits, I called him and said, "Hey! Let's go to Las Vegas!"

I packed a few clothes and necessaries, including the big wool sock I kept silver dollars in for gambling. Back then you could still gamble with silver dollars instead of chips, and I loved the clink-chink sound they made. I only had eight or ten of them, but I kept them safely under the driver's-side seat.

I picked up Larry about 1100 at night, and we took off in the Magic MG, top down and radio blasting, bathed in the light of a full moon, tear-assing down Highway 91, a two-lane blacktop, bound for that place where wise decisions go to die. Las Vegas.

"I used to make this trip all the time—alone," I shouted to Larry over the wind noise. He was hunkered down trying unsuccessfully to light a cigarette.

"At night? Jesus, why?"

"Traffic. The road's deserted. There's nothing out here but jackrabbits and road runners this time of night. There goes one now." I pointed at the roadside where a jackrabbit disappeared into the sagebrush. "And it's cooler."

Larry gave up and tossed the unlit cigarette aside. "You're right about that. It's fucking cold."

We topped a small rise, and a pair of red truck taillights came into view up ahead.

"And the big semi-trucks like that one." I pressed the accelerator pedal. "I want to get around this one. There's a big hill coming up, and I want to be in front of him before we start the climb."

The little MG's four-cylinder engine whined loudly as we overtook the big semi. I waved at the driver as we went by, but Larry raised his hand and flipped the driver the bird. The trucker angrily blasted his air-horns and yelled, "Fuck you!" out the open window.

"Larry, what do you think you're doing?"

He took a pull from his flask. "I just gave that son-of-a-bitch something to think about."

"Yeah, you gave him running us off the road to think about."

I jammed the MG into a lower gear and accelerated away from the truck.

The big-rigs were powerful as hell, but they were slower to pick up speed. I'd heard stories of people—especially young women—being run off the road by some truck jockey torqued up on Dexedrine.

"Larry," I shouted over the road noise, "you are a prize-winning dumb fuck."

He saluted me with his flask. "Thank you so much. What's the big deal anyway?"

"All he needs to do is nudge us off the road with that monster. If we roll over, we could be killed or injured, and nobody'll find us for weeks."

He thought about that one for a minute. "Well, he can't catch us…right?"

We had sprinted out ahead of the truck by a mile or so, but the long grade was coming up.

"This little car doesn't do well climbing steep grades. I'm getting a running start at the hill now, but so is he. Take a look."

Larry looked behind us. I saw in the rearview mirror the semi's exhaust stacks belch an enormous cloud of black diesel smoke. I could hear the roar of his engine as his headlights grew larger.

"Holy shit," Larry muttered under his breath.

We struggled up the hill, the little English sports car against the big brute of a truck.

"Hey, Baby Joanie," Larry said, apprehension in his voice, "we are not winning this race."

"Nope, thanks to you. You really screwed the pooch this time."

Larry turned to me. "Where'd a young girl like you learn to talk like that?"

"From you, genius."

The semi's headlights were growing larger by the second in the mirror. I could see a steady stream of smoke billowing from the stacks in the moonlight. The crest of the hill seemed hopelessly far away. I began to prepare myself for the inevitable impact of the truck tapping the MG's fender and flipping us off into the sagebrush.

We were close to the top of the hill when the trucker made his move and swung the big rig into the left lane. He was gaining fast as the truck came along side. It was only a matter of seconds until he ran us off the road.

Just as we reached the top of the hill, a pair of automobile headlights came barreling toward us in the opposite lane. The trucker locked the big semi's brakes and the rig began to skid, barely missing the MG's back fender. The truck's tires howled as he fought to keep it on the road and avoid jack-knifing. The oncoming car narrowly missed him, veering onto the highway's shoulder.

Safely over the top of the hill, I held the MG steady as we picked up speed. The last I saw of the truck, it had skidded to a stop blocking both lanes, the driver standing next to it shaking his fist at us.

I was quivering from the adrenaline rush. Larry was gasping for breath. He held his flask toward me, and I shook my head. He immediately tipped it up and drained it.

"Pull over, Barney Oldfield. I need to take a piss."

"Not on your life." My voice was shaking, and I was drenched in sweat.

"I'm not taking any chances that asshole might get that thing going again.

See that sign?" I pointed toward a highway sign that read: *Las Vegas 95 Miles.* "We're not stopping until we get there."

We rolled into Las Vegas just after 4:00 a.m. I was bleary-eyed and still shaking from jousting with the semi-truck. Larry had slept off his booze and was nursing a headache. We checked into the El Rancho Vegas, got ourselves a bungalow, and got ready to sleep before hitting the casino.

The El Rancho Vegas was the original hotel-casino on Highway 91 just outside of Las Vegas. The highway would later be renamed Las Vegas Boulevard, eventually to be widely known as the Las Vegas Strip. I had stayed at the El Rancho with my parents since I was eleven. Several times a year the three of us would decamp to the rustic, Western-themed El Rancho so my dad could play the crap tables, while my mom and I lounged by the swimming pool.

The owner of the El Rancho Vegas was Jake Katleman, who ran the place with his nephew, Beldon Katleman. The two of them took a shine to me and allowed me to kibitz while my dad shot craps, even though I was underage to be in the casino. I would sit on a bar stool and roll the dice for my dad, who considered me his lucky charm. Often, he won with me shooting the dice. I was lucky. You might say I learned the crap tables pretty well at my father's knee.

Larry and I settled into the bungalow and took showers to wash off the road grime and diesel exhaust. I was desperate for some sleep before hitting the crap tables, but when I came out of the shower, Larry was sporting a large erection. We slipped into bed and put it to good use. As we both drifted off to sleep, Larry mumbled, "God, but I love fucking you."

It was dark when I woke. I had to look at the clock twice to orient myself. I was positive it was 9:00 a.m., but I couldn't understand why it was dark outside. When I connected both sides of my sleeping brain, I realized we had slept through the entire day, and it was now just after 9:00 at night. Larry was snoring loudly, still oblivious to the world. I quietly got dressed, dug out my silver dollar sock, and headed for the casino.

Though the El Rancho Vegas was only a few years old, it had the look and feel of the Old West. The casino was noisy inside, the air blue with cigarette smoke. It was not unusual to find horses tethered at hitching posts outside, and the gamblers inside might be sunburned tourists sprinkled with a few cowboys and farmers.

On one of our early Vegas trips with my parents—I was maybe fourteen years old—I was shooting craps with my dad. When we took a break, a well-dressed, dark-haired man at the bar approached me and said, "I've been watching you shoot craps. You're good." He offered his hand, "My name's Nick Dandolos, but most people just call me Nick the Greek." It started an unlikely friendship between the world famous—even notorious—gambler and me. Nick's advice was to always bet with the house at the crap table.

I knew the Katlemans would look the other way, even though I was underage to be in the casino. I found a crap table that wasn't too crowded and put a silver dollar each on the Don't Pass/Don't Come lines. I won several dice throws with a shooter down the table. When the dice changed hands, I changed my bets to the Pass/Come lines and won again, and then again. By the time was my turn to throw the dice, I had won fifty dollars or so over my original two-dollar bet. Each time the croupier pushed my winnings toward me, I slipped them into my sock.

It was an era when women seldom played the crap tables except to lucky-charm some high roller's dice, let alone a young girl who looked barely old enough to have a driver's license.

Bystanders began to gather and cheer me on. I kept rolling sevens and elevens. The other players were winning big each time I rolled. A high roller from down the table moved closer to me. I was still only laying my little two-dollar bets. The high roller took a stack of his chips and pushed behind my silver dollars. I rolled another seven, and the croupier pushed a larger stack of chips in front of me.

And then I looked up and saw Larry striding toward me through the casino with his Dillinger face on.

"Oh, shit," I muttered.

Larry pushed through the crowd in time to see my new friend push another stack of chips behind mine. I rolled another seven, and everyone at the table cheered. Except Larry.

"What the fuck?" Larry barked. "Why are you taking money from this piece of shit?"

"Hey, fella," the high roller said, "don't make such a fuss. She's only—"

"Shut the fuck up!" Larry punched him in the jaw, and he fell back into the crowd.

"Larry!" I shrieked. "Stop it!"

The high roller struggled to his feet ready to fight back, but the bystanders kept the two apart. Security guards arrived almost immediately. I was so furious I took a swing at Larry myself.

I slipped the last of my winnings into my sock and ducked out of the crowd. I was fuming as I hurried back to the bungalow. I began throwing my things into my suitcase, raging at what a dope I thought Larry was.

In a few minutes Larry came back to the bungalow accompanied by Beldon Katleman.

"Joanie," Beldon began without preamble, "I got everyone quieted down. I can't have any police called over this because you were a minor gambling in my casino. I essentially bribed the customer to be quiet about the incident. He's got free room, food, and alcohol for a couple of stays." He motioned to Larry. "Mr. Tierney here has offered to pay for any damages, but I've declined to accept that."

"We're leaving right away, Beldon," I interrupted. "I'm so sorry about this."

He smiled. "I know, Joanie. You and your family have been longtime guests of the El Rancho, and we appreciate that. I hope you'll continue. However, I have asked Mr. Tierney to choose another hotel the next time he comes to Las Vegas."

Larry nodded contritely. Beldon patted me kindly on the shoulder. "Have a safe trip back to LA. Be careful, I understand there's a good bit of rain between here and there."

Beldon left and closed the door behind him. I wanted to yell at Larry, but I was exhausted from all the excitement. I only wanted to get in the car and go home.

"Look, Joanie, I'm—"

"Shut up, Larry. Go to the front and pay our bill." I tossed my money sock on the bed. "Take some money out of there for it."

Larry turned toward the door. "I've got it."

We packed our things in the MG, and I drove across the street to a gas station and topped off my gas tank. The air was chilly and smelled of rain. We put the top up and carefully fitted the side curtains in place. It took a bit of finesse to get the curtains in place properly so there would be no leaks. I made sure all the tires were filled and that the little car was shipshape for meeting some weather.

The rain began an hour outside of Las Vegas. Before long, it got heavy, and I turned the windshield wipers up to full speed. Gusts of wind buffeted us now and then. We stayed more or less dry inside.

I concentrated on my driving, but there was a knot in my stomach and a sinking feeling of sadness. I was too angry to speak except in monosyllables. And I was heartsick knowing that I had to tell Larry that we'd come to the end. We rode in silence. Larry didn't smoke or take out his flask. It was a long six-hour drive.

When we got into Los Angeles and drew near Larry's apartment, he spoke up, "Joanie, I think—"

"Don't talk, please."

"No, I need to have my say, kiddo. I really fucked up big time tonight, I know. And I've fucked up a few more before this. And I know we've reached a crossroads." He shifted in the seat to face me. "I've told you before that I think you've got possibilities—talent, chutzpah—a big future in movies. There are some serious opportunities on the horizon for you. But not with somebody like me around."

I stopped in front of Larry's apartment. Suddenly my head began spinning. "Larry, I'm very—"

"Shush, Baby Joanie. Just listen. We've never mentioned it between us, but for quite a long time really—I realized that I love you."

"Me too!" Tears were suddenly streaming down my face. "I—I love you too."

"Yeah. We were lucky as hell that day you found me at the Tail o' the Cock. We've had fun and a lot of laughs and many, many sweet moments. But you, my dear, are going to be called soon. Destiny is going to change your world, and very soon. You're the silver slipper, Joanie. I'm a worn-out old combat boot. You're going to dance, and I don't want to get in the way."

The rain was coming down harder, the windshield wipers flop-flopping a losing battle against the downpour. Larry opened the door and kissed me on the lips, softly and deeply. "I'm going to miss you."

"Larry," I sobbed, "I don't want this."

"I know, not now, but you're smart, and before long, you'll see it's the right thing. Bye."

He got out and closed the door. He walked through the rain into his house without looking back.

Coda

Fast-forward to Warner Brothers Studios circa 1957. Little Joanie Olander underwent a metamorphosis, and out of the cocoon came Mamie Van Doren. In 1953, amid much hoopla, I was signed to an unheard-of seven-year contract by Universal Studios. (Most starlets signing with Universal got six-month contracts if they were lucky.) I left Universal in 1956 when my son was born. Uni's management felt that so-called sex symbols shouldn't be married with children. Universal was always prudish about such things. Despite that, I quickly signed a three-picture deal at Warner Brothers. *Untamed Youth* was the first one.

This was a particularly big day on the *Untamed Youth* set. I would be filming the dance scene for "Oobala Baby," a song written for me by Eddie Cochran. Dance production numbers take time and patience with master shots, medium shots, and close-ups—especially when there are a couple dozen dancers.

By the time we finally got to the end of the day, we were exhausted. I'd heard the "Oobala Baby" playback so many times that I now loathed the song. When the director called, "Cut! That's a wrap!" everyone groaned in relief. The soundstage lights came on, and the crew began packing up. Wardrobe people began gathering up stray pieces of costumes. Actors and dancers headed for the makeup areas to clean up.

Then, from somewhere out in the soundstage a familiar voice boomed, "Oobala Baby Joanie! Nice job, sweetheart!" A tall figure came striding toward me.

"Larry!" I shrieked, throwing myself into his arms. We embraced hard and close, like lovers long separated. "Larry, what are you doing here?"

"They know me here. I heard you were shooting this today, and I wanted to see if all the hype about Mamie Van Doren was for real."

We embraced again. “I’m so glad to see you! What did you think?”

“I think Mamie Van Doren is going to be a big star.”

I took him by the hand, and we walked toward my dressing room. “Let me change, and we’ll go have dinner.”

“Thanks, baby, but I can’t stay. Let me just tell you that there are more and bigger things ahead for you. Take it from this old gangster.”

I pressed my face to his chest as tears began to flow. “I still cry when I remember that rainy night. But you were right, Larry. My heart broke, but it healed again.”

“Fucking right, I was right. It always heals but leaves a little scar. I’ll always love you, Joanie.”

He turned and walked away into the soundstage.

“I’ll always love you too,” I said to his back. He waved without turning. I never saw Larry again in the flesh.

Chapter Six

Ten Days with Quincy

The music had just stopped, and my ears were still ringing. Lionel Hampton's orchestra had wrapped up the first set of their opening night at Club Oasis. His musicians were straggling down off the bandstand, and the audience members were heading for the exits and the restrooms.

Everybody seemed to be lighting a cigarette or a cigar, and I could smell a whiff of the occasional reefer. The room was covered by a thick blue haze, and my eyes were watering as I sipped the last of a glass of orange juice.

The small showroom of the Club Oasis was packed. People—White and Black—came from all over to see and hear orchestras like Hampton's or performers like Billie Holiday or Thelonious Monk. The Club Oasis building had once been a residence, not originally suited for a nightclub venue.

You might call it intimate or cozy, or you could just call it what it was: cramped. But whatever you called it, the Oasis on Western Avenue had some of the best jazz and bebop music in LA. And there were many other jazz clubs nearby on Central Avenue, where greats like Duke Ellington and Dizzy Gillespie performed with their orchestras. It was a three-square-mile area that was ground zero for the jazz scene on the West Coast.

I dreamed of being a movie star, but in my heart of hearts I also longed to be a singer. Like my idol, Lena Horne. I styled my singing voice, my delivery, and my movements after everything Lena did. She had headlined at the El Rancho Vegas, and I watched her religiously every night.

Lately, I began making the rounds of the South Central jazz clubs in hopes of getting a chance to sing just a little in front of a live audience.

Concentrating on my ambitions as a singer had eased the pain of my breakup with Larry Tierney. I had decided I was through with moping. It was time to take some action and follow my dreams.

I ordered another orange juice and checked my lipstick in my compact mirror. As I was putting on my lipstick, I saw the reflection of a handsome face in the mirror looking down at me. I turned to look at him. He had an impish smile and smart eyes set in a light brown face.

"I like the color," he said. "It suits your skin."

I was taken aback.

"Thanks," I managed. I covered my discomfort, putting my compact in my purse.

"My name's Quincy. Are you alone? Do you mind if I sit for a moment?"

I said, "Go ahead, yes. I'm Joanie. Pleased to meet you."

"Pleased to meet you too. I can only stay a minute. I play trumpet for Lionel. We'll start our next set pretty soon."

I was impressed. He couldn't have been much older than me—seventeen, maybe eighteen. This was 1949, pre-civil rights, only a year after President Truman desegregated the armed forces. I felt myself liking Quincy in spite of the obvious cultural drawbacks.

"Do you come here often?" Quincy asked.

"I've been coming here for a month or two. There's always great music—like tonight. It's wonderful."

"Thanks. I'm Hamp's arranger too. I write all the parts for the different instruments."

"That's really cool, Quincy." I thought, *He's so young. He must be really good at it to have so much responsibility.*

"Hey, Joanie, do you like bebop?"

"Love it. And boogie-woogie. And the blues."

"Have you been to Jack's Basket Room over on Central? My friend Charlie Parker's playing there tonight."

"No."

There was a moment. Neither of us spoke. Then Quincy grinned shyly. A little sweat was beading on his upper lip and forehead. "Say, are you busy tonight? After our second set, I was thinking about going over there. They have great Southern fried chicken. If you'd like to come along, we can have some chicken and listen to Charlie Bird."

I was warming to the whole situation now. And I was getting hungry. But I held back. "I dunno. Let me think about it, okay?"

"Okay. I'll talk to you in a few minutes." Quincy got up and ambled toward the bandstand. After a few steps, he turned and came back. "Tell me, Joanie, are you Swedish?"

"Yeah, both sides of my family. Why?"

"I love Swedes, that's why."

The musicians took their places on the bandstand. Their second set began with "The More I See You." Quincy stood up and played a solo, his trumpet pointed directly at me. It was a very sweet sound, crystal clear trumpet piercing through the blue haze with a subversive message.

I got it loud and clear. But I didn't know what I would do with it. I hesitated because of the ideas—bad ideas—that get ingrained in your mind, trained into you the way a circus elephant learns to balance on one foot. It's the baggage we all carry, the biases we might not consider—ever—until prejudice comes up against desire.

After the song, Quincy sat down. I sipped my orange juice and watched the second set. Thinking. *What's it going to be, Joanie? Your mother's voice in your head? Or a handsome trumpet player?*

I was getting hungry, and Southern fried chicken was sounding better by the minute. And then Lionel Hampton's second set was over, and Quincy was walking toward me, that jaunty smile on his face. He pulled up a chair and sat down.

"How about that chicken, Joanie?"

"Yes, I'm starving."

"Me too. I'll go borrow a car from one of the guys."

"No need, Quincy. We can take my car."

"Then let's go eat."

Outside in the parking lot, Quincy looked at the Magic MG in astonishment.

"Now that is a cool car! What kind of car is it?"

"It's English, an MG TC."

"Jesus, it's got spoke wheels. And you drive on the wrong side."

"I know, I love it. Get in."

I drove us the three or so miles over to Central Avenue, and we parked on the street in front of Jack's Basket Room. The aroma of fried chicken wafted out into the street. Before we got out, Quincy put his hand on my arm.

"Look, Joanie, I understand."

"What?"

"This the first time you've ever been out with a colored man, right?"

I hesitated. "Yes."

"Well, don't worry. Nothing bad's going to happen. We're going to have a good time listening to the Bird, and we're going to have a good dinner."

Jack's was crowded with after-hours patrons who were noisy and hungry, and smoking, laughing, and drinking from pint bottles. We squeezed into a small table elbow to elbow with others. Waitresses were hustling trays of mixers and ice and baskets of fried chicken, weaving between the tables.

"You want a drink, Joanie? They don't have a liquor license. They only serve mixers, but I can step down to the liquor store on the corner and buy a pint."

"Just orange juice for me, thanks."

"You'll probably have to make do with a Nehi Orange soda, okay? They don't have very sophisticated mixers here. Let's get some chicken."

Quincy ordered two baskets of chicken with shoestring fries, a Nehi Orange soda for me, and a coke for himself.

"How long have you known Charlie?"

"A year or so. Seems like I've known him forever. He's been a mentor to me. Great guy, but he's got problems. Heroin, booze. He's been in and out of hospitals for treatment. I hear he's back from his latest bout and feeling good. You've heard him play, right?"

"Records, yes."

"A genius. Wait'll you hear him up close like this. I swear it's a whole different experience. He's got technique other sax players can't even imagine. You listen to how he takes chord progressions…."

Quincy went into a discussion of Bird's ingenuity and artistry. As a wannabe professional musician, it was over my head. But I loved looking at Quincy as he talked about his craft—animated, gesturing, altogether charming. He had silky smooth skin. The intensity in his eyes made you feel he was talking directly to your soul. I was developing a crush on this young man.

Quincy looked up. "Here he comes!"

The whole place broke into applause and cheers. Bird smiled and waved at the crowd. A drummer and a standup bass player took their places onstage. Bird counted them in, "One, two, three, four…" And he played—restless, melodic, dissonant, drawing up from somewhere in him music that took over your toes and made them tap. I didn't know about the chord progressions Quincy tried to explain, but I knew Charlie Bird Parker's shiny bebop sax was now part of me.

At the end of the set, Bird stepped off the bandstand and moved into the crowd. There was a lot of embracing and back slapping. Other musicians shoved each other aside to pay their respects. They stood close in hopes of catching some of his magic. He took time to speak with Quincy, and he smiled when Quincy introduced me. Quincy made a point to tell him he looked great. I overheard him tell Quincy, "I feel like I'm strong again. I feel fuckin' great."

"I hope he can stay that way," Quincy said as we made our way back to my car. "Smack is easy to come by in these parts."

"I really had fun. Thank you for asking me."

"It was my pleasure, Joanie. Can we do it again sometime?"

"Yes. Where do you live? I'll drop you off."

Quincy rented an attic room in a house a short distance from the Club Oasis. We stopped in front of a two-story frame house.

"This is it," he said. "You want to come up? The apartment's not much, but I have some good weed we can smoke."

"I'll take a rain check." I wanted to go upstairs with him, but I hesitated again. I didn't want him to think I was a pushover for a chicken dinner and a Nehi orange soda. I found a scrap of paper and scrawled my number on it. "Call me if you feel like it."

He grinned. "I will."

It was well past my usual curfew when I got home. My mother was waiting for me.

"I was worried," she said accusingly. "Where were you?"

"At the Club Oasis listening to Lionel Hampton. Good show."

"Yeah, he's good. Who were you with?"

"Just by myself. Then I went to Jack's Chicken Basket and saw Charlie Parker play."

Skeptically, she said, "Umm hmmm. So, who did you meet? Someone interesting?"

"Nobody." It hung there for a moment.

"Jo, I know you better than you know yourself. You'll tell me when you're ready."

I turned toward my bedroom. "'Night, Mother."

I had drama school classes the next morning. I was groggy from the late night, but I managed to get there. When the class was over, I went straight home to take a nap.

"Jo," Mother said when I walked in the door, "you had a call from someone named Quincy. He left a number for you to call back." She handed me the number. "Is Quincy who you met last night?"

"Yes, he is."

"He sounds colored."

"He's first trumpet for Lionel Hampton's orchestra, and he arranges all their music."

"And?"

"He's very nice, quite handsome, obviously very talented."

"And?"

"Okay, yes, he's colored. I like him."

"I just don't understand you, Jo. First you go out with that nut case, Larry Tierney—"

"Don't say that about Larry!"

"And now you're going out with a colored man."

"At least he's my age, Mother."

"Well, I guess that's progress. But, Jo, what you're doing is very dangerous. Don't you realize that? If your father found out—"

"We stayed in the jazz clubs," I said lamely. "He's very nice. Why don't you meet him? Why don't I invite him over? You'll see."

"That's not going to make any difference, Jo. It's just not a good idea to mix and mingle races."

"Mother," I said in consternation, "I don't think about this the way you do. And I hate hearing you say it. Quincy's very nice and every bit a gentleman. He's very talented, and I'm sure that someday he'll be a big star."

"And you want to be a star too, Jo. What happens if someone at a studio sees you hanging around in Negro neighborhoods and nightclubs?"

I hadn't gotten that far with my thinking. Race was a growing problem in postwar America. Black veterans were being discharged from the racially integrated armed forces, where they had grown accustomed to being treated more or less equally. However, after being discharged, they discovered very quickly there was no such thing as integration or even equal treatment in American civilian life. Everything from voting, going to the toilet, buying a house, getting a drink of water, or eating in a restaurant was circumscribed by skin color. Some parts of the Jim Crow South were nothing short of apartheid states, like South Africa.

I had never thought about the problem of race, because it was never a problem for me. My experiences in dating had been with White men and boys only. In confronting the everyday racial bias in my country, I was suddenly entering unpleasant new territory.

"I like him, Mother. What am I supposed to do?"

"Far be it for me to tell you what to do, Jo. You always do as you please, no matter what I say."

It was time Quincy and my mother met. I called Quincy and told him so.

"Tonight's my night off, Joanie. I called earlier to see if you wanted to have dinner tonight. How about then?"

"I'd like to do that. After you and I have dinner."

Mom was miffed that I was going to dinner with Quincy before she met him, but I was not ready to manage a meet-and-greet with Quincy and her. I just wanted a quiet dinner somewhere with him. And whatever happened between us after that would just happen.

I picked up Quincy, and we drove to an upscale restaurant in Malibu called The Point. It had a great view of the ocean and the sunset. There were a few occupied tables, but it didn't look like a busy night. We were seated by a window and looking at menus when a stocky guy in a dark suit came to our table.

"I'm afraid that you'll have to leave," he said.

A look came over Quincy's face, part anger, part disappointment, and part fear.

"Why?" I asked a little louder than is polite. Other diners looked our way.

"Because, miss, we do not serve colored people in this establishment."

"What is that supposed to mean?" My anger was about to spill over.

"Please keep your voice down, miss. That is our policy. You'll have to go."

Quincy pushed his chair back and stood up. He took my hand. "Let's go. It's no good making a fuss."

"This is bullshit!" My face was burning, and tears were running down my cheeks. Quincy guided me to the door and out into the parking lot. "How can they get away with this shit?"

"They're White. Believe me, it's not my first time, and I doubt it'll be my last."

We got into the MG, and I started the engine. "I'm so fucking mad I could bite this steering wheel in half."

Quincy chuckled.

"What are you laughing at?" I snapped.

"I'd pay admission to see you bite that steering wheel. But that's no substitute for dinner."

We both laughed hard. The anger, embarrassment, shame of what happened eased a little. I had felt one inch high as we walked out of The Point, all the patrons' eyes following us to the door.

"Let's find another place to eat," Quincy said softly. "I don't feel like going to another restaurant."

Quincy squeezed my hand. "Let's hit the Club Alabam. Dinah Washington's singing tonight. And they've got fried chicken *and* Chinese food. But we'd better hurry. I don't want you getting so hungry you eat your steering wheel."

I gave him a playful slap on the shoulder. "Wise ass."

I put the MG in gear, and we drove back to South Central.

Club Alabam was the queen bee of the South Central LA jazz clubs. It was next door to the Dunbar Hotel, an upscale destination for colored celebrities. Club Alabam was where you went to see and hear Duke Ellington or Billie Holiday. Dinah Washington was one of my favorites.

Her recordings of "Cry Me a River" and "September in the Rain" were nearly worn out on my little record player. Dinah and Lena Horne were inspirations to me as I tried to figure out how to become a jazz and blues singer. I was thrilled by the prospect of seeing and hearing her in person.

Quincy ordered fried wontons, egg rolls, and beef chow mein for us. I was starting to like Nehi Orange soda, so I had one of those too.

I leaned toward Quincy and said, "What happened tonight, I feel awful about it. I know you must too."

Quincy smiled. "Yeah, I feel like shit. You can fight them if you want, but alone—like we were tonight—it's just a ticket to jail. The restaurant calls the cops, we get arrested—or worse. Then your mama is mad at me for getting you involved, even before I meet her. No, it's best to retreat and fight another day. I keep my feelings to myself, otherwise I'd be angry all the time. Brothers like that lawyer, Thurgood Marshall, and athletes like Jackie Robinson, they're doing the heavy lifting for us. Imagine, Jackie's the first colored guy out there playing an all-White sport and traveling to some of the most God-awful segregated cities in the country. Now *he's* taking a lot of shit. People aren't just telling him he can't eat in a restaurant, they're telling him that if he plays ball in their city, they'll pick him off on first base with a deer rifle."

I shook my head. "How about when Lionel goes on tour? Don't you all have the same problems?"

"Once in a while. Most of the time we're playing venues where the audiences all really dig jazz, and our audiences are mixed—colored and White. On the road, we keep to ourselves, mostly. My job is to play music that makes people smile, bob their heads, tap their feet, and snap their fingers. Folks respond to that just about anywhere. They laugh and drink and sometimes get up to dance. When I see that, I get a rush. Until tonight, I thought California was a pretty easy-going place. Live and learn."

By the time the food came, we were as hungry as lumberjacks. We listened to Dinah Washington's set while we ate. Here and there couples danced on the small dance floor. When she started "What a Diff'rence a Day Makes," Quincy and I looked at each other, put down our chopsticks, and got up to dance. Her velvety voice was like a sugary blanket around us—a wrapping for sweet thoughts. We danced very close, thinking the same things, feeling our bodies fitting together.

When we got back to our table, Quincy smiled wistfully. "Hey, Joanie, why don't we take this vibe and go to my place?"

"Okay."

I drove us to Quincy's little apartment. It was an attic—little more than a rented room really—but adequate for a young musician on the road. There was a sink and mirror, a wardrobe with a couple of suits and some pressed shirts, and a futon.

We sat on the edge of the futon and kissed long and hard. We necked for several minutes and laid back on the futon. Quincy lit a joint and offered it to me. I shook my head. "I don't smoke, and I've never smoked marijuana."

"No lie? It won't hurt you, you know?"

"I just know it's illegal, and we could go to jail for twenty years."

Quincy comically twisted his head from side to side. "I don't see any cops in here, do you? It's probably safe to give it a try."

"No thanks."

"You know, Joanie, it starting to look like you and I are gonna make love. Take a little hit, just one puff. This is very good shit. I promise it will make it all very special."

"You are seducing me with pot, sir."

Quincy grinned. "You are right, madam."

I took a hit off the joint and coughed a couple of times.

"Smooth, huh?" Quincy quipped.

"Fuck you," I said, laughing.

"Exactly what I had in mind."

Very quickly my body began tingling. A warm rush washed over me, and I encircled Quincy's neck with my arm. We slipped out of our clothes, holding on to each another with one hand, unbuttoning and unzipping clothing with the other. Quincy entered me—an erotic jolt—an electric sensation up my spine. All nerve endings seemed to terminate in the interior of my vagina. It was as though the rest of my body had said goodbye and gone on vacation, leaving my pussy in charge until further notice.

Time spun out of control, and we fucked very hard. At some point, we turned over, and I mounted Quincy astride. Deep sensations brought me quickly to an orgasm that lasted longer than any I had ever experienced. It felt like it would never end. The random thought entered my mind that this orgasm would be my life's work, a cross between the Sistine Chapel and a porn movie.

I collapsed on Quincy's chest, covered with sweat, and went to sleep.

When I woke, I was curled up under a blanket. It was still dark outside. Quincy was next to me, his head propped on a pillow.

"What time is it?" I asked.

"Two-fifteen."

I jumped up. "Shit, I've gotta get home. My mom'll kill me."

"Yeah, I figured. I wish you could stay."

"Me too," I said, "but I can't."

"You okay to drive home?"

I threw my arms around him. "Yes. No thanks to you, Mr. Jones."

"My pleasure, Miss Olander." He bowed and helped me into my jacket. "Better keep the side curtains closed on that Magic MG. It's cold."

"Tomorrow, my mom. You've got to meet her, okay?"

"Okay. Bring her to the late show at the Club Oasis. We can have dinner there after."

"Got it." I kissed him and dashed out the door.

It was almost 3:00 a.m. when I stopped in front of our house. I was prepared for the worst when I walked in the front door. The light was on, and my mother was sitting in the front room, almost asleep in my dad's big easy chair. When I came in, she got up and walked toward their bedroom.

"At least you're alive," she said coldly. "Go to bed."

"Mother, I—"

"Go to bed." She closed their bedroom door.

I got undressed and got into bed. The spots where Quincy had touched me, my private parts, still tingled with the memory, pleasurable sensations, contented. I knew my mother would still be angry in the morning. I fell into an untroubled sleep.

When I woke, I showered and got dressed. I had drama classes in the early afternoon. Mom was in the kitchen when I went in to pour myself a cup of coffee.

"Good morning, Mother."

"Are you going to your classes this afternoon?"

"Yes."

"If you keep staying out all night with this…Quincy, you won't be able to continue your drama school. You're throwing away your opportunities."

"I won't be staying out all night. He's leaving in seven days to continue touring with Lionel Hampton. You'll meet him tonight. You'll see he's really a nice guy."

"No, I won't. I'm not going to meet him."

"Why?"

"Because I'm not. There's no reason to. You'll keep seeing him, whether or not I want you to. I think you're making a mistake, Jo. You're not mature enough to understand what you're doing. And you don't give a damn what I say."

"That's not true, Mother. I do care about what you say. But I've got to make my own decisions sometime."

"Jo, look, your father and I aren't prejudiced against Negroes. And we never taught you that people are different because of their skin color. Perhaps we should have."

"What does that mean?"

She took a moment to answer. "Just this. What's in your heart may be innocent, but the outside world isn't innocent, and it's not going to change for you. It's not easy to go against the tide. And it's not easy to accept the verdict of the majority. But the world you are so ambitious to enter will have strong feelings about you crossing racial lines. Just know what you're getting into."

"I understand."

"But you're still going to see him?"

"Yes."

My mother nodded resignedly and went back to the kitchen.

That evening I pulled up in front of our house with Quincy in the passenger seat of the Magic MG. He looked at me apprehensively.

"I hope this works, Joanie."

Me too, I said to myself.

"It'll be fine," I told Quincy. "Just be your usual charming self."

"Oh, brother," he said under his breath. "Let's go. I gotta get back for the second set, or Lionel will have my ass."

We went to the front door, and I rang the bell. Mom opened the door and her jaw dropped.

"Mother, this is Quincy Jones. Quincy, meet my mother."

Before she could speak, Quincy extended his hand and shook hers. "Missus Olander, it's a great pleasure to meet you."

Still in shock, she said, "Nice to meet you too, Quincy."

"I can see that Joanie inherited her beauty naturally." Mom blushed.

"Why, thank you. Won't you come in?"

We walked into the living room, and I took over. "We're kind of in a hurry, Mother. We've come to pick you up."

"I'd like for you to be my guest at our second show, Mrs. Olander."

"Oh, no, no. My goodness, it's so late," Mom demurred. "I don't have any makeup on."

I put my arm around her and guided her toward her bedroom. "Then you better get cracking because we're taking you with us, made up or not. I'll tell Daddy that you'll be home late."

Half an hour later, the three of us were figuring out how to seat three in a two-passenger car. At my direction, Quincy climbed into the passenger seat and mom sat on his lap. I got behind the wheel and pulled the starter.

"Everybody ready?"

"Are you comfortable, Mrs. Olander?"

Mom nodded. "Yes. And Quincy, if we're going to ride to the Club Oasis like this, I think you should start calling me 'Lucille.'"

At the Club Oasis, Mom and I sat at a table close to the stage while Lionel Hampton's orchestra played their second set. Quincy played his solos to us. Mom smiled the whole time, more than I'd seen her smile in a long time. I doubt she knew any more about jazz than what little she heard played on the radio, but I could tell she was taking in all of Hampton's set with rapt attention.

When the set was over, Quincy joined us at our table. We ordered fried chicken and biscuits. Quincy produced a pint of whiskey, and he and mom had whiskey and coke highballs, while I sipped a Nehi Orange. Quincy kept up a stream of witty banter, which mom found increasingly charming as she moved to her second highball. By the time we finished dinner, I knew mom was a big fan of Quincy's.

I decided to be a good girl tonight. Mom gave Quincy a hug and thanked him for dinner and the drinks.

"Good night, Lucille," Quincy said, holding the car door for her.

"Good night, Quincy. And by the way," she continued boozily, "you can call me 'Lulu.'"

I kissed Quincy goodnight and whispered, "Good job, baby. See you tomorrow."

Mom was feeling no pain, humming off key "The More I See You," as I drove us home.

"Jo," she said, "thank you for inviting me tonight. I had a great time. And I enjoyed meeting your Quincy. I can see why you feel the way you do about him. He's very handsome and talented."

"Thanks for saying that, Mother."

"I don't feel any differently about you seeing him, mind you. You're still at risk to run afoul of other people's expectations." She turned and looked at me directly. "But I know you'll do what you damn well want to. You'll be taking your chances."

"I know, Mother. But he won't be here long, only for the next six days, then they're off to the next tour stop."

I stopped the MG in front of our house and cut the engine.

"I know this isn't a long-term thing, Mother. I'll probably never see him again. And it makes me sad."

We went inside the house.

"It was fun having you along tonight. We'll do it again sometime, just you and me."

"I'd like that, honey. Good night, Jo."

"I'm going to be spending a lot of time with Quincy between now and the time he leaves. I've made arrangements to put my drama classes on hold for a week or so."

Mom shrugged and closed her bedroom door.

I went to my room, undressed, and got into bed, thinking about my mother's life. She got pregnant with me at sixteen. My dad was barely twenty. Two kids who suddenly brought into the world their own kid, with not the slightest idea of how to raise her. Their solution was to farm me out to mom's parents, who also didn't want me. I grew up painfully aware of that feeling of abandonment. I couldn't wait to see Quincy again.

***

Time is a subjective thing. Waiting for something pleasant, like Christmas or a birthday, time is slow. But waiting for an event that you dread, like separation from one you love, time races. As the time approaches, it feels like a slide down a steep slope, with disaster at the bottom.

Quincy and I barely left each other's side during the remaining days of his gig with Lionel Hampton in LA. We holed up in his little attic apartment by day, indulging ourselves in one another. At night, we emerged to make the rounds of the South Central clubs in the Magic MG, with time out for Quincy's sets at the Club Oasis with Hampton's orchestra. The other musicians looked at us with amusement. They ribbed Quincy about his new girlfriend. "You gonna pack her in your suitcase, Quince?" It was good-humored teasing, and he laughed off their off-color kibitzing. But it got my hackles up—I don't tease well.

"They don't mean anything by it, Joanie. If they didn't like you, they wouldn't bother. They'd just ignore you. Besides, they're just musicians." He added in an accent, "They ain't got no couth. And they know we've got good lovin' together."

"How would they know that?"

"They only have to look at the satisfied expressions on our faces when we show up at Club Oasis every night."

"I didn't know it showed."

"Joanie, good lovin' is written all over us."

We laughed hard and fell into each other's arms again.

We tried to hold off the last day, but it inevitably came. It was Sunday. It always has to be a Sunday, melancholy in the evening rain. We sat in the MG at the bus station, rain pattering on the cloth top, staring at the band bus.

"Quincy, there's so much I need to say before you go—but I can't find the words." I began to cry.

Quincy put his arm tight around me. "I know. No matter how long we have, we'll never get it all said."

The musicians were boarding the bus. A couple of them waved to us. One shouted, "Better come on, Quince. Lionel will be here any minute."

Quincy waved back. "I'll be right there."

"You'd better go," I said through my tears. "You can write me if you want."

"I'm not too good with letter writing, honey. We'll meet up again, for sure," he said lamely. My heart sank, realizing that Quincy would be no better at letter writing than I would.

"Yes, of course. But you never stop touring."

"Something good will happen for you, Joanie," he said, his voice cracking.

"And I know something good will happen for you too, Quincy. We had a very good thing between us, don't you think? We'll see each other again down the road—when we've both become somebody."

Lionel Hampton appeared at the door of the tour bus. "Hey, Quincy," he called, "let's go."

Quincy kissed me long and hard, and then he opened the car door. "Bye, Joanie."

He trotted through the rain and ducked into the bus. The door closed and a black cloud of diesel smoke belched from the tailpipe. The bus lumbered out of the station and onto 6th Street, and disappeared into the rain.

Coda

In 1954, my telephone rang and the voice on the other end said, "Hi, Joanie, didn't I tell you something good would happen for you?"

By now I had a contract with Universal Studios, I was Mamie Van Doren, I had made *All American* with Tony Curtis, and my picture was in every movie magazine and newspaper.

"Quincy," I shrieked, "is that you?"

"The one and only, Miss Mamie Van Doren."

"My God, what a surprise. Are you in LA?"

"Yeah, I've been here a while. How about I take you to dinner?"

Oh, shit, I thought. "I'm sorry, Quincy, but I'm dating someone—Ray Anthony."

Ray was one of the most popular band leaders in the country and well on his way to becoming Capitol Records bestselling recording artist.

Quincy chuckled loudly. "I know. I'm doing some arrangements for Ray Anthony Enterprises. I got your number off his secretary's desk."

"You sneak! God, I wish we could go have some of that Jack's Basket fried chicken."

"They're still open. You just say the word, Joanie—I mean, Mamie."

I gave it some thought for a second. "I've never been a cheater, Quincy. I just can't."

"I understand," Quincy said with a sigh. "I respect you for it. Disappointed, but respectfully."

"My God, but it's great to hear your voice!"

"You too."

When we hung up, I was shaking. I had thought of Quincy many times since we said goodbye at the Greyhound Bus Station that Sunday. Dating Quincy had profoundly changed me. His easy manners and quick smile had made every minute with him special. And his effortless ability to move between Black and White worlds was to me a lesson on how everyone should get along.

Quincy's career grew in many directions over the years. Much of what happened in American pop music was the result of Quincy's influence. Quincy's obvious talents were spotted by Frank Sinatra, who hired him to be his full-time arranger and conductor. Quincy was gifted as an arranger, conductor, songwriter, and record producer. He produced albums for Sinatra, Celine Dion, Michael Jackson (*Thriller* is still one of the biggest-selling record albums of all time), and many more. He produced Lesley Gore's "It's My Party." "We Are the World" shined a light on compassion for the world's children. The fact is that anybody who was anybody in pop music had sung Quincy's songs or been produced and arranged by him.

When I was told I would receive an Icon Award during the Oscars in 2020, I started kicking around names of people to present me with the award. The one that kept popping up was Quincy. When I told my publicist to contact him, he discouraged me, saying that Quincy wasn't in good health. I said ask him anyway and see what he says.

Quincy said yes.

Quincy didn't want to go out, but his daughter, who is a video producer, recorded his brief but moving speech, which was played onstage for the presentation of my award.

I watched with tears streaming. It was so long ago that we'd been lovers, but it felt like it was yesterday. At the end, Quincy patted his heart and said in Swedish, *"Mamie, I love you deep down."* And I will always love him the same.

Peace, Quincy. Until we meet again in heaven.

Chapter Seven

Tony Curtis

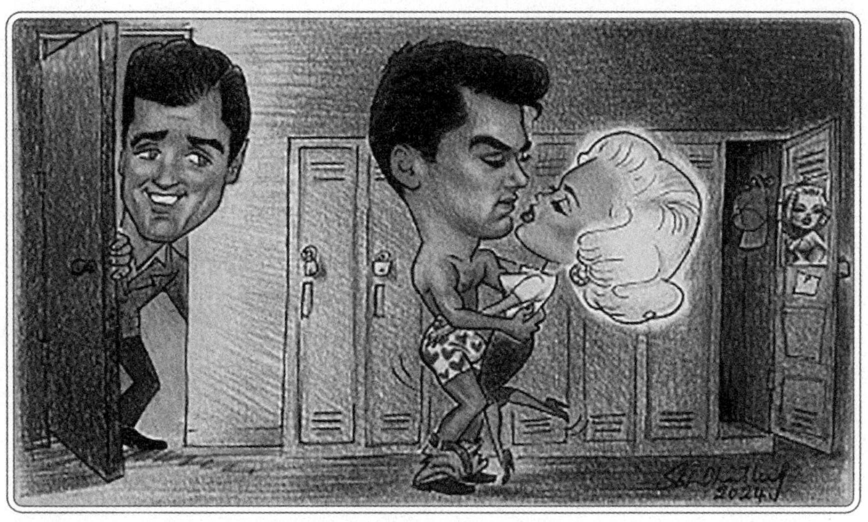

Two nervous manicurists were working feverishly on my fingernails. One clucked, "Just look at these chewed-off nubs."

The other one snipped, "And she's got to smoke a cigarette on camera, for chrissakes."

A hairdresser was fussing over my platinum coiffure, admonishing a stray curl with hairspray: "Stay there, dammit!"

Bud Westmore, chief makeup artist at Universal International Pictures, was finishing my makeup. "They'll be ready for you in five minutes, Zaba. The director wants you to have long eyelashes, so I need to apply these pronto. Please try to hold your eyelids still. Oops, hold still, try again."

It was a cold January morning, and the makeup department was poorly heated. In addition to shivering from the cold, I was shivering from pure terror. My eyelids wouldn't stay still, my hands were shaking so that the manicurists could barely glue on the fake nails, and my knees were knocking, even though I wasn't out of the makeup chair. It didn't help that the shoes I was wearing were too large—six and a half when I wore a six. They were Joan Crawford's shoes, borrowed from Warner Bros at the last minute because in all of Hollywood, there were apparently no size sixes.

Forty-eight hours ago, I had no idea any of this would be happening. I was minding my own business, studying acting, performing the role of Marie in a showcase production of *Come Back, Little Sheba* at the Bliss-Hayden Theatre. The whole point of appearing in a so-called showcase was to attract the attention of casting directors and talent scouts. That's what happened.

My phone rang the next morning with a call from my manager, Jimmy McHugh.

"Zaba," he said, using the name he had helped me choose to replace my more boring given name: "Joan."

"Zaba," he continued, "I just had a call from Phil Benjamin, a talent scout at Universal. He saw you in *Sheba* last night. Rudy Maté is directing a picture over there with Tony Curtis and Joanne Dru, called *Forbidden.* He wants you to come in and meet Maté and Ted Richmond, the producer. They're interested in casting you as a singer in an exotic nightclub in Macao. It's a small role, but Benjamin thinks you'd be a natural for it."

"Jimmy, that's fantastic!"

"Yes it is, Zaba, but we've got to move fast. They want to see you tomorrow morning at 7:00. If they like you, you'll get a wardrobe fitting and they'll give you the song lyrics. You'll be working over the weekend with a choreographer on your blocking. You'll be lip syncing 'You Belong to Me' in the scene, so you'll have to learn the lyrics over the weekend. You'll shoot your scene on Monday morning."

"Oh, my God, Jimmy," I groaned, "I can't do all that in two days."

"Yes, you can! Just do it, Zaba! If you think this is hard, wait until you become the star you want to be. This is what you've been waiting for. And this is only the beginning."

"Okay, Jimmy," I said sheepishly.

"And don't be late!" he barked.

The next morning, I drove to Universal and met with Phil Benjamin and Ted Richmond. Richmond looked me over like I was a side of prime beef.

"Zaba," he said kindly, "you have come along at just the right time." He turned to Benjamin. "You were right, Phil. She's perfect. Let's go meet Rudy."

Rudy Maté was on the nightclub set explaining a scene to Tony Curtis and Joanne Dru. Richmond spoke briefly in his ear. Maté immediately excused himself and followed Richmond to where I was standing. Maté gave me an appraising look. He led Richmond and me behind the giant white scrim that surrounded the nightclub set.

"Very good, Ted," he said to Richmond. "Can you sing, Zaba?" he asked.

"Sure," I said and burst into "I Can't Give You Anything but Love, Baby." After a few lines he stopped me. "Terrific, Zaba. You've got the part. Ted, take her to wardrobe and get her fitted for the gown. Better let Bud Westmore know. Monty's got all the makeup he can handle here."

Richmond escorted me to the wardrobe department and turned me over to the wardrobe supervisor for *Forbidden*. She was a stocky and no-nonsense middle-aged woman with a twinkle in her eye. She stuck out a hand and said, "Zaba, I'm Faye."

"Nice to meet you, Faye."

"Mutual. So, you're probably nervous about all this, right? First movie? First really big screen exposure?"

"Yes, yes. I could scream."

"Okay, don't do that. It frightens the seamstresses. Sit down over there." She motioned me into a tall director's chair. "Now, Zaba, the truth is this will be very easy. Remember the *I Love Lucy* episode where Lucy and Ethel go to a beauty spa and Ethel says, 'Do you think they could make a glamour girl out of me?' And Lucy looks at the brochure and says, 'Sure, it says right here, "We work miracles."' Well, *you* don't need a miracle, Zaba. You brought the goods with you. You're beautiful right down to the bone. All we need to do is frame you like a beautiful painting."

I found myself smiling and breathing easier. I nodded. "Okay, Faye."

"So, let's take your measurements and see what we can find."

After measuring me in minute detail, they handed me off to a choreographer named Kenny Williams. Kenny and I became instant friends, and he quickly became one of my biggest allies at Universal.

"You'll need to come work with me on Saturday and Sunday, Zaba," he said. "We'll rehearse your movements to the song on the Macao set."

"Okay," I said. I must have looked intimidated.

Kenny patted me on the shoulder. "Don't worry. We'll work it out. You're going to be fantastic."

"Okay," I repeated, trying to sound more confident.

"I'm sending you home with the lyric sheet and a recording of the song so you can get the lip syncing down. It'll need to match with the recording. Rehearse it in front of a mirror."

I spent the weekend singing "You Belong to Me" in front of the big mirror next to our front door. After my first session with Kenny Williams, I rehearsed the movements at home along with the song.

My mother shook her head in astonishment. "Jo, I can't believe you. This is so hard. You're going over and over this. It's driving us crazy."

"It's got to be perfect, Mother. Repeating it is the only way I know to get it right."

By the time Sunday night rolled around, my mother and father knew all the lyrics by heart too. After a few hours, my dog, Mitzi, got bored with following me around through my routine. Lighting a cigarette, walking and singing while holding it, finally depositing it in a strategically placed ashtray, then slinking over to the piano where the pianist accompanied me.

When Kenny and I rehearsed my blocking, he made me repeat lighting the cigarette and moving while holding it.

"You don't smoke do you, Zaba?" I shook my head. "Do it again, please. And relax with it. You're holding that cigarette like it was a lit stick of dynamite."

By the time we were done, my stomach was churning from the cigarette smoke, but I could pass for a real smoker.

***

Monday morning, Faye and couple of seamstresses sewed me into a gorgeous, slinky, white satin gown. Jean Harlow had worn it in one of her early movies. The feel of that heavy satin caressing my skin sent a thrill up my spine. Harlow had been my idol and inspiration since the morning I saw the pictures of her in the Sioux City Journal the day after she died.

I struggled with the first blocking rehearsal on the set, but Kenny coaxed me through it. After a few tries, I had the moves. It was time to shoot.

Faye fussed with the gown and whispered to me. "You look absolutely stunning, Zaba. You're going to knock 'em dead." She patted my arm and stepped away.

Kenny Williams checked to make sure I was on my mark. "They've never seen anything like you, Zaba. Show 'em what they've been missing."

Ted Richmond said in my ear, "You look sensational!"

I looked out at the table where Tony Curtis, Joanne Dru, and Lyle Bettger were seated looking at me, waiting for the scene to start. There was an impish twinkle in Tony's eye. He was truly one of the most beautiful men I'd ever seen: darkly handsome, sinfully blue eyes, a wise-ass grin that morphed easily into a smirk, pouty lips and white-white teeth, and an insolent curl teasing at his forehead.

Tony was famously married to Janet Leigh. They embodied the wholesome American family ideal promoted by the Hays Office movie censors in the 1950s. Their photogenic marriage was just what movie magazines loved, pictures of them sitting by the pool, playing tennis, or attending premiers. But in reality, despite the gushy family images of Tony and Janet, Tony was completely uninterested in being faithful.

I was slapped back into reality by the playback of "You Belong to Me" and Rudy Maté shouting, "Action!"

My nightclub singer scene was a blur. Retakes. Coverage. Close-up. Closer close-up. Coverage of reactions from Tony, Joanne, and Lyle with me singing in the background.

Then at the end of a long take, Rudy Maté said with finality, "Cut and print! That is a wrap for Miss Olander! Great job, Zaba."

The crew applauded. People began congratulating me. My pals, the wardrobe ladies, were hugging me; the hairdresser was patting my shoulder with tears in her eyes; Bud Westmore grasped my hands in his. "That was amazing, Zaba. You looked like you'd been doing this all your life."

Tony pushed his way through the crowd around me. "Who's this amazing little actress no one's seen before?" he shouted, dancing around happily. He grabbed me in a bear hug. "They told me your name's Zaba. You lit this whole place up, Zaba."

He planted a big kiss on my lips.

I managed to stammer, "Thank you!" My legs went a little weak. That kiss lit up my tingle motor.

Tony went on, "We need to talk, Zaba. Sometime soon. I want you to meet my agent, Herb Brenner. Herb, come over here and meet Zaba."

I shook hands with Brenner, and Kenny Williams hugged me like a long lost relative. "I knew you could do it, Zaba. You put it all together. Not many experienced actresses could have done this on such short notice. You made it look easy."

"Ha! It wasn't easy at all!"

"It never matters whether it's actually easy or not, Zaba. The pros—the real pros, like Crawford, Gable, Jimmy Stewart—they all make it all *look* easy. Mark of the pro, honey. Talent and technique sweep the hard part under the rug. What's left is the real stuff."

I hugged him. "Thanks, Kenny, I couldn't have done it without you."

Tony shouldered his way back in to plant another big kiss on my lips. "Remember we need to get together, okay?"

Tony walked away, and Kenny Williams said quietly, "Zaba, I think Tony likes you. Did you notice the people watching you from the back of the soundstage?"

I shook my head. "I didn't notice anything but my blocking and handling that damned cigarette."

He chuckled. "Good concentration. There were six suits in the back watching you, big shots from UI corporate in New York. One was none other than Milton Rachmil himself."

"Who's that, Kenny?"

"He not only owns Universal International, but Decca Records as well. The scuttlebutt is they're out here to evaluate the CinemaScope process. Word on the street is it'll soon be in all the theaters." He looked around conspiratorially and lowered his voice. "But they couldn't stop talking about you."

"Wow! Great!"

"I overheard one ask, 'Why is this girl not under contract?' Richmond and a couple of them were huddled up thick as thieves."

I was thrilled to say the least. "What should I do?"

Kenny grinned. "Have lunch."

"Lunch? Are you kidding?"

"I'm dead serious. All the execs are having lunch at the commissary right now. They don't know it, but they need to see you again. I'll escort you over there. Wear your slinky satin gown. Keep your makeup just the way it is. It's cold out so wear your coat, but make sure you take it off to give the execs a full dose of what their newest starlet will look like."

"Oh, come on, Kenny."

"No bullshit, Zaba. This is how things get done in the big leagues. Are you ready for it?"

I took all of two seconds to decide. "Okay."

The commissary was crowded, but it was a day for miracles: We found a table near the visiting executives. I followed Kenny's instructions to the letter. Slipped off the coat. Made sure I posed without posing. It was a busy working lunch.

I was exhausted by the time I got home that night. Mom asked me how it went.

"I think it went well. Everyone congratulated me. They all said they liked it. I didn't get fired before it was over."

She made tomato soup and a grilled cheese sandwich with sliced tomato for my dinner. I took a bath, then a shower, and fell into bed.

The next day the world turned over.

Tuesday morning the telephone woke me, and Jimmy McHugh brayed in my ear, "Zaba, get over to the UI business office first thing tomorrow morning! Seven a.m.!"

Much louder and he wouldn't have needed a telephone.

Wiping the sleep from my eyes I mumbled, "What are you talking about, Jimmy?"

"I'm talking about a seven-year contract with two-year options for $260 a week."

"Wait a minute—Universal? Two hundred sixty—a week? Dollars? You're kidding me, right?"

"I am not. I just negotiated the contract not fifteen minutes ago."

"Jimmy, you *are* my gold-plated Svengali! How did you make it happen so fast?"

"Good things happen fast," he said with a chuckle. "UI is really high on you. Most of their starlets are getting fifty dollars a week on six-month contracts. Now, tomorrow—"

"I just can't believe this—"

"Don't interrupt me, Zaba. Here's what they want. They'll do a photo shoot immediately after you sign the contract. They want the pictures to look like they're your personal photos. They can get away with them being a little more risqué without the Hays Office objecting."

The Hays Office was Hollywood's self-censorship watchdog. Since the Hollywood scandals in the 1920s, the mission of the Hays Office was to ensure that the morals of unsuspecting moviegoers would not be corrupted by the glimpse of a naked body, the utterance of the mildest profanity, or movie plots that it deemed "unwholesome." (This was only the beginning of my interaction with Hollywood censors.)

Jimmy went on, "James Bacon from the Associated Press will interview you after the photo shoot and use the pictures for his article."

"Geez, Jimmy, I don't know about the interview—"

"Just do it, Zaba. You'll have a chaperon from the publicity department to make sure it goes smoothly. After you sign your contract, you'll go to the makeup department where they'll do your face and hair, then to the wardrobe department to select some outfits for the photographs. And by the way, they'll be giving you a new name tomorrow."

"New name? What's wrong with Zaba?"

"Nothing's wrong with it. But they want you to have a new name. Piper Laurie, Tony Curtis, Rock Hudson—nobody has their real name in Hollywood. Seven o'clock sharp, Zaba. And don't be late."

I was early.

Just before dawn, I showed up in my dad's old Ford at the front gate of the Universal lot. The gate guard sternly held up his hand. "You can't come in here, miss."

"Oh, please," I implored, "I just got a contract, and this is my first day! I've got to get to the business office to sign it!"

For a moment, he didn't say anything, and my heart sank. Was he going to turn me away and make me park outside the gate? Then he broke into a broad grin.

"First day? Park over there by the commissary, and good luck."

I thanked him and parked where he told me. As I walked the short distance to the business affairs building, I marveled that the place was busy so early in the morning. People were bustling from place to place, equipment was being rolled through the streets, trucks were unloading, and extras and bit players in costumes and makeup were heading for soundstages. Everybody was absorbed in their day-to-day, and the sun wasn't even up yet.

I was trying to get my head around that I was really here. For me, just a few days ago walking on this lot was the stuff of fantasy—maybe even delusion. I had wanted to be a movie star forever. I thought and talked about nothing else since I could remember. My parents never failed to supply a steady stream of disapproval. "Millions of girls are trying to get into movies," my father groused. "What chance could you possibly have?" My mother chimed in with, "You need to get a job, Jo. Stay in school." And as if that didn't dampen my spirits enough, she added, "Learn to type and take shorthand so you can get a decent job."

I didn't listen. And here I was.

For the business affairs guy and the lawyer who witnessed my signing, it was just another day at the office, but for me it was a dizzying, indelible memory. It was the culmination of the dream I'd had since I was six years old to become a Hollywood movie star. And suddenly, with the stroke of a pen, I was a movie star in the making, under contract to a major Hollywood movie studio. Of course, all I had to do now was prove I could actually do it.

As the ink dried on my dream, I was ushered down the hall to the makeup department. Heads turned when I came in—everybody checked out the new kid on the block. I was greeted by Bud Westmore, who had done my makeup on *Forbidden*. "Hi, Mr. Westmore."

"Bud. Hi, Zaba, welcome aboard. Have a seat and let's get to work."

A couple of hours later I was made up—facial and body makeup—my hair had been coiffed, and I had selected some outfits from the wardrobe department upstairs. They escorted me across the lot to the photo gallery and introduced me to Ray Jones, one of Universal's journeyman photographers. I didn't know it then, but Jones had photographed many of the glamorous greats: Marlene Dietrich, Ava Gardner, Yvonne De Carlo.

He was the photographer's photographer. For an aspiring glamour girl, he was the perfect mentor to show me what to do in front of the camera.

He shot a few tests to get a feel for what I could do. "Excellent, Zaba. You're naturally relaxed in front of the camera. That's a good start. You'd be surprised at the big stars who're intimidated by the camera." He moved a white oval mirror into position in front of the camera. "Can you see yourself, Zaba?"

"Yes, I can."

"Okay, that's how you check your pose. Dietrich used that very mirror for every photoshoot I did with her. Try it."

I was awkward with the mirror at first, but after a few minutes I began to get the hang of it. Jones was patient, coaxing me into the pictures he wanted.

We shot a lot of setups. Each one needed a wardrobe change, a different hairstyle, and a makeup change. Near the end of the shoot, we took a break. One of the publicity guys came in and asked if James Bacon could watch the last few shots. I said okay.

James Bacon was a short, compact young man with a disarming smile. He watched from the shadows behind the lights while we finished shooting.

We sat down for the interview and immediately got along great, as though we'd known each other forever. The interview went smoothly. It was lucky it wasn't radio or TV because my stomach was growling like an angry bear.

When we said goodbye, Bacon commented offhandedly, "You know, Zaba, I think I've got just the name for you."

"Really? What is it?"

"I can't tell you right now, but you'll find out soon enough."

I didn't pursue it. By then I was too hungry to care about a new name. I hurried over to the commissary and ordered a big lunch. I had wolfed down nearly an entire cheeseburger and fries when someone from the publicity department came to my table and handed me a folded note.

"It's your new name," he said.

I took a deep breath and unfolded it.

The note read: *Mamie Van Doren.*

***

I rushed home to tell my mother, agonizing over it the whole way. I'd glance at the note on the seat next to me and think, *Is anyone going to remember a three-word name?* I'd look at it again and think, *Yeah, maybe it's pretty cool.* But I didn't know what to think. It was like waking up one morning and being told you were adopted. *Who the hell am I now anyway?*

I burst in the front door and told my mother my new name.

"Oh, Jo!" she exclaimed. "What a beautiful name! It's so elegant and unique."

She was laughing and hugging me as I told her about the photo shoot and my interview with the Associated Press.

"My God, Jo, they must really like you, with special photos and an interview. You really are on your way."

"But you like the name, right?"

"I love it. That name will be very special—historical even. You respect that name. It's going to serve you well. You just wait and see."

I slumped on the living room couch. "I'm exhausted, Mother."

"Go take a hot bath and a shower. Wash off all your makeup and get into bed. You're going to have to get used to getting up early. Are you hungry?"

"I had a cheeseburger and fries not long ago."

"Get ready for bed. If you're hungry, I'll fix something."

I went to bed without supper and slept ten hours.

The next morning before daylight, I drove through the studio entrance. The smiling gate guard waved me through with a salute.

I parked outside the talent department. I was going inside to begin my first classes when I ran into Tony.

"Hey!" he boomed, hugging me like a long-lost brother. "Welcome to the family, Mamie." He kept a hand on my arm and stood close to me. "They gave you a terrific name. I love it."

"How'd you know it? Publicity hasn't released it yet."

"The jungle telegraph. By now even the gate guard probably knows your new name."

"I like it, but it takes some getting used to."

"You'll get the hang of it." He winked. "Now that you've got the contract, you need a movie. Keep your eyes open. I hear something good may be on the horizon."

"What do you mean, Tony?"

He put a finger to his lips. "Shhhh. Stay tuned. Gotta go. Janet's rehearsing a dance number with O'Connor in the gym."

Tony's wife, Janet Leigh, was just beginning to work on *Walking My Baby Back Home,* starring opposite Donald O'Connor.

Tony walked toward the gymnasium next to the talent department. As he reached the door, Janet Leigh came out and threw her arms around him. They kissed for a moment before Donald O'Connor came outside. They exchanged hellos, and Donald ducked into the men's dressing room next door.

The gymnasium was mostly a dance studio, with a ballet bar and a scattering of workout equipment. Dance rehearsals were held there. The dressing rooms for the men and women were adjacent to it, just outside.

Even as I watched Tony and Janet walk away hand in hand, I felt the same tingle I did when Tony kissed me after my scene in *Forbidden.*

If you've been paying attention throughout these pages, you know that for me, a tingle often signals the onset of yearning, which for better or worse, will likely manifest itself as good old-fashioned lust. But this was just too dangerous to act on. It was one thing to track down John Dillinger and ignite an affair with Lawrence Tierney. I was a cheeky teenager with little to lose, looking for adventure. Now I was just beginning the career I had dreamed of, and I had everything to lose.

There was another danger to my career as well. The bitch-goddess of Hollywood columnists, Louella Parsons, was Jimmy McHugh's girlfriend. She was notorious for sabotaging the careers of stars she didn't like, and because Jimmy was my manager and mentor, she was not likely to pass up a juicy bit of gossip about me.

I warned myself not to get too chummy. It is safest not to meddle with American apple pie. Tony and Janet looked like the perfect modern American couple, constantly on the pages of every movie magazine in town, their home life played up as the model for mid-century America. If I got involved with Tony, and we became an item in one of the magazines, it would ignite a huge scandal that would end my career and damage Tony's.

Universal had strict rules about fraternization. The rules might not apply as strictly to an honest-to-God star like Tony, but for a newly fledged starlet like me, it was a line that could not be crossed. At least not without sufficient planning.

As I entered the drama department to begin my classes, I thought about what Tony said. I needed a movie, and soon. A starlet without a movie is like a speedboat without an ocean.

But a young woman named Susie Ward was about to intervene. Susie wasn't even a real person yet, but she would emerge soon from the pages of a movie script, and she would be everyone's favorite football girl. The girl who would push Tony Curtis to be the *All American*.

***

When I drove in the gate on Monday of my second week, the guard saluted twice and said, "Good morning, Miss Mamie Van Doren!" That put a smile on my face right away.

Inside the drama department, there were newspapers spread out on the couch and contract players avidly poring over them. Clint Eastwood looked up when I came in. "She's here! Hi, Mamie!"

Lori Nelson turned around. "Mamie, have you seen all this?"

"No," I answered, looking over her shoulder at the *LA Times* front page. The headline read, "Mamie Van Doren: the answer to Marilyn Monroe."

"Oh, my God," I said.

There was a huge spread of the photos we'd shot last week. I had a hard time believing the girl in those pictures was me.

"You look fantastic, Mamie," Clint said. He was lanky and handsome back then too.

Richard Long peeked out from behind the *LA Times* entertainment section. "Great article too, Mamie. You really hit the jackpot with this one."

All the excitement had my head spinning. Suddenly there was a new me with a new name. Zaba had been a short-term tenant in my head. Joanie had seniority in there, but now this Mamie Van Doren was pushing out the boundaries of my head space.

Tony Curtis came in and scooped me up in his arms. "It's little Mamie! She's the girl with the answer!" Tony put me down and headed down the hall toward the classrooms. "See y'all later. Got a diction class."

"Me too," I said, following Tony.

"Mamie," he said when we were out of earshot of the others, "we've got to get together."

"What do you mean, Tony?"

He pulled me close. "I mean *get together*. I've wanted you like crazy since the first day I saw you on the set of *Forbidden*."

I felt his sudden erection and stepped away. I glanced around nervously. "Tony, we can't. If we get caught, I'll be out on the boulevard before you can say, 'morals clause.'"

"We won't get caught."

"Look, I'm really attracted to you, but…no. I've got to get to my class."

I walked away and left Tony and his erection standing in the hallway.

***

Meanwhile, back on the farm in South Dakota:

My grandfather, Pa Bennett, walked down to the square newspaper box on the shoulder of the dirt road and retrieved the local newspaper, the *Argus Leader*. It was barely light out, so he had a hard time making out the big picture on the front page above the fold. He squinted at the page and froze for a moment, his mouth open.

"Ma! Ma!" he shouted, dashing into the farmhouse. "Look, it's Joanie!"

He held the paper up to the kerosene lamp. My grandmother looked over his shoulder and exclaimed, "Oh, my goodness! It is Joanie!"

The headline read, "Local Rowena girl makes it big in Hollywood."

Pa jammed his battered old cap on his head. "I've got to go show everybody down at the pool hall."

"You'll do no such thing. There's work to be done around here, and the sun's not even up yet. You sit and have your breakfast."

Pa set his jaw defiantly. "I'll have breakfast when I get to the pool hall."

Pa drove the bumpy two miles to Rowena. He waved the *Argus Leader* front page with my picture in the face of anyone who would stand still. "You see? You see? My little Joanie's made it. She's a movie star!"

The denizens of the pool hall bought a lot of beers for Pa that day. When he finally came home gloriously drunk, my grandmother made him sleep it off in the attic. He curled up on a little cot in his Union suit, snoring, clutching his beer-stained copy of the *Argus Leader* to his chest.

While I sweated out the wait for my first movie role, I bided my time taking classes in the Universal Talent School. In particular, I doubled up on diction lessons. Jimmy McHugh had humiliated me often enough for me to realize that I needed to learn to speak better. He delighted in ridiculing me as a "dems and doze" girl. It was one of his less-than-endearing traits. I also enrolled in a ballet class and, of course, a scene study class.

Many of the other contract players poo-pooed at the talent school classes, but to me it looked like a fantastic opportunity. I was getting paid to study things that I would otherwise never have had access to—things that would make me more valuable as a performer. I was a regular in the drama department's classes.

To my great relief, I got the call from Jimmy McHugh that I was up for *All American,* a college football movie, directed by Jesse Hibbs, a former All American when he played football for the University of Southern California Trojans. He had directed some westerns at Universal, and he was considered a natural to direct a movie about college football. Tony Curtis was set to star in the role of a USC student from the wrong side of the tracks, who would, in the final reel, lead the team to victory, but only after overcoming a world of troubles with help from sexy Susie Ward.

I was to test for the role of Susie—gulp—in four days. It was panic time. I dashed over and got the script from the drama department and hurried to the wardrobe department to be fitted for a waitress's uniform.

My pal, the wardrobe mistress Rose Marie, helped me with the costume. First, I tried on Shelley Winters's waitress costume in *A Double Life.* Rose Marie shook her head.

"Too big," she growled. "And not the least bit sexy. Forget that one."

We went through more waitress outfits, none of which lived up to the ideal Rose Marie had in mind. Finally, she threw up her hands. "You need sexy, Mamie. You need something that'll..." She groped for the word. "Something that'll sing. Fuck this, Mamie. I'm going to make you a waitress outfit that'll knock their jockstraps off."

Rose Marie quickly put together a butt-hugging short skirt and a white silky blouse. Underneath the blouse was the first iteration of what would become known as the "bullet bra." It did all the right things for my curves. Maybe it looked a bit upscale for the little beer bar and burger joint where Sally worked, but as Rose Marie said, "Mamie, this'll double Sally's tips." She smiled slyly. "I hear there'll be a bunch of USC football players working as extras. That outfit'll make all those big gorgeous football players stand at attention."

I nodded enthusiastically. The football player I was thinking about was Nick Bonelli, Tony's rebellious character. We would be working side by side—even playing love scenes. Tony was cocked and loaded at all times, ready at the least provocation, a fact that was bound to put a real strain on my ability to say no...and mean it. Even though Janet was making a movie on the same movie lot, Tony was undaunted—obsessed with fucking. And if my tingle comes along at just the right moment, I might dare to do the nasty too.

Mid-afternoon on a Wednesday turned out to be the right moment. Tony and I were rehearsing my screen test in the gymnasium next door to the drama department. The scene is when Tony and Susie begin dancing in the bar and have a very sexy conversation:

We've just met, and I've served him a beer. We get up to dance and I say, "What are you afraid of?"

Nick replies, "You."

"Why?" I ask.

Nick looks at me, "Because I know trouble when I see it."

I cuddle up to him and say, "How could I cause you trouble?"

In the finished movie, it's a very sexy scene. In our rehearsal, it became damn near pornographic. When we danced and Tony held me close, I could feel his erection throbbing against my leg.

Tony's breathing was suddenly raspy. "Look, Mamie," he said, "I've just got to have you. Let's do it."

I was tired of holding back too. "But where? We're sure to get caught in here."

"Next door. The men's dressing room. Nobody ever uses it this time of day. It's deserted."

I nodded enthusiastically. My tingle was raging like an electric current. We hurried out the gymnasium door and into the men's dressing room. Tony quickly checked to make sure no one was inside.

"It's empty. Get in here."

I brushed past him through the door. As soon as I was inside, he locked it, grabbed me in his arms, and kissed me hard and deep. Our bodies pressed against each other. Tony unbuttoned his trousers, and I hiked up my skirt. He grasped my butt cheeks and crushed me against him. It was rumored around the studio that Tony possessed an enormous cock. I was now in the position to confirm that those rumors were true. He was about to enter me when there was a discrete knock at the door. We froze.

"Is anyone in there?" a small feminine voice asked. "I'm looking for Rock Hudson. The business office has a message for him."

She was one of the bicycle couriers the studio employed to deliver messages around the sprawling campus.

"No," Tony said, "sorry, Rock's not here. Probably on the backlot filming *Taza, Son of Cochise.*"

There was a pause. "Is that you, Mr. Curtis? It's me, Sheila."

Tony's eyes darted to me. I was trying not to laugh.

"Oh, yes, yes, Sheila. You'd better go find Rock. You can't miss him. He'll be wearing an Indian headdress."

We heard the messenger get on her bike and pedal away.

"So that's how you knew this was a good place to hide? Little Sheila?"

"No, no, that's not what you think."

"I think we'd better get down to business, *Mr. Curtis.*"

I reached for his flagging erection and gave it a helpful tug. We started squirming against each other again, grinding our hips. As he grabbed my butt cheeks again and lifted me, someone loudly rattled the locked door. Tony and I jumped. After a couple of seconds, there was a loud knock.

"Anybody in there?" It was Richard Long.

"Yeah! Hi, Richard," Tony said through the door. "What's going on?"

"Well, nothing special, Tony, I just wanted to take a leak."

"Right, Richard. Just a minute." Tony growled under his breath, "Christ all mighty, it's like Grand fucking Central Station around here. Hide over in the corner away from the door. I'll get rid of him."

I stepped into the shadows, and Tony unlocked the door. I could see Richard Long's face through the crack next to the hinge. "Hi, Richard. I'm kind of busy right now. Could you use the bathroom over in the gym? Just this once?"

Tony was known for his womanizing, and Richard immediately understood. "Sure, sure," he said, trying to hold back his laughter. "Just this once, Tony?"

"Okay, Richard, thanks—" Tony looked over Richard's shoulder and stopped dead. "Holy shit! Janet just came out of that soundstage, and she's walking this way."

That terrified me. I would have wet my pants, if I had been wearing any.

"Richard," Tony said, "wait right here. Don't move. Let's you and I walk down to meet her."

Richard was openly chuckling now. "Sure, Tony, but you'd better hurry before she gets any closer."

Frantically, Tony ducked back inside. "Mamie, Janet's walking this way. Richard and I will walk down to meet her and steer her into the drama department building. When the coast is clear, get out of here fast."

Tony tucked in his shirt and went outside. I could hear their voices as they walked away.

"So, what have you got going in there, Tony?"

"I can't tell you, Richard."

"Not even a hint?"

"Not even. Jesus Christ, I've got such blue balls."

"You're going to owe me for this one, Tony."

Their voices faded away. I stuck my head out the door and looked around. Tony, Janet, and Richard were just entering the drama department. No one else was around, and it looked safe. I slipped through the doorway and walked as nonchalantly as I could to my car. I started the engine and drove out the front gate. Outside on Lankershim Boulevard, I breathed a sigh of relief.

***

The next day was my screen test for *All American*. I had agonized over it all night. If I got this part, how would I deal with Tony? Nearly all our scenes were romantic. And once the camera stopped rolling, Tony's overcharged libido would tempt him to move our scene to someplace private. And my own roiling hormones had already coerced me into cooperating once. But, I told myself, no more hiding in locker rooms or anywhere else on the Universal campus.

Tony looked sheepish on the soundstage the next morning. I was not a little pissed off. Our little romantic tryst wasn't exactly Charlotte Brontë, but more like a cross between D. H. Lawrence and the Marx Brothers. I was embarrassed to have gotten involved in such a ludicrous situation, regardless of a what a sexy hunk Tony was.

We avoided eye contact as the director, Jesse Hibbs, finished setting up the shot. When he was out of earshot Tony said, "Sorry about yesterday, Mamie. We'll do better next time."

"There won't be a next time, Tony. Not on the studio lot."

The cameraman leaned in to check a light. We shut up until he leaned back out.

"I understand, Mamie—"

"I hope so, Tony, because I was in real jeopardy the other day. If we'd been caught humping against that dressing room door, I'd have been fucked in more ways than one—"

Jesse Hibbs interrupted, "All right, Mamie, Tony, let's shoot one."

After the screen test wrapped, Hibbs took me aside. "I've got to test one more girl for this role this afternoon, so you'll probably get the decision tomorrow morning." He gave me a fatherly pat on the arm and winked. It left me feeling that I had a good chance of getting the role.

I sneaked back onto the soundstage later that afternoon and watched Marisa Pavan test for the Susie role. Marissa was a lovely girl, the twin sister of Pier Angeli. She did an okay job, but clearly she wasn't right for the part of an all-American girl like Susie.

Jimmy McHugh phoned me that evening and said, "You've got the part, Mamie. Congratulations, Jesse Hibbs loved you."

It was unlike Jimmy to be so effusive with congratulations. Usually that meant that something else was on the way.

"Just be careful," Jimmy continued. "Tony Curtis is notorious for being a womanizer."

"Really?"

"Yes, really. Steer clear of him. There are rumors that he's not very faithful to Janet."

"No kidding. Is that so?"

"Don't risk getting involved with him—and he'll try, I'm sure. You get caught, and your career will be over before it starts."

"Okay, Jimmy, I'll be careful."

"One last thing. Jesse Hibbs wants to see you in his office at 8:00 a.m. sharp tomorrow. Don't be late."

***

I wrote in my 1984 autobiography, *Playing the Field*, about my relationship with Jesse Hibbs. It was a classic example of the predatory environment in the movie industry during the so-called Golden Age. A new starlet in her first movie was like blood in the water to the male sharks at the studio. Since Hibbs was going to be directing me, he took it as an opportunity to try for a little action.

All of a sudden, I was in the middle of a bizarre situation. On the one hand, the star of the movie, Tony Curtis, was ardently trying to have an affair with me, and on the other, Hibbs, the director, was using his position to do the same thing.

It was a scenario so common in Hollywood as to be a cliché. And I couldn't see a way to do anything about it. If I spoke up and rang the bell on Hibbs, I might as well turn in my gate pass too, because my career at Universal or any other studio would be toast.

Eventually, I couldn't avoid a summons to Hibbs's office for a "rehearsal," without getting into trouble. Luckily for me, he was only interested in having me put my hand on his penis, perhaps because he understood the trouble we could get into. Or maybe he felt just the least bit creepy. But to get along, I went along and gave his tiny penis a friendly tug. He didn't need much. It brought back memories of my encounter at the beach with Hank the Yank, the creep that Nils Thor Granlund had fixed me up with when I was a teenager. Welcome to Hollywood, Mamie.

The football action sequences in *All American* were shot at the Rose Bowl in Pasadena and featured bit players and extras recruited from the University of Southern California Trojans football team. Because the movie was scheduled for a fall release to coincide with football season, we shot in the Rose Bowl throughout the summer.

The publicity department thought it would be a good idea to send me to the Rose Bowl for a photo shoot. The wardrobe department dolled me up in short shorts, a tight sweater, and high heels—I mean, who doesn't play football in heels? My wardrobe did not fail to catch the attention of the team. Every time I turned around, there were handsome guys in helmets and tight pants jostling to get into the picture with me. Among the USC hunks were Frank Gifford, Tom Harmon, Donn Moomaw, and Jimmy Sears, all of whom went on to illustrious careers in professional football. (Gifford had an annoying habit of hugging me and tossing me into the air every time we met. It was a frightening reminder of the incident at LA High School when a group of senior boys grabbed me while I was having my lunch and threw me into the air over and over.)

Tony and Richard Long sweated along with the real players through drills and mock game sequences. It was tough for them. They were older than the college players and definitely not in game shape. Tony and I eyed each other a few times, but Janet was often nearby. Meanwhile, my ardor for Tony cooled considerably in the presence of a squad of so many good-looking alternatives.

Let's see: eeny, meeny, miny, moe. But I didn't. Or did I? I might have. It's a secret. Hey, a girl's got to have *some* mysteries in her past.

***

All American was more than just my introduction to the silver screen. It was a baptism of fire and a master class in being a movie actress, and, ultimately, a movie star. Aside from some acting coaching at the showcase theaters where I'd worked (Aaron Spelling was one of my acting coaches—only so-so!) and a few scene study classes in the Uni drama department, I'd had little training as an actor. But once the movie was under way, I was immersed in the how and why professional actors do what they do. (And, boy, did I need to know it.) Watching character actors like Paul Cavanagh and Donald Randolph prepare for their scenes and then work in front of the camera was a revelation and an education. And working with skilled and talented actors like Tony Curtis and Richard Long who carried the movie on their shoulders—especially Tony, of course—was a first-rate apprenticeship.

All American also initiated me into the real "donkey work" of making movies: multiple scene takes; hitting your marks; finding your key light; doing the scene the same way each time; doing the scene the same way, only with the changes the director wanted; and interminable waiting for lighting changes, set adjustments, and film reloads.

And getting up early. I was lucky. My mother made sure I got up on time and made breakfast for me. After work, she'd have dinner ready so I could shower and get to bed early.

"My God, Jo," she said one early morning a few weeks into *All American,* "you work so damned hard. Are you sure you want to do this?"

I nodded with a mouth full of oatmeal. "It's all I ever wanted, Mother. That's what you get for parking me in the Orpheum Theatre while you were working. But I admit that being in movies looked a damn sight more glamorous from the front row of the Orpheum than it does from here."

When *All American* was ready to open, Universal sent Tony Curtis and me on a national publicity tour. Naturally, Janet Leigh tagged along to make sure Tony stayed out of mischief. A few weeks on the road might have been the perfect opportunity for Tony and me to consummate our lust. But with Janet along on the tour, ix-nay on the ucking-fay. I was saddled with a Universal-employed chaperone named Midge, presumably to guard my virtue and to make sure I said the right things in press interviews. (Universal was *that* old fashioned.)

Tony and I had barely spoken for weeks until we found ourselves alone in the same hotel elevator the day of the premier. As soon as the door closed and the elevator started, Tony took me in his arms and kissed me.

"I hope it's a slow elevator," I said, coming up for air.

"Not slow enough," Tony said. "Why don't we go to your room? Janet's in the hotel beauty salon having her hair done."

I reluctantly pushed myself away from his embrace. "No. I never know when Midge will show up. Too much risk to enjoy it."

"Yeah," Tony groused. "Janet and I will be on our way to New York after the premier tonight."

"I'll be going on a tour of the South for a couple more weeks."

The elevator stopped on my floor, and I stepped out.

"See ya," said Tony.

I blew him a kiss as the elevator doors closed. It would be a long time before Tony and I met up again.

I continued promoting *All American*, making the rounds of movie theaters and press interviews in Ohio, Texas, Alabama, Georgia, and Louisiana—places where folks take their college football seriously, and where they took their racial segregation seriously too. It was my first exposure to the Jim Crow South.

Growing up in California, I had seen racial discrimination firsthand when Quincy Jones and I tried to have dinner in a Malibu restaurant and were turned away. But California's racism was nothing compared to the rigid apartheid in the southern states. I was shocked by separate drinking fountains, restrooms, train station waiting rooms, and public facilities.

The not-so-subtle message was: *The South may have lost the Civil War, but you are still not free.* Under Jim Crow laws, Black people were meant to be invisible, except when performing their slave-like service roles. The slightest disobedience could bring on grave punishments—harassment, beatings, or, worst of all, lynching. The dark side of the genteel South frightened me, and I couldn't wait to leave it.

I felt let down when the publicity tour ended. I missed the excitement of traveling to new places, talking to the press, and meeting fans who seemed to really accept me as, well gee, a movie star. And though I could do without the smug reality of Southern racism, I also missed the genuine friendliness of Southern hospitality.

And I truly missed the charm of New Orleans. The city seemed to say, "Never mind tomorrow. Dance and have another sloe gin fizz. Tomorrow will arrive right on schedule." I told myself that I'd visit there again.

New studio contract players all suffer from the same obsession: What's my next movie? If producers and directors are not thinking about how you'll fit into their next project, the chances are you're going to be looking for a new job.

It was most definitely on my mind during the long trip back to LA. But fortunately, audiences, reviewers, and theater owners had reacted enthusiastically to Susie Ward. My bosses back at Universal were pleased, and producers and directors on the lot began discussing what movie their newest so-called sex symbol was going to appear in next. *Yankee Pasha*, directed by Joseph Pevney, came along with the role of Lilith for me opposite Jeff Chandler, Rhonda Fleming, and Lee J. Cobb. I got down to work on it. Tony Curtis, lovely as he was, faded into the background. For a while.

***

Fast-forward seven years. There had been a lot of changes: I got pregnant, married band leader Ray Anthony, had a baby (my beloved Perry, the light of my life), and got released (read: fired) from Universal. In that order.

Just days after Perry was born, the only female executive at Universal, Donna Holloway, visited me in the hospital to deliver the most priceless firing statement ever. "Mamie," she said with a straight face, "sex symbols don't have babies." That was just the kind of dumbass prudishness you might expect from a corporate giant. But I admit I was fearful that I'd never work again.

The pregnancy was a tedious ordeal: big belly, growing bigger all the time; morning sickness; and the whole panoply of pregnancy ailments, mood swings, and depression. Then it was labor, false start, labor again, a universe of pain—and it was over.

I confess that I possess very few maternal skills. I needed lots of help from a parade of nurses and nannies, but I got myself back into shape with surprising speed. The wonderful Earl Leaf took pictures once I was skinny enough.

And suddenly, the jobs began to come in: *Untamed Youth; Girls Town; Born Reckless; Guns, Girls and Gangsters;* and more lined up to become the second phase of my career.

Then came *The Private Lives of Adam and Eve,* the brainchild of my old friend, producer Al Zugsmith. It would be shot in my old neighborhood, Universal. The prospect of going back to the studio where I got started was exciting. Instead of being a contract player, I was returning as a star in my own right. And instead of a dreary makeup room, I had a bungalow all to myself, newly redecorated, with a comfy bed, a makeup table and mirror, and a kitchenette. It was a quiet place to retreat from the noise and confusion of the set while the next shot was set up.

As the fates would have it, *Adam and Eve* was being shot at the same time as the newest sword-and-sandal spectacular, *Spartacus. Spartacus* was directed by Stanley Kubrick, starring Kirk Douglas in the title role, and co-starring none other than Tony Curtis. As an added temptation, my bungalow was situated between Kirk's and Tony's.

Uh-oh. This could be trouble. Tingle time.

When Tony paid a visit to our set one morning, he was like visiting royalty. Always one to look his best, Tony was clad only in his loin cloth, short shorts, (provided for modesty's sake by the wardrobe department), and Egyptian #1 makeup. That was the lovely thing about Tony's role: his wardrobe was very simple and very tingle-worthy. The loin cloth left little to the imagination. He looked every inch the movie star.

After a few minutes of schmoozing, the crew dispersed to their own jobs. Tony sidled up close to me.

"You look sensational, Mamie," he said softly.

"You too, Tony. It's so good to see you. If you keep looking like that, you'll have men all over America wearing loincloths."

"You think so?"

"Look at what Brando did for wife-beater T-shirts."

He leaned in to whisper, "Can we see each other sometime?"

In the seven years since our close call in the men's locker room, Tony and I had been model citizens—at least when it came to each other. I'd had an assortment of lovers and so had Tony, but we had never sought out each other. Still, tucked away in the back of my mind was always the unfulfilled memory of Tony. And if you have an adventurous spirit like mine, the allure of the one mountain yet to be climbed is powerful. Karma was serving up a special plate of temptation.

We broke at noon, and I went back to my bungalow. The commissary had laid out my food—a shrimp cocktail, the specialty of the house. I was looking forward to a quick lunch and a nap. But my plans were about to be changed.

I had just eaten the first shrimp when there was an authoritative knock at the door. When I opened it, Tony was standing there, still wearing nothing but his loin cloth.

Tony grinned. "Hi," he said. He was sporting a major erection. "Surprise," he added.

"No surprise to me," I said. "You'd better bring that thing inside before somebody gets hurt."

He stepped inside and closed the door. He took me in his arms, and we kissed deeply.

"We'd better not waste any time. Lunch is already half over."

I slipped out of my skimpy Eve costume. "You're right."

He lifted me onto the bed and entered me.

"Oh, oh, wow! My God!"

Tony groaned and pushed deeper, in rhythm—steady, deep, slow.

The talking was over. We fucked in earnest, hard and fast. I am not a size queen, but Tony's member was as large as any I'd ever had. He moaned loudly, our rhythms matching, painful and beautiful and erotic. We were gasping for air, sweat rolling off of us. My orgasm started, the rumbling of a freight train off in the distance, racing inevitably down the track. Tony was the engineer, driving the locomotive, hell-bent for the train to be on time. And then it was.

My orgasm was well under way by the time Tony reached his. It was explosive. He let out a loud groan, and semen gushed everywhere, on and on. By the time his climax subsided, Tony, the bed, and I were covered in sweat.

Tony dashed into the bathroom and brought back towels. "Sorry for the mess. We'll do better next time."

I'd heard that one before. "Right," I replied, already knowing that there wouldn't be a next time. You couldn't help but love Tony. He was charming, gorgeous, and sexy, but he was a lot of extra work.

There was a knock at the door. "Miss Van Doren, they'll be ready for you in five minutes."

"Thank you! Tony, I'd better get cleaned up."

He leaned over and kissed me. "Me too. See you soon." He slipped out the door. I hurriedly put myself together for my next scene, thinking of how the callow young starlet who barely knew where to park her car had morphed into the current version of Mamie.

Coda

Tony Curtis and I remained friends for the next seventy years. Though we often saw each other at Hollywood parties and at the Playboy Mansion, we never went to bed again. But no matter where it was, no matter who was around, as soon as he laid eyes on me he would bellow out: "Little Mamie!" and wrap his arms around me in a giant hug.

In the early 2000s, American Cinematheque in Los Angeles had a special showing of *Guns, Girls and Gangsters*. I came onstage for a Q&A. Before I could answer the first question, a courier brought me a giant bouquet of flowers from Tony. It meant so much to me that he remembered and thought of me.

Tony was married and divorced four more times. His fifth wife, Jill Vandenberg, was a keeper. Jill was an animal-rights activist dedicated to rescuing horses that would have been otherwise destroyed for food. Jill just seemed to "get it" about Tony. And for his part, Tony looked upon her as his anchor. Jill never felt threatened or jealous when Tony was around me. She took his flirtations and ego in stride. Tony was the way Tony was, and Jill was smart enough not to try and change him.

A few months before Tony died, we met at an autograph signing in Palm Springs. I was promoting a line of wines bearing my name. Tony had a booth where he was exhibiting and selling his paintings. He was sitting in a wheelchair, looking shockingly weak and infirm. When he saw me, he let out a shout. We embraced for a long time, tears flowing.

The years had not been kind to Tony. He was a lifelong heavy smoker and suffered from chronic obstructive pulmonary disease (COPD) and a host of other health problems. He died on September 29, 2010.

In 2013, I participated in a documentary about Tony. When it was completed, Jill invited me to be one of the guests of honor at the premier at the Jewish Community Center in Hollywood. Being a guest of honor meant that I would be one of several to go onstage after the documentary and answer questions from the audience. My husband Thomas and I attended.

The documentary had been approved by Tony, and he had recorded a running narration, often on camera. I found it a little unsettling to watch him. Then he began to talk about his girlfriends—Marilyn Monroe, Gina Lollobrigida, Piper Laurie, and me. As he spoke about us being lovers, I sank lower and lower in my seat. I hid my face against Thomas' shoulder. All the pages of this book notwithstanding, I am a very private person, particularly about my sex life. (I know, I know, what have I done for the last umpteen pages but talk about my sex life? Suffice to say, it's been a long life, sex and otherwise, and, well, it's complicated.)

When the lights came up and Jill called my name to come on stage, I wanted to hide under my seat. But instead, I sat on a high stool with Jill and three others, took the microphone, and answered questions. As we talked about our experiences with Tony, I had the strangest feeling that he was part of the audience, watching from somewhere, smirking that insolent smirk, and laughing along. If there was one thing that Tony loved, it was being the center of attention. Tony was definitely in there with all of us. It was as though I could reach out and touch him.

I could feel the tingle.

Chapter Eight

Jack Webb—Just the Facts Ma'am

Author's Note: There is no introductory cartoon for this chapter. For reasons that will be clear as you read on, he doesn't deserve one.

The story you are about to read is true. No names have been changed to protect anyone.

Television in the 1950s produced some enduring and iconic characters. Lucy Ricardo (Lucille Ball), Ozzie and Harriet, Gunsmoke's Marshal Matt Dillon (James Arness), Lassie, Rin Tin Tin, and Dragnet's Sergeant Joe Friday all became household names. Few of those characters have endured in people's imaginations as pervasively as Sergeant Joe Friday, the alter ego of Jack Webb, Dragnet's creator, producer, and director. While Dragnet became part of popular culture, the program and Jack Webb seeped into the culture of the LAPD.

Dragnet's first incarnation was a successful radio show that made its debut in 1949. From its beginnings, *Dragnet*'s story lines were drawn from LAPD case files. Webb's insistence on the authenticity of the stories and police procedures endeared *Dragnet* and Jack Webb to both the LAPD upper echelon and its rank-and-file officers. *Dragnet*'s popularity on NBC radio led the network produce the program for television where it quickly became one of the most popular TV shows in America.

Like most people, my parents and I faithfully tuned in every week to watch Sergeant Joe Friday's deadpan police work bring murderers, drug dealers, car thieves, and rapists to justice. Remember that—rapists. By today's standards, the series was almost quaint, devoid of car chases, sexual innuendo, and fight scenes. But it was the kind of conservative, crime-doesn't-pay sort of cop show that post-war America wanted.

LAPD was often under fire from community groups for police brutality and shoddy investigatory work. *Dragnet* conveniently ignored the department's flaws. The show presented the LAPD as starched and pressed, shaped and trimmed, and trusty and loyal. You could sleep well at night knowing that Joe Friday-type cops were on guard. Joe Friday became LAPD's standard bearer and patron saint.

My parents and I had recently moved from the house on Harvard Boulevard to the San Fernando Valley, the epicenter of post-war middle-class resurgence. My mother had been critically injured in an automobile accident five years before, broadsided by a drunk driver running a red light. Her right leg was shattered, and fragments of bone nicked an artery. She would have bled to death but for the quick thinking of a passing soldier who applied a tourniquet and stopped the bleeding. The soldier left without a word. When the emergency medics arrived, they insisted that the anonymous Samaritan soldier had saved her from certain death from loss of blood. She was taken to Queen of Angels Hospital for treatment. It was touch and go for a while whether or not they could save her leg, but in the end, save it they did.

As my mom recovered from her injuries, the medical bills became overwhelming. I took it upon myself hire an attorney to get compensation from the drunk driver, who was clearly at fault. With typical teenage chutzpah, I picked the name of LA's first superstar attorney, Jerry Giesler. When I told my father that I was going to have Giesler take my mom's case, he scoffed, "Why would he see you? How could we possibly pay him?"

"Just watch, Daddy."

I marched into his office and told him my story of Mom's accident. Whether it was out of pity or admiration for my sheer guts, he took the case and won a large settlement for us. My parents used the money to buy a new house in the Valley. It would turn out to be a fortunate choice of location. It was a short drive from Universal International Studios, where I would soon be a contract player.

I had only been under contract at UI for a short time when I got a telephone call from my friend, Carolyn Jones. I had known Carolyn and her partner Aaron Spelling since we were all players at Ben Bard Theater, a local acting school and talent showcase. Aaron had managed to get a good part on *Dragnet*, and Aaron and Carolyn had become friendly with Jack Webb.

"Mamie," Carolyn said, "Jack very much wants to meet you."

Publicity was beginning to hit from my introduction at UI. My pictures were showing up in newspapers and the trades, and columnists' interviews with me were being published in movie magazines. Webb would've seen me all over. "He's really interesting, but he's married, isn't he?"

"Yeah," Carolyn softly drew out the word to make it sound sexy. "But he's separated and on his way to a divorce. I wouldn't sweat that. When he found out that we knew you, he right away wanted an introduction. Aaron's shooting a scene tomorrow afternoon. Why don't you come by and watch the filming? You can meet Jack after we wrap."

"Okay, Carolyn, I'll do it." We agreed on a time, and I hung up the phone.

I was flattered. Jack Webb was really good-looking—dark and handsome, the strong silent type. Everyone knew that Sergeant Joe Friday was as straight an arrow as you could find. Plus, Webb was then probably as well-known as anyone in Hollywood. A fledgling starlet like me could do worse than be seen around town with an important and popular personality. In my mind, it was a good career move, possibly with exciting benefits.

I showed up at the *Dragnet* soundstage on the Disney studio lot the next afternoon. Carolyn ushered me into the soundstage where a scene with Aaron playing a convicted drug dealer was about to be shot. The set was considerably lower budget compared to the studio-built sets on UI's soundstages. Lights were set, makeup checked, and Webb said, "Action!"

Aaron looked into the camera with a remorseful hangdog look as the judge handed down his twelve to fifteen-year sentence.

"Cut!" Webb said loudly, "And that's a wrap everybody." The crew began packing up the camera gear and lights. Webb sauntered over to where Carolyn and I were standing.

"Hi, Mamie," he said. "Welcome to our humble workshop."

I extended my hand. "Thank you, Jack, it's a pleasure to meet you." Up close he was not as handsome as I had thought. I had been expecting a buttoned-down version of Joe Friday. Instead, the real guy didn't quite measure up to my expectations. "I'm a big fan of *Dragnet*. It's fun to peek behind the curtain."

He smiled at that. "Thanks. Mamie, I'd like to take you to dinner sometime. Would you give me your number?"

"Sure. That sounds like fun." He offered me a pencil and the back page of his shooting script, and I scribbled my number.

"Thanks. I'll call you soon, okay?"

"Okay, Jack. It's nice to meet you."

Carolyn walked me back to my car. "Well, what do you think, Mamie? Is he handsome or what?"

"Umm hmm."

"Let me know what happens, okay? I bet you two will have a lot of fun."

Webb called a couple of days later and asked me to dinner. He picked me up at my parents' new home, and we drove to a nice steakhouse in the Valley. We made small talk over dinner. He described some of his plans for other shows, and I talked about life at UI. When we finished dinner, he drove me home and we said goodnight on my doorstep. It wasn't even dark yet. I didn't even kiss him.

I didn't hear from Webb for the next couple of weeks. I thought it was just as well. He didn't seem to be that enthusiastic about being on a date with me. He just appeared to be a guy who was seriously lacking in charm. I made up my mind not to go out with him again.

However, I was surprised when he called me about two weeks later. We had an amiable conversation for a few minutes before he asked me out.

"Mamie, I'm going my producer's house for a barbecue next Sunday. He and his wife have a beautiful spread out in the country with horses and stables. I've got to talk some business with him after we have an early dinner, but it'll be fun for you."

He sounded more charming this time, and I wasn't doing anything on Sunday anyway. I reconsidered and said I would go.

We had a pleasant dinner with Jack's producer and his wife. When they retired to another room to talk business, I took a walk down to their stables. They had a number of handsome horses, and I took some time to get acquainted with them. When I wandered back to the house, Jack was preparing to leave. It had been an agreeable Sunday afternoon outing, but it was clear that our personalities didn't mesh. It cemented my resolve not to kindle a relationship with Jack Webb.

On the drive back, Jack said, "Before I take you home, Mamie, I need to stop by my house and pick up some things."

"Okay," I said. I didn't think much about it, since I knew Jack and Julie London were recently separated. I thought perhaps he needed to pick up some clothing for the week ahead.

When we pulled into his garage, I said, "I'll wait in the car."

"No, c'mon in. It might take a few minutes. You can have a drink." Reluctantly, I got out of the car and went into the house.

Jack waved me toward the sofa and disappeared into the kitchen. He came back with a glass of wine.

"I don't want anything to drink, Jack. Thanks."

He insisted on handing me the glass. "Go ahead and try a sip. It's a brand-new Chardonnay and it's really tasty. Just a sip."

I sipped the wine. I'm not much of a wine drinker, but it tasted like just another white wine to me.

And then I blacked out. I managed to open my eyes, and I could see Jack hovering in front of me. He took the wine glass out of my hand and said, "I've got to go to the garage and get some rope." I blacked out again. This time when I opened my eyes, I was tied to a kitchen chair. My ears were roaring, and the room was spinning. I could see Jack doing something in the living room. Panic set in, but it was like I was in a dream—I tried to scream but nothing came out.

"Wha—what are you doing...? Please untie me." I passed out again.

When I regained consciousness, I was spread-eagled on a bed, tied hand and foot. Webb climbed on top of me, forcibly entered my vagina, and began having hard sex with me. I tried to scream, but no sound came out.

I couldn't move my arms to fight him off or close my legs to prevent his entry. It was painful, but when I tried to protest, words wouldn't come out.

Again, I lost consciousness. I was jolted awake by the animal growl of his orgasm. I opened my eyes to the nightmare image of a crazed-looking Sergeant Joe Friday thrusting himself into me, his teeth bared in a grimace and a manic look in his eye. I was overcome by terror and blacked out again.

I don't know how much time passed before I came to again. I could hardly breathe, but I could smell leather. I was lying face down on the passenger seat of Jack Webb's car. I tried to sit up, but I was too dizzy. I slumped in the seat again.

The next thing I remember is pounding on our front door and sobbing for my mother to let me in. When she opened the door, I fell into her arms.

"Good God, Jo! What's wrong? Are you drunk?" She half carried me into my bedroom, and I collapsed on the bed. "My God, look at your clothes." Webb must have tried to dress me enough to get me home, but my blouse was on inside-out, and my skirt was on backwards. "Answer me, Jo. What's happened to you?"

I blinked at her, unable to focus my eyes. I could barely form the words to speak. "Oh, Mother, I've been doped and raped."

She turned toward their bedroom and called my dad. "Warner, get in here!" She told my dad what I had said. "She was out with Jack Webb, and the son-of-a-bitch slipped her a Mickey Finn and raped her."

My dad bellowed, "That bastard! I'll kill him!"

"No time for that now, Warner. We need to take care of her."

They looked me over carefully. My legs were still wet with semen. "Help me get her into the bathroom. We need to take care of this right away."

They sat me on the toilet, and Mother douched me with vinegar and water. "Warner, while I'm doing this, fill the bathtub with hot water." When she finished, they eased me into the hot bath, and Mother washed my body and hair.

I was still groggy from the drug, and my head was pounding as Mother rinsed me. "All right, Jo, we're going to help you stand, and I'll turn the shower on. You're going to feel a lot better after a hot shower."

She was right. The pounding hot water soothed me. I finally stopped crying.

When she had me washed and dried, and a towel wrapped around my wet hair, she got me into some pajamas and sat me on the edge of my bed.

"You need to get some food in you. Towel dry your hair while I make some scrambled eggs and bacon."

The smell of bacon cooking made me realize I was hungry. I wolfed down the food when she brought it. My headache was subsiding, and I felt profoundly exhausted, but my mind was clearing.

Mother tucked the blankets around me. "Sleep for now, Jo. We'll talk about all this in the morning."

"Mother, Daddy, listen. Please don't say anything to anyone. If news of this gets into the papers, I'll be finished at UI. They'll boot me out, and no other studio will touch me. And it'll be his word against mine. Jack Webb is very tight with the LAPD. Even if I went to the cops, who do you think they'd believe? Joe Friday or some movie starlet?" I slumped back on my pillow, completely spent. "Just don't do anything. We can talk when I wake up. I'm just going to have to live with this."

The next day was Monday, and I slept past noon. The studio called to find out why I hadn't come in, and Mother told them I had a bad case of the flu. I stayed out for a week.

When whatever drug Webb had given me finally wore off, my nerves were jangled and on edge. Violent nightmares kept me from sleeping soundly. I woke screaming from the repeated vision of Jack Webb's demented face hovering over as he violated me.

My mother thoroughly checked my body for bruises, but apparently he had not injured me in any other way. My vagina was swollen and painful. It would be a week before I could walk without pain. My worst injuries were not physical. The real trauma was to my psyche.

I was panic-stricken that I might get pregnant. I spent the next three weeks sweating out my period. When it finally came, I cried from relief, but my tears didn't last long.

I was furious and frustrated. I had been seriously wronged, and I was helpless to do anything about it. There was no one I could confide in outside of my parents. In the backstabbing world of movie studio politics, my fellow contract players at UI would be happy to whisper this latest bit of dirt to a studio head or movie magazine. The gossip queens, Louella Parsons, who loathed me, and Hedda Hopper, who liked me, would claw each other's eyes out to run my sordid little story as the lead in their next columns. And I couldn't trust Carolyn Jones or Aaron Spelling, even though they had gotten me involved with Jack Webb to begin with. They were good friends, but not that good. A scandal like this was too good not to gossip about.

When I was at my most outraged during my hiatus, I picked up the telephone and dialed *Dragnet*'s production office. I asked to speak to Jack Webb, but I was told that he wasn't in. I asked when he would return and the secretary said, "I don't know. Would you like to leave a message?"

I wish I could truthfully say that I told her, "Tell him I said, 'Fuck you, and fuck Sergeant Joe Friday, you phony piece of shit.'"

But I didn't.

Coda

That's all ancient history, seventy-odd years ago. But if you are a rape victim, I don't need to tell you that the memories will return unbidden, often in the dark mid-watches of the night, to reignite the terror and anger. When they do, it feels like it happened yesterday.

And sometimes there's a trigger.

In 1997, I was invited to an awards gala for the Los Angeles Police Protective League at the Beverly Hilton Hotel in Beverly Hills. My long-time friend, Hollywood talk show host and raconteur, the late Skip E. Lowe, had received the invitation for me. He volunteered to be my escort if I wanted one, since my husband, Thomas, is infamous for dodging Hollywood parties. I checked with Thomas, and, sure enough, he passed.

It was the year of the LAPD shootout with two bank robbers in North Hollywood streets; the Rampart scandal, where seventy officers were implicated in beatings, drug dealing, perjury, and planting evidence; and the drive-by shooting murder of Notorious B.I.G. on Wilshire Boulevard, about two and a half miles from where I was standing. LA Mayor Richard Riordan and Police Chief Willie L. Williams thought it was high time for some good press for the LAPD. What better event than a Hollywood awards banquet?

Arm in arm, Skip E. and I rode the escalator up to the Hilton's glitzy main ballroom, prepared to make an entrance. I was wearing a glamorous new outfit, a Jean Paul Gaultier metallic silver jacket and skirt—jacket with ample décolletage with nothing underneath, skirt butt-hugging, shoes Chanel, heels sky-high.

But as we reached the top of the escalator, my glamorous entrance was ruined. The sight of a twenty-foot poster of Sergeant Joe Friday hanging from one wall made my blood run cold. I hung onto Skip's arm to keep from fainting. The scene from more than forty years before replayed in my head.

It took a few minutes for me to calm down. If I had been alone, I would have turned around and gone home. But I didn't want to explain the whole traumatic story to Skip, so I stayed.

Much of the program that evening consisted of celebrities on the dais singing Jack Webb's praises, droning on about Jack Webb the humanitarian and policeman's friend. I left my food untouched and drank champagne.

When the evening was finally over and everyone began heading for their cars, I was well-oiled and furious. I was stewing as Skip and I rode the escalator down to the main floor and the waiting paparazzi. Halfway down my anger got the best of me. I popped open my jacket and flashed my breasts. There was a gasp and some cheering from the spectators. Some of the quicker photographers got the shot. I closed my jacket, smiled at everyone, and went to my limo. I am told there are still copies of that photo circulating among the LA paparazzi underground. I understand that even Mayor Riordan had his own copy. The Police Protective League never invited me back.

It is a blessing that Jack Webb died fifteen years before that night. If he had been there in the flesh…I don't know what I might have done.

I asked Thomas what he thought might have happened, and what he would have done if he was my escort. We've been married for more than fifty years, and he's known about the incident since the early years when we met. Here's a transcript of his answer.

"I would have wanted to get you out of there as soon as possible. I know how you get when you've had some champagne. Of course, you are completely justified to be pissed off at someone who committed such a grievous crime on you. But because you are the owner of a hair-trigger temper, I would have removed you from the situation before you injured yourself or someone else."

Predatory brutes like Bill Cosby and Harvey Weinstein have been outed, tried, and punished by the Me Too movement. Women can—and should—feel empowered by the support of their sisters. Every woman has been the victim of some form of harassment—bullying, being passed over for promotion, pay discrimination, unwanted touching—the whole shitty spectrum of aggravation that we've come to expect. Young women being preyed upon and seduced by rapacious Hollywood producers, stars, and studio heads is a tired cliché, but like all clichés, it is based on reality. The casting couch was, and is, part of Hollywood's shameful legacy. But through all the tears and fears, I am living proof that it is survivable.

Chapter Nine

Three Dominant Divas

"You have to be self-reliant and strong to survive in this town. Otherwise, you will be destroyed."

—JOAN CRAWFORD

Joan Crawford

If I possessed magical powers, held sway over the powers of darkness, the second thing I would do is bring Joan Crawford back. We met a few times when she had become an elder stateswoman of the movie business. She made her last film, *Female on the Beach,* at Universal Studios with my favorite producer, Al Zugsmith. Crawford was complicated, willful, and often demanding. She was also a consummate professional—a fact which even her enemies, like Bette Davis, admitted.

I wrote in *Playing the Field* about my first meeting with Crawford. We sat at the same table for the 1953 *Photoplay* Awards. My date for the evening, arranged by the studio, was Rock Hudson. It was a date contrived to make both Rock and me look good. Me, to add to some glamour and bright lights to my young career, and Rock to counter the growing rumors that he was gay.

Marilyn was cavorting on stage that night in a skintight gold lame gown, while Crawford watched in disgust, drinking herself into a stupor. I didn't see the end of the night for her, but most likely the young man who was her escort had to help her to her limo.

It must have been difficult for her to witness the changing of the Hollywood talent landscape. Joan Crawford had been in movies since 1925—before talkies. That she had survived in an industry so unforgiving of growing old is a monument to her determination and sheer cussedness.

It saddened me to sit with her at the *Photoplay* Awards and endure the snide remarks she directed at me and the other starlets.

However, one day, two years later, I was coming out of a soundstage on the Universal lot and saw a white Lincoln Continental convertible parked in front of one of the star bungalows. The initials "J.C." were painted in cursive script on the driver's side door beneath the window. To my surprise, Crawford emerged from the bungalow, leading her two white miniature poodles.

She waved. "Hi!"

I was a bit dumbfounded that she even waved. "Hello, Miss Crawford."

"Where are you going?" she asked.

"To the drama department at the top of the hill."

"I'm taking my two babies for a stroll. I'll tag along."

The two poodles were pacing excitedly in anticipation of their walk. We set off in the direction of the drama department.

"What are their names?" I asked.

"Stinky and Pupschen."

"They're awfully cute."

"Thank you. What happens up in the drama department?"

"We take classes—scene study, diction, horseback riding, that kind of thing."

"We had some of that at MGM, but this sounds more organized."

At the drama department, I introduced her to the contract players and to our teacher and sometimes keeper, Estelle Harman.

On the way back down the hill I said, "I never really introduced myself—but my name's not really Mamie Van Doren. My mother was absolutely crazy about you. She saw every movie you did, I think. She named me for you: my real name's Joan Lucille Olander."

"I'm flattered," she said simply.

"Now that you've met the stars and starlets back there, did you see anyone destined for real stardom?"

We took a few steps before she answered. "No."

Al Zugsmith invited me to the set to watch her film a scene from *Female on the Beach*. I slipped into the stage and watched her play a love scene with her co-star, Jeff Chandler. In the scene, Jeff asked Crawford, "How do you like your coffee?" And she curtly replied, "Alone." I had worked with Jeff on *Yankee Pasha,* my second role at Universal. Jeff was the sweetest, most helpful co-star I ever worked with before and since, but to me, he was not a romantic lead.

Monte Westmore had always been my go-to makeup man at Universal. He had done my makeup since my first small role in *Forbidden*. Monte was a member of the Westmore family dynasty of studio makeup artists and cousin of Bud Westmore, the head of Universal's makeup department. Monte told me that when Crawford took the role in *Female on the Beach,* she said she wanted Mamie Van Doren's makeup man. He said the hardest part of the job was her eyelashes. Crawford took short twenty-minute naps throughout the day. She would wake up refreshed, but she required a new set of lashes after every nap. Monte said he spent most of his time preparing her next set of lashes.

I am not one who subscribes to the *Mommie Dearest* version of Joan Crawford. The book her daughter authored was, by many accounts from people who knew Joan Crawford, a pack of lies. The terrible behavior her daughter wrote about, which became a major part of the movie, just didn't happen.

She supported her mother and younger brother Hal throughout their lives. She tried to get them work in the movie business, but they only managed to get parts as bit players and extras. When Hal took sick and died, Crawford paid for his funeral.

Her former husband, Franchot Tone, remained her friend after their divorce. When Tone became ill with lung cancer, Crawford paid for his medical expenses and allowed him to stay in her home. When he died, she oversaw the funeral arrangements and had his ashes scattered in a place he requested.

After eighteen years as a huge money maker at MGM, Louis B. Mayer unceremoniously dumped her. When she drove out the studio gate, there was no one to say "Goodbye."

***

My one-time boyfriend, Steve Cochran, once modestly bragged that he had slept with every leading lady he ever worked with. I didn't pursue it. I have a few notches in my gun too. Past lives are personal, in my book, except in this one. Of course, since Steve had slept with me too, I felt that one question was justified. Joan Crawford was my namesake and a major influence on me.

"So, when you made *The Damned Don't Cry* with Joan Crawford, you went to bed with her?"

"Yes," he answered. "More than once, actually."

"Yes, and?"

"And how much more do you want to know?"

"What was her body like?"

"She had a fantastic body. And she was in her fifties then."

"And how was she as a lover?"

"Fantastic."

"So, you fucked all thirty-nine of us? That makes me just one of the pack, right?"

"No, Mamie, you're different. I never told the other thirty-eight I loved them. I love you."

That stopped me in my tracks. I was not in the market for true love at that stage of my life. Especially one as jealous and volatile as Steve Cochran. I had already decided to gently put on the brakes of our relationship. When he asked me to do another movie with him, part of which would be shot on his sailboat on the way to Mexico, it was the perfect excuse for me to pass. I was a single mom with a young son who needed me, and I had another movie on the horizon.

A short time later, Cochran set sail on his boat, Rogue, with three girls he recruited in Mexico. When he fell ill during the voyage, his condition quickly worsened, and he ultimately died. Because none of the girls knew how to sail, they drifted aimlessly while Cochran's body rapidly decomposed. After ten days, they were rescued by a passing fishing boat. It was trip I was glad to miss.

***

Because of a serious back injury in the last year of her life, Joan Crawford did not leave her house. As a result, her health steadily declined. Four days before she died, she gave her dog, Princess Lotus Blossom, to a friend. Mother's Day was two days before her death, but none of her children visited. She spent the day alone. The day before she died, she told her nurse, "I'm not needed anymore." She died on the fourteenth anniversary of her marriage to Alfred Steele, about whom she said, "He was the only man I ever really loved."

Joan Crawford paid her dues in the movie business. She worked hard, knew her lines, and hit her marks. Always an absolute professional when the director said, "Action!" Crawford delivered the goods in her own inimitable way.

Warning—cliché ahead: *They don't make them like that anymore.*

Joan Bennett

"I don't think much of most of the films I made, but being a movie star was something I liked very much."

—JOAN BENNETT

I had dozed off in Monte Westmore's makeup chair. It was early morning, and he was applying the makeup to transform me into Susie Ward in *All American*. I was due on the set in a half hour. There was a gentle tap on my shoulder and I opened my eyes. I looked up into the face of an angel.

"Hi, Mamie," the angel said, "I'm Joan Bennett."

I sat up so fast that Monte smeared my lipstick. I knew that lovely face as well as I knew my own.

"I know who you are! What a pleasure to meet you, Miss Bennett."

Joan Bennett had been one of my movie idols since I was eleven. She had been an honest-to-God movie star since the silent era. I was a new starlet at Universal, barely dry behind the ears, and she was tapping me on the shoulder and calling me by name. She was one of only two screen stars over whom I was starstruck—the other, of course, was Jean Harlow.

Joan Bennett was born into a show-business family. Her sister, Constance Bennett, was a movie star in her own right, as beautiful as Joan; her other sister, Barbara Bennett, was famous on stage and in movies, an actress and dancer. Her father, Richard Bennett, was one of the most famous leading men in silent films. Her maternal grandfather was the Jamaican-born Shakespearean actor Lewis Morrison, whose career began in England in the 1860s.

"I've got a tip for you, Mamie," she said holding up a folded magazine.

"There's a story in here that would make a perfect movie for you—a strong feminine role that could be a huge boost for your career." She handed me the magazine.

"Thank you so much, Miss Bennett."

"Read it and see what you think. Get this to one of the studio writers and have them create a script for you. This story will make you a huge star."

I thanked her again. When she left, Monte said, "Do it, Mamie. She's been around a long time and knows her stuff."

I can't recall all the details of the story. It involved a young woman overcoming a bad start in life and other obstacles to become a successful actress. I took the magazine story to Jimmy McHugh, my manager.

"No," he said gruffly, tossing the magazine aside. "Under no circumstances do you take this to the studio writers. Your studio will decide what movies you should make."

It was typical of the advice I had learned to expect from Jimmy McHugh. His assumption was always that I was too young and too stupid to make my own decisions about my career. Perhaps in a way he was partially right. I was too inexperienced to trust my own instincts to pursue Joan Bennett's suggestion. I never took the idea anywhere, a decision I've always regretted.

Part of my fascination with Joan Bennett was that we share a family name. My mother's maiden name was Bennett. And we share a direct ancestral connection to America's first president, George Washington.

Joan's career was tepid when she was a blonde. She got movie roles, to be sure, but real stardom eluded her until her third husband, Walter Wanger, convinced her to become a brunette. She became a darkly sultry femme fatale. She starred in a number of Fritz Lang's noir films and became a star in her own right, playing opposite such leading men as Gregory Peck, Robert Ryan, James Mason, and Spencer Tracy. My two favorites among her films were *Woman in the Window* and *Scarlet Street*, both of which co-starred Edward G. Robinson and Dan Duryea. Both very noir.

Her career was nearly scuttled by a scandal involving a rumored affair with her agent, Jennings Lang, head of MCA's west coast television division. Her husband, Walter Wanger, saw them arriving at Lang's office, in Lang's car, and flew into a jealous rage. When Bennett got out of Lang's car, Wanger pulled a gun and shot Lang in the groin. Lang survived, and Wanger was tried for attempted murder.

Hollywood glamour attorney Jerry Giesler defended Wanger, entering a plea of temporary insanity. (In addition to handling the case of my mother's hit-and-run auto accident, Giesler successfully defended Errol Flynn and Charlie Chaplin in rape cases, and he handled Marilyn Monroe's divorce from Joe DiMaggio. He would later become my attorney too, handling a lawsuit against a drunk driver who ran a red light and nearly killed my mother. Giesler also got me out of my onerous contract with my manager, Jimmy McHugh.) Wanger, at Giesler's recommendation, waved a jury trial and threw himself on the mercy of the court. It worked. He served four months at the LA County honor farm at Castaic, California.

After the shooting, Bennett was blacklisted by the major studios. Movie roles quickly dried up, perhaps because the powerful Hays Office that imposed censorship codes on the studios disapproved of a woman involved in an affair in which her lover had his balls shot off. In fairness, Bennett always denied there was a romance between her and Lang, but the staunch Puritans in the Hays Office didn't want to hear it. Note that the philandering Errol Flynn and Charlie Chaplin did not face such stern treatment. Duh. They were men.

Joan Bennett continued to have a successful stage career. Eventually, she began to get roles on television, ultimately landing an iconic five-year run on the Gothic soap, *Dark Shadows*.

I met Joan Bennett a second time at an award ceremony a year or so before she died. She was given a lifetime achievement award. She was frail, but still beautiful. I reminded her of the recommendation she gave me for a movie script, and she pretended to remember. She died of a heart attack on December 7, 1990, at age eighty.

Of the scandal that derailed her promising career, she once said, "If [the shooting] happened today, I'd be a sensation. I'd be wanted by all studios for all pictures."

Joan once said: *"Few people remember good women. They don't forget bad girls."* Namaste, beautiful Joan.

Gloria Swanson

"Writing the story of your own life is a bit like drilling your own teeth."

—GLORIA SWANSON

Not long after I got involved with Howard Hughes, I received a call from his secretary. This was a direct command from "The Boss," as she put it. I was to go to an address on Sunset Boulevard, a new European designer's boutique.

His secretary went on, "She'll make a special swimsuit for you that the Boss wants you to wear at the christening of his newest TWA airplane. The ceremony's next Saturday. Don't be late."

I went to the designer's store, and she took my measurements. A few days later, a black and silver one-piece swimsuit was delivered to my house.

When I arrived at the airport, on the appointed day, there was a large gaggle of press photographers firing off flashbulbs at Gloria Swanson, who was posing with Howard Hughes next to his new airplane. Swanson was tiny next to tall and gangly Hughes, barely visible behind a giant bouquet of four dozen roses.

I was part of a group of girls, some in bikinis and some in one-piece suits like mine. They positioned me near the top of the boarding stairs, while Swanson and Hughes chatted and admired the airplane.

An aide removed the giant rose bouquet from Swanson and handed her a bottle of champagne. She posed as if to break the bottle on the airplane's fuselage, though Hughes would never allow such a trauma to his new aircraft.

When the photos were done, one of Hughes's aides took me aside and said, "Miss Swanson would like a word with you."

I followed him to where Hughes and Gloria were standing, and Howard introduced me.

"Is that your natural hair color?" Swanson asked. I had begun bleaching my hair a creamy platinum color. No one else was wearing it, and it made me stand out.

"No," I replied, "I'm a blonde, but I bleach it up lighter and add a platinum rinse."

"It's stunning," she said.

"Thank you, Miss Swanson."

Hughes took my arm and steered me back to his aide. "Thank you, Joan," he said dismissively.

I went back to where the other girls were waiting. "What did she want?" they asked. "What did she say?"

"Oh, she just wanted to know about my hair."

A couple of years later I went to visit a girlfriend who was staying at an upscale hotel on Sunset Boulevard. I went into the hotel by a side entrance through a narrow path in the hedge. As I walked in, I bumped into Gloria Swanson, hurrying out in the opposite direction. She was wearing a turban and a dressing gown, and she had an assistant and a hairdresser in tow.

"Oh, gosh! Miss Swanson, I'm so sorry."

"It's okay," she replied, hurrying past.

"Do you remember me from the TWA photo shoot with Howard Hughes? You asked about my platinum hair color."

She was momentarily taken back by my cheeky question. She was, after all, Gloria-fucking-Swanson, and unused to being questioned by a strange young woman.

Her assistant began to shoulder past, but Gloria said, "No, wait.... Yes, I do remember that lovely hair of yours. Good to see you again, but unfortunately, I'm in a hurry to get to a location."

"You're shooting *Sunset Boulevard*, right?"

News of the production of *Sunset Boulevard* had been in all the trade papers for months, in addition to the rumors of Swanson's torrid love affair with her handsome co-star, William Holden.

"Yes," she said.

"Could I come watch you work, Miss Swanson? I promise to stay out of the way."

"No, my dear, it's a closed set." She thought a moment, "But if you'd like to just take a quick peek inside, it would be all right."

"Oh, Miss Swanson, I would love that."

"I'll leave word with the assistant director."

She turned to her assistant. "Give her the address."

I made my way to the address on Wilshire Boulevard. The location was known as the Jenkins mansion, which had been built in the extravagant silent era of the 1920s. I had to park on a side street a couple of blocks away because studio trucks and vehicles lined the curb along Wilshire. I was stopped at the gated entrance by a security guard. I told him I was expected by Miss Swanson, and he cleared me through the assistant director.

"You can come in for a few minutes, but you'll have to leave when they start shooting."

The crew was setting up a shot by the swimming pool, in which William Holden climbs out of the water and dries himself with a towel while having a conversation with Swanson.

As I watched the crew making final adjustments to the lights, William Holden walked onto the set, shirtless and in bathing trunks. Holden was, to me, the most gorgeous man ever to be in movies. Watching him chat nonchalantly with the crew, I understood that the rumors about him and Swanson must have been true. Gloria Swanson would never let a dazzling specimen like that get away without putting her stamp of approval on it.

***

In 1970, I did the play *See How They Run* at Chicago's Drury Lane Theatre. Swanson had appeared in a play there not long before. The publicist for the theater told me the following story.

While in Chicago, Miss Swanson gave an interview to a young reporter from one of the local papers while riding in her limo. Cruising down busy Lakeshore Drive, the interview was going well until the reporter asked Swanson her age. Because Swanson had been born in Chicago, the reporter did her homework and looked up the actress's birth records. When the age Swanson told her differed from the one on record, the reporter challenged the star with the discrepancy.

Swanson's eyes went steely. "Stop the car!" she barked at the driver. They skidded to a halt, and she threw open the limo door. "The interview is over! Now, get out!" And she kicked the stunned reporter out of the limo in the middle of Lakeshore Drive traffic.

Swanson was not to be fucked with.

I recently re-watched *Sunset Boulevard.* It seems impossible that Swanson did not win the Academy Award that year for her performance as Norma Desmond. It is so tight, so disciplined, so perfectly balanced—a master class of acting, dammit—one of the best performances on film I've ever seen. To the Academy's shame, the Oscar that year for Best Actress in a Leading Role went to Judy Holliday in *Born Yesterday.* Alas, not the first time—nor the last—that a big studio (Columbia) crossed the Academy's palm with silver to garner an Oscar. (Ironically, William Holden co-starred in *Born Yesterday* too.)

But if you watch Swanson in *Sunset Boulevard,* a diminutive little beauty of a munchkin, fill that fucking movie screen with her energy, you realize you have been in the presence of something great.

JOE GILLIS

You're Norma Desmond! You used to be big.

NORMA

I am big. It was the pictures that got small.

Yes, she was. A giant talent paired with the role of a lifetime. Who among us wouldn't trade their soul for that moment when Norma throws off her last lifeline to reality and looks directly into the camera.

NORMA

All right, Mr. DeMille, I'm ready for my closeup.

Peace, Gloria, my Swedish sister.

Chapter Ten

Jimmy Stewart

"When it came to kissing, Harlow was the best."

—JAMES STEWART

The first time I saw Jimmy Stewart in person was on the dance floor at Ciro's nightclub. I was on a date with Conrad Janis. The King Cole Trio was playing "Nature Boy." Jimmy was dancing with Gloria, who would eventually become his wife. As Conrad and I danced, I gradually edged closer to Jimmy until we were within arm's length of them. I was all of fourteen, trying to look twenty-four. As we danced with our respective dates, Jimmy turned in my direction and our eyes met. We held our gazes for the longest time. There was something in his eyes that held me. Kindness.

I had already seen all of Jimmy Stewart's movies, and I confess to having a long and inexplicable standing crush on him. That moment when our eyes locked seemed perfect to me.

If only, I thought, *I could meet him, I would be a perfect wife for him.* This was a very un-Joanie-like thought for me. However, we would never meet. I never had a chance to have his children, make his home, or grow old with him. As karma would have it, our paths did not cross again.

Until…

In the mid-1980s, I was invited to a birthday party for Martha Raye at the Friars Club in Beverly Hills. Martha had made numerous trips over the years to entertain the troops in WWII, Korea, and Vietnam. She had been given many accolades in that time, including an honorary officer's commission—much as I had been awarded for my tours in Vietnam. Because Martha's health had been failing, this might be the last opportunity we would have to celebrate her.

There was a bit of pomp and circumstance to the occasion too. The Marine Band escorted the color guard and played the national anthem. Several high-ranking officers and local dignitaries paid tribute to her. Bob Hope spoke of her long and brave service.

Among the dignitaries on the dais with Martha were Bob and Dolores Hope, and Jimmy and Gloria Stewart. My table was directly in front of the dais. Jimmy kept casting puzzled glances in my direction, trying, I imagine, to place my face. After a few people made speeches, we all formed a line to file past the dais and pay our respects. Gloria Allred, the attorney, was next to me in line, and we chatted about this and that. When we passed behind Jimmy and Gloria Stewart, I put my hand on Jimmy's shoulder and said, "Hi, Jimmy."

He turned and looked into my eyes, and it was like that night years ago on the dance floor at Ciro's. A sweetness shown out of his eyes, a certain grace and tenderness that threatened to sweep me away.

"Hi." He smiled but couldn't place my face.

I leaned in closer. "It's Mamie Van Doren, Jimmy."

His eyes got wide and he gasped. He grabbed my hand and pressed it to his lips. He held it there for a few ecstatic seconds. I was seized by an overwhelming desire to lean over and kiss him on the lips. Unfortunately, his wife, Gloria, saw what was happening and gave me a disapproving frown. I thought better of it. Jimmy reluctantly let go of my hand and whispered, "Mamie, it's a pleasure."

I wished Martha a happy birthday and went back to my seat, but I was so stoned on Jimmy Stewart, I could barely keep from giggling out loud. It was a magical moment. The lips that kissed Jean Harlow had kissed my hand.

The two things I'll always remember about Jimmy Stewart are that kiss on my hand at Martha Raye's birthday party and his reading of the poetic tribute to his dog, Beau. I watched him read the poem on *The Johnny Carson Show* in 1981, and I couldn't stop crying. I have loved dogs the way Jimmy loved Beau. It made me love Jimmy all the more. I am certain that Jimmy Stewart was the kindest man in Hollywood. His kindness stole my heart, and he never knew it. And he stole the hearts of millions of fans too.

Jimmy was a womanizer, to be sure. He had numerous affairs throughout his career, which Gloria apparently accepted. Jimmy had a small part in a Jean Harlow movie, but since he never kissed her in their short scene, he must have kissed her *outside* of the movie. How else would he have known she was the best kisser? Not only had he kissed Harlow and then kissed my hand, but Clark Gable had also kissed Harlow's lips and mine too. How is that for romantic synchronicity?

Jimmy was one of the most courageous men in Hollywood. He came from a family in which military service was viewed as a part of citizenship. His father served in WWI, and both his grandfathers served in the Union Army during the Civil War. Jimmy had learned to fly in the 1930s, even buying a surplus military aircraft to train in. At the outbreak of WWII, Jimmy was first in line at the draft board. When he got his draft notice, Jimmy cheerfully commented that he had won the lottery. Refusing the safe, cushy military jobs that other Hollywood stars were given, Jimmy became a bomber pilot and flew dangerous missions over Germany from a village in East Anglia. Jimmy was discharged from the Army Air Corps as a colonel but eventually rose to the rank of brigadier general. He actually flew a bombing mission in Vietnam. Sadly, he lost one of his adopted sons there. Fortune is never fair or comprehensible.

Years after I appeared in *Teacher's Pet,* I heard that Jimmy had originally been offered the Clark Gable role. Had Jimmy played that part, there might have been an alternative future for Mamie. There would most certainly have been some off-camera action on the set.

Oh, Jimmy, the stars were not on our side. But next life, let me have the Harlow role, and I'll give you a real kiss to seal an alternate future for the two of us.

Love you, Jimmy.

Chapter Eleven

Make a Left at Argentina—Che Guevara

The chauffeured car stopped in front of an upscale mansion in the toniest part of Buenos Aires. It looked like a castle from a fairy tale. The grounds were festooned with lights. Music from a string ensemble wafted into the night.

Jean-Pierre Aumont and I went inside. I was shooting *The Blonde from Buenos Aires,* and Jean-Pierre was my leading man. We were welcomed by a liveried butler and ushered into the party. The guests were done up in formal attire. Jean-Pierre was wearing a suit and tie. I was glad I had changed into a gown before I left the movie studio.

"I told you it would be a fantastic party," Jean-Pierre said over the strings. "These are wealthy industrialists—"

"Obviously," I put in. "What a house!"

"Wait'll you see the grounds. They have a pool house that would house two families. The pool looks like a small lake. And they have huge stables and a full-sized polo pitch."

"Do they have any food?" I was starving.

The shooting days on *The Blonde from Buenos Aires* were long. There were no unions to limit the time actors and crews worked. We wrapped shooting at 9:00 p.m. because the director, George Cahan, thought it was a good political move for Jean-Pierre and me to attend the party. Financing help often came from industrialists like the ones here.

Jean-Pierre pointed to a large adjacent room. "In there. That's the dining room."

I slipped into the dining room and looked over the table settings. My place card was at the head of the table, wide enough to seat two people side-by-side. Jean-Pierre was to be seated next to me.

Back in the main room, Jean-Pierre and I circulated. Jean-Pierre was well-known among the partygoers. It was a largely left-leaning crowd, politically speaking. He had been a member of the French Resistance during WWII. He had harassed the Nazis with sabotage and helped many French Jews to escape. He had a price on his head back then, and he was lucky to have survived.

We worked our way around the room and ended up near a handsome stranger dressed in fatigues. He embraced Jean-Pierre with a wide grin. Jean-Pierre said, "Comrade Che, let me introduce you to the American movie star, Mamie Van Doren. Mamie, Generalissimo Ernesto Che Guevara."

His mustache was a bit sparse and scruffy, connecting with his beard on each side of his chin, with a large gap under his nose. It looked like a mustache not quite ready for prime time, but I found it intriguing. He had an engaging boyish smile and white teeth.

I extended my hand, "A pleasure to meet you, generalissimo."

"Call me Che," he said in heavily accented English. "It is certainly a pleasure to meet you. I read in the papers that you're making a movie. I've seen your pictures. What's the title?"

"*The Blonde from Buenos Aires*," I said. "We're almost finished. Just a few more days for my scenes."

"And, of course, you are the blonde in question?"

"None other."

He toasted with his champagne. "Salud." We sipped, eyeing each other.

I thought: *Charming smile, soft Spanish accent, an altogether dashing presence in fatigues. What could go wrong?*

Other guests interrupted our moment and introduced themselves. Che returned their greeting graciously, then turned back to me.

"A pleasure to meet you. Perhaps we could talk more later."

"I would love to."

By the time the dinner bell rang, I was famished and dizzy from too much champagne. Pierre and I straggled with the others into the dining room. I took my seat where I had seen my place card. I turned, expecting to see Jean-Pierre, but instead Che sat down. He was holding a large Cuban cigar between his fingers.

"I hate to say it, Che, but if you're expecting to smoke that thing, I'm afraid I'll have to move," I said.

He looked fondly at the cigar for a moment. "Then the cigar will have to go."

I hate cigar and cigarette smoke. An unattractive man with a cigar is a non-starter; an attractive man with a cigar is the beginning of a negotiation.

"Now we can talk," he said, slipping the cigar into a pocket of his khaki jacket.

I found myself totally charmed. "Do you live in BA, Che?"

"No," he replied, "my home is in Cuba. I miss it terribly, but I'm not going home yet. Tomorrow, I leave for the Congo."

"Why there?"

He thought for a moment, making some internal decision. "There's a revolution brewing in Africa. The Congo is ripe for it to begin. My job is to help it."

A server filled our glasses. We sipped champagne.

"I hope you don't mind my little subterfuge. I asked our host to switch my placard so I could sit next to you."

"No, no," I said, "I'm happy to have a chance to talk to you."

Across the table, Jean-Pierre was giving me a wry grimace. A matronly lady sitting next to him was busy chattering in his ear. He waved half-heartedly and emptied his champagne glass. He grabbed a passing server by the arm and held out his glass for a refill.

"Have you known Jean-Pierre long?" I asked.

"We've met a number of times. I was very much aware of his bravery in the French Resistance. He's a friend of the movement but not active. I understand his wife passed away recently."

"Yes. Maria Montez. He took the part in this movie because they spent their honeymoon in Buenos Aires. He wanted to revisit their favorite places."

"Ah, a love pilgrimage."

"Yes. He's a joy to work with—a wonderful actor and a good man."

"I confess," Che said, "that I once wanted to be an actor. I was an extra in two movies."

"And why didn't you stay with it?"

"Too much waiting."

I laughed out loud. "That is the story of my life. Movie acting is ten percent acting and ninety percent waiting for everyone else to get ready."

"I couldn't take it," he agreed. "I have to be *doing* something."

"I've been working in movies since I was sixteen. Waiting is second nature to me now. Do you like American movies?"

"Oh, yes."

A server came to take our orders: Steak or chicken? I ordered steak and Che ordered chicken. He must have seen the puzzled look on my face.

"In Argentina, chicken is a very expensive delicacy. Beef, on the other hand, is a large export commodity and is quite cheap. When a host offers you chicken, it is a sign of your VIP status."

I turned to the server. "Change my order to chicken."

The champagne had been flowing, and the guests were getting louder. I had to raise my voice to be heard over it.

"Who's your favorite American movie star?"

"You."

"A very clever gambit, generalissimo."

He smiled and shrugged. "One tries."

"And other than me?"

"Gene Autry. I love American cowboy movies."

That made me laugh. "You're kidding."

"Oh, no. You know Argentina is famous for its cowboys—here they are called gauchos. Gene Autry movies are classic blueprints for revolution."

"I don't understand," I said.

"Gene Autry rides into a town where there is trouble. The townspeople's cattle are being stolen. They're being forced off their lands. They're being overcharged for their food, and they are being underpaid for what they produce on their farms and ranches. A corrupt judge, a crooked sheriff, and the town mayor are conspiring to bleed the people dry.

"If any of the victims speak up or protest, they are targeted. The corrupt trio keeps armed thugs on salary to intimidate the people into silence. If they refuse to cooperate, they are killed.

"Gene Autry uncovers the plot. He exposes the plotters and cleans up the mess, fighting off the hired guns with a rain of bullets. He makes citizen's arrests of the bad guys, then turns them over to a federal marshal. The corrupt officials give back their ill-gotten gains, and the townspeople get justice."

"I never thought of it that way. Wouldn't the singing cowboy be surprised to find out he's a Marxist?"

"Yes, he would. He'd deny it, of course. And it is an oversimplified example. But you could say that Mr. Autry and I are in the same business—getting justice for the helpless and the weak."

"There are so many starving and helpless people in this country. We drive past a giant garbage dump on the way to the studio every morning. Dozens of children are digging through the filth looking for food. There was a dead horse in the road when we started the movie. Someone moved it to the side of the road, but it has stayed there rotting the whole time."

"It is a world-wide problem, Mommie. Hunger spawns desperation—and revolution."

"It's Mamie."

When we finished our dinners—excellent chicken, by the way, crispy and spicy and flavored with fruit—exhaustion began to set in. Crêpes Suzettes were flaming at other tables, but I was too weary to consider dessert. Jean-Pierre caught my eye and mouthed, "Let's go!" even while the matron continued bending his ear.

"Che, I think I'd better say goodnight."

"So soon? Where are you staying? Can I give you a lift? I have a car and driver."

"Thanks, but-Jean Pierre and I have a driver too. We're staying at the Alvear. It's not far."

Che flashed an impish grin. "I would be honored to take you to your hotel, Miss Van Doren."

I smiled. *Honored* was a nice touch. And if you've been paying attention reading these pages, you've learned that a girl makes up her mind about these things early.

I waved Jean-Pierre over. "You go on. Che's giving me a ride to the hotel."

He gave me a surreptitious wink. "See you tomorrow."

Che's driver brought the car, and we got in. It gave me pause that in addition to the driver, he was also accompanied by an armed bodyguard. When I asked about it, he said, "In my line of work, it's often useful to have some backup. This is Alberto."

The burly guard was in khakis like Che. He had a pistol holstered on his hip and behind the heavy beard and mustache, his hooded eyes said, "Don't fuck with my boss or me."

At the hotel, Alberto scanned the nearly deserted lobby, motioned us to the elevator, and rode with us up to the penthouse. When he walked us to the door, I glanced at Che, and he read my mind.

"He waits outside."

They exchanged a quick look, and it occurred to me that Alberto might not have always waited outside. There are love scenes, and there are love scenes. Nearly always, they are spiced by the promise of the unexpected. An armed guard at the bedroom door was about as unexpected as it gets.

Che and I wasted no time. He took me in his arms and kissed me. My tingles merged into a cosmic jolt and I was instantly aflame with desire. As almost always happens, my lips began to swell. Before I realized it, we were naked, and Che was carrying me to bed.

Che possessed an unusually shaped penis, very large at the end. As he entered me, it created an ecstatic expansion, first physical, then psychic. Champagne in the proper quantities will do that to me—a tidal ebb and flow, setting me adrift from all reality except sensation.

In short, Che was a wonderfully heart-stopping fuck.

My earlier fatigue melted away. I closed my eyes and gave myself up to his strength and agility. We orgasmed simultaneously more than once. I can't remember the delirious words either of us spoke. I closed my eyes in ecstasy.

When I opened my eyes again, it was daylight. My first thought was, "I have to get to work."

No sooner did I have that thought than I felt Che's penis stirring against my thigh. I sat up resolved to get in the shower to wash away the pervasive smell of sex that stuck to me like perfume. Instead, I straddled Che's erect cock and gasped.

"Oh, yes!" Che said.

"I have to get to work," I said, working my hips instead. "I'll never get to work like this."

Che laughed as he matched my rhythm. That was all it took to launch both of us into a towering, noisy orgasm.

"Olé! Olé! Che-Che!" I shouted.

"Olé! Mommie!" Che answered. "I love your Spanish accent."

I collapsed on top of him a moment later. I wondered numbly if we woke Alberto outside the door.

"I'll never get to work this way," I groaned. "Never in hell."

Che gently massaged my naked butt. "You earned a day of rest, Mommie."

"It's Maaamie, honey."

He playfully slapped my butt. "I like Mommie better."

I rolled out of bed and pulled on a robe against the morning chill. I picked up the telephone and dialed Jean-Pierre's room. "I need a favor," I said when he answered. "Can you get George to work around me and shoot your scenes today? I'm a bit under the weather this morning."

He chuckled wickedly. "You naughty girl! You're not under the weather, you're under the Guevara."

"Very funny. I *was* on top a couple of times."

"Good girl. Rest up. I'll take care of changing the shot list with Cahan."

"You're an angel, J.P. Ciao."

I turned to Che. "Okay, I'm off the hook. Do you want some coffee and brioche?"

"I'd love it, but I'd better tell Alberto so that he doesn't shoot room service."

He padded barefoot and naked to the door, opened it a crack, and spoke in Spanish to his bodyguard. He had the beginnings of an erection as he walked back to the bed. He pulled me onto the bed, and we made love again. It was leisurely enough that Alberto had to make room service wait outside.

When we finished our breakfast, Che said, "I must go soon, Mommie. There are people waiting to spirit me off to the Congo. Things are not going well there."

"Is it dangerous?"

"All revolutions are dangerous. Many civil wars are about to start in Africa."

"Will you be careful?"

"Of course. Alberto and others will protect me. In a civil war, one can never tell today's enemy from tomorrow's. When I'm done in the Congo, I will go back to Bolivia. Would you like to come visit me? Bolivia is a beautiful country."

It was an invitation I did not expect. I opened my mouth to speak, but nothing came out. The prospect immediately appealed to my sense of adventure. And yet…

"I don't know," I finally said. "What would it be like?"

"I have an encampment in a remote area of the rainforest. There is dense jungle in places, many beautiful flowers and birds, an occasional jaguar perhaps, but we are in a safe area—and well-armed."

"And snakes?"

He shrugged. "It *is* the jungle, Mommie. But it will give you a taste of the revolutions and how we fight for them."

"But the people on the other side of the revolution are out to get you, yes?"

Che scratched his beard. "Revolution means the overthrow of one form of government and the establishment of another. Sometimes that means violence. But I am only suggesting that you visit for a few days. I will make sure you are out of danger."

Warning bells were clanging in my head. But an adventure conjoined with a lover, whether breaking studio rules with Tony Curtis or tracking down John Dillinger in the person of Lawrence Tierney, never failed to activate a reckless tingle in me.

The phone rang, and I picked it up. The chirping little voice on the other end said, "Hi, Mom! It's me!"

"Perry, my love! How are you?"

"Good, Mom. Just missing you. When are you coming home?"

"Oh, baby, I miss you too. I'll be done with my part at the end of the week. Then I'll be on my way back to you."

He began to cry. "Oh, I'm so glad, Mom. I miss you something terrible." He sobbed hard. "Please don't leave me again. Please? You can take me with you. I promise I'll be good."

I felt my heart break and my eyes filled with tears. "I promise, Perry. I won't leave you. Ever. Please don't cry. You have to be a big, strong boy for me, okay?"

"Okay, Mom, I will. Call me soon."

"I will, honey. Bye."

I hung up the phone and dried my eyes on my dressing gown sleeve.

I looked at Che. He already knew my answer. He nodded his head in understanding.

"I have a young son who needs me, Che. I also have a career with movies lined up to do. Infatuated as I am with you, I couldn't risk my life because I'd be risking my son's too."

"Even just for a short time?"

I went to him and kissed his cheek. "Revolution is temporary. A bullet is forever."

Chapter Twelve

The Pole Position—Graham Hill and Bruce McLaren

Sydney, Australia, circa February 1963

I was occupying a giant penthouse suite in the Chevron-Hilton Hotel, with floor-to-ceiling windows overlooking Sydney Harbor and Rushcutters Bay. There was a large well-stocked bar within reach—with an iced bottle of pink Cristal champagne—and an oval Jacuzzi the size of a fish pond with a clear skylight affording a stunning view of the night sky and the Southern Cross.

It was my thirty-second birthday, and there were two dashing race car drivers infatuated with me, waiting in the living room for the checkered flag.

Two days earlier, however, I was alone and lonely. I didn't know a soul in Sydney, and I was missing my son terribly. I had just arrived in Sydney for a week of shows in the Chevron-Hilton's Silver Spade show room. It felt like an eternity before I could fly home. My thirty-second birthday was shaping up to be bleak.

Mind you, there was excitement in Sydney that week. The Australian Grand Prix was in town, to be run at the Warwick Farm Raceway just outside of Sydney. Droves of tourists were crowding into the city, and I was playing to packed houses. But when the applause was over and I went back to my room, it was just me and cricket matches on television.

But to my surprise, on the night of my birthday, the hotel threw a party for me after the show. There was music and there were lots of well-wishers and there was lots of drinking. After all, it was Australia.

Among the audience members who stayed for the party were a table full of Grand Prix drivers who had been sitting ringside for my show. Everyone was toasting and chatting and getting acquainted. Two in particular—Graham Hill and Bruce McLaren—took a shine to me.

Graham Hill was the prototypical British race driver. Tall and thin, in his thirties, he had a shock of brown hair, a well-groomed mustache beneath a distinguished nose, and a raffish smile. He told me his birthday was in February too, so tonight it was only fitting that we celebrate together. Bruce McLaren was a New Zealander, in his twenties, boyish, with a charming Kiwi brashness about him. He loved racing cars and, even at this early age, was making plans to build his own. Both of these men touched off a serious tingle along my spine.

Get in gear, Mamie.

At some point in the party when everyone was pretty well-oiled, Graham turned to me and said, "Look, Mamie, Bruce and I are going to the Chequers Nightclub to catch Shirley Bassey's late show. Why don't you come along with us?"

Shirley Bassey was Welsh and not well known outside the UK and the Commonwealth in those days. But she possessed a powerfully expressive voice which would soon catapult her into international stardom with her recording of the theme from the James Bond movie, *Goldfinger*.

I said yes.

"We'll take my car," Graham said. "McLaren, you drive. Mamie, you'll have to sit on my lap."

Parked in front of the main entrance to the Hilton was a sleek, red Ferrari Testarossa. It was the most beautiful car I'd ever seen.

"Wow, that's a gorgeous car, Graham."

"It is that, but it's a bother to drive in street traffic. Doesn't like to go slow."

Bruce McLaren didn't even try to drive slowly to the Chequers Nightclub. My heart was in my mouth most of the way.

Graham asked, "Have you had a chance to see Sydney, Mamie? Did you take a dip at Bondi Beach?"

"I was supposed to have a publicity layout with the Bondi Beach muscle boys until I heard about the shark attack."

"Oh, my God, yes!" said Bruce, "I read it in the papers. A tiger shark attacked a woman in thirteen inches of water."

"Absolutely horrible," Graham put in.

The newspaper accounts said that the shark had tried to drag her under, but her boyfriend jumped on the shark's back and pounded its head until he let her go. But her leg was severed.

"Jesus, what a nightmare," Bruce said.

An ambulance drove near the water's edge to pick her up but became stuck in the wet beach sand. Bystanders pitched in to push it out, but it was too late. She bled to death.

Graham shook his head. "Those things happen around here this time of year. Sometimes the sharks get through the barriers that are supposed to keep them out. Better to stay out of the water."

Shirley Bassey put on a first-class show at Chequers. Her voice was remarkable, and she did multiple encores. After the show, I said it was time for me to go back to my hotel. The three of us piled back into

Graham's Ferrari, Bruce driving again and me on Graham's lap. It wasn't long before I felt Graham's excitement growing.

I was beginning to feel that tell-tale tingle by the time we reached the Hilton. Graham said, "Shall I see you up?"

"I'd like that."

I turned to Bruce, who looked crestfallen in the driver's seat.

"Do you want to come up too, Bruce? My suite has room for three and a well-stocked bar."

Bruce broke into a broad grin. "Sure!"

Riding the elevator to my suite, I looked at the three of us in the reflection of the mirrored wall. My face looked tipsy, and I was. The two of them fidgeted with their wrist watches and stared at their shoes. The elevator door opened. We stepped out and went into my suite.

"Great Scott!" Graham exclaimed, looking around. "Mamie, this isn't a hotel suite, it's an estate. It covers the whole top floor. And what's this at the far end? Damned if it isn't a Jacuzzi. You could damned near do laps in that thing. Have you been in it?"

"Every night," I said, loosening the combs in my hair and letting it fall to my shoulders. "It's heavenly—especially with that skylight."

"Bruce," I said, motioning toward the bar, "why don't you open that bottle of pink Cristal and let's all go for a dip? Graham, turn on the hot water tap."

The cork made a pleasing *pop*, and Bruce poured three glasses.

"Sorry, Mamie, but we didn't come prepared with bathing trunks."

I raised my glass. "So what? Here's to a skinny dip."

"Jolly good," toasted Graham.

"Here! Here!" said Bruce.

"Will you have enough time to recuperate before the race?"

"The race is four days away on Sunday," Graham said. "We'll be fine."

Silence. Each of us was wondering what was next. Who would make the first move?

I unbuttoned the top button of my blouse and looked at Graham. I unbuttoned another and exposed my breast. Graham emptied his glass to bolster his courage. He touched my breast, then my nipple, and it sent a thrill through me. He kissed my lips, and his mustache tickled. It made me think for a moment of Clark Gable. Everyone's breath was quickening, but both men suddenly hesitated.

"Mamie, is this all right?" Graham asked.

"Yeah," repeated Bruce, "you sure this is all right?"

I looked at them directly.

"Guys, it's my birthday, and this is my present. I've never done anything like this before, and I probably won't do it again. I broke up with a serious boyfriend a year ago, and I haven't had a man since. This is what I want."

Graham answered by picking me up in his arms. As he turned to carry me into the bedroom, I took Bruce by the hand.

"Come along, Bruce. You'll be lonely out here."

Bruce followed and closed the bedroom door behind us. Graham eased me onto the bed. I slipped off my blouse and wriggled out of my skirt. The boys undressed, and we positioned ourselves to get down to business. A lock of Graham's hair fell over his forehead as we kissed. I felt Bruce's hands on my hips. I closed my eyes and gave in to lust.

A lot of women probably fantasize about having two men at once. I had. Most don't act on the fantasy, and, honestly, I never thought I would. In spite of all my sexual adventures, I have a pretty conventional approach to doing the nasty. But thanks to the champagne, a lonely birthday far from home, and two handsome men I would probably never see again, the sweaty and sometimes awkward reality of a *ménage à trois* had a certain appeal.

At one moment, I looked at Bruce's still rock-hard erection and giggled in spite of the seriousness of the moment. "Is that what they call the 'pole position' in racing?"

Bruce only groaned and returned to the task at hand.

I lost all track of time, but when at last the three of us were satiated and drenched in sweat, Graham gasped, "Mamie, what an amazing race week." He got off the bed and wandered naked into the living room. I could hear the slushing of the ice in the champagne bucket as he poured himself another glass.

I touched Bruce's cheek and went into the bathroom. I sponged off my body and gave my hair a quick brushing.

When I came out, Bruce said. "You know, I don't want to leave you."

"I know, Bruce. Maybe we'll meet again. Who knows?"

He kissed me again, and we got dressed and joined Graham in the living room. I embraced them both.

"Gentlemen, it's been a wonderfully memorable evening."

"Would you like to be our guest at the race on Sunday?" Graham asked. "We can get you into the pits to see everything up close."

"Thank you, guys. I would love that, but I'm leaving for home on Sunday morning. My son is waiting for me in Hawaii. Next time?"

"For sure," Bruce said.

"Good night," they said, walking out the door to the suite.

"Drive carefully."

When they were gone, I went into the bedroom and sat on the edge of the bed. The sky was getting lighter over Sydney Harbor. Small pleasure boats were beginning to move around.

"Happy birthday, Mamie," I muttered to myself. "Alone again, I see."

I reflected on that. I had spent many birthdays blowing out the candles by myself. This was not a new experience, but why do I keep ending up this way? Answer: I prefer my own company to that of most other people. Maybe I am too exacting in my selection of friends. Perhaps my trust issues are too finely tuned.

One of my companions this evening—Bruce McLaren—was someone I might have spent more time with, given the chance. Handsome, young, dashing in a dorky sort of way, he seemed inclined in the same way toward me. Graham Hill was older, more refined, but more calculating. A David Niven-type, handsome enough to be a leading man. Our tête-à-tête was an adventure, a dalliance. He'd had many and so had I. Bruce had been on the verge of developing a crush. I would find out later that both were married but neglected to volunteer that information. Both men went on their way to their next race. Tomorrow I would be on my way to my next gig.

I looked around the room again. Yep, still empty. Except for memories.

Coda

The following month, Graham Hill won his first Monaco Grand Prix. He would go on to win it four more times. For all its dangers—narrow, winding streets; rough pavement; and a crowded field, he had figured the race out and won it in 1963, 1964, 1965, 1968, and 1969. Newspapers were splattered with photos of Princess Grace presenting him with the winner's trophy, looking enthusiastic to try the pole position herself.

Ironically, Graham Hill would not lose his life on the race track but in his private plane. In 1975, he was flying his Piper Aztec back to his home field after testing a new car. Five of his key crew members were on board. Attempting to land in dense fog, Hill crashed short of the runway, killing everyone on board. He was forty-six.

Bruce McLaren founded a Formula One team that was the second most successful in championship history. He was a brilliant and charismatic auto builder and race driver. The car company he founded had a showroom half a mile from where I'm writing. He won the 24 Hours of Le Mans, Monaco, the Can-Am, the Argentine Grand Prix, and many more.

McLaren died at age thirty-two while testing a new car. Some of the rear body work broke away at high speed, the car spun and left the track and hit a bunker. He was killed instantly. His family continues the work of his company.

My interest in Formula One racing faded pretty quickly. As a child, I tagged along with my parents to the Saturday-night midget races. My mother even drove in a powder puff race and won a trophy. The races were noisy, smelled of exhaust fumes, and I usually ended up sleeping under the bleachers. With all due respect to the complexities and huge expense of international Formula One racing, and with a nod to the giant egos of the drivers, I feel like I might curl up under the seats, snoozing like I did when I was a youngster.

Chapter Thirteen

Apocalypse Then: Vietnam 1968—1971

"For neither good nor evil can last forever, and so it follows that as evil has lasted a long time, good must now be close at hand."

—DON QUIXOTE

Every true story about Vietnam begins at the end. Real life, if you were a grunt, ended when you stepped off the plane in country. Once there, life became like serving a sentence in a maximum-security prison—part boredom, part life-and-death struggle, and part simply bearing witness to unimaginable suffering. When your tour was over, that was when your story began. If you were lucky enough to return home, you faced a new struggle against the hostility of the American public over the Vietnam war, hostility directed not only toward heads of state, politicians, and bureaucrats, but to those who had the least control over the war—the men and women who served in it.

This is also a story of unintended consequences—consequences that sometimes have great significance.

I've entertained audiences on stage, on TV, and in movies for the better part of seventy years. During that time my focus has been, understandably, on my performance—remember my lyrics, sing on pitch, hit my marks, find my key light. But a chance contact with a Vietnam veteran on social media refocused me on the other side of that transaction.

That other side is represented on these pages by the eloquent words of John Huddleston, a combat medic who, as you will see, crossed my path all those years ago with his friend Rick. John has kindly allowed me to reprint some of his messages describing the life and perils of a grunt in Vietnam.

***

John Huddleston

> You entertained the real grunts in Vietnam and became an important part of their lives. I remember you clearly over fifty years ago. That is half a century. There are other grunts who remember you too. For Rick, seeing you was a big moment in his life. It was one that he often referred to up to the time of his death. There were others like Rick.
>
> Your entertaining troops, in the firebases, made you one of us. As I wrote you before, the grunts would have died

> for you. Many have loved you and many desired you, but think about the ones who would have died for you.

***

Quang Tri was the first stop on my newly begun tour in Vietnam. I had arrived at Tan Son Nhut airfield in Saigon just ten days before. I checked in with a lieutenant colonel, who had me fill out paperwork, saying that if I got killed, the Army wasn't responsible, and I couldn't sue them. I got my dog tags to wear at all times so that I could be identified if I was killed.

The army was responsible for ferrying me around the country to entertain at various places. When I lined up this tour, I said I wanted to visit the places where USO shows and Bob Hope didn't visit. When I asked if I would be traveling by Jeep, the colonel laughed.

"You kidding? You wouldn't last half an hour on these roads. You'll be traveling by helicopter to these firebases."

I must have looked perplexed. "It's dangerous out there, Mamie," the colonel said. "Too dangerous for you to travel on the roads."

"I see." There was a sudden knot in the pit of my stomach.

"If you have misgivings about doing this, Mamie, now's the time to say so. There's an honest-to-God war going on out here. No one would blame you if you said no to the smaller outposts and just played the larger bases."

I had come to Vietnam because public opinion in the US had turned against the war. Protests had grown in size and intensity. The young soldiers fighting and dying in the jungles and rice paddies were made out to be villains by celebrity activists like Jane Fonda. I had seen news footage of American soldiers being paraded through the streets of Hanoi in tiger cages, jeered at and spat upon. I called my agent and took on the Quixotic mission of bringing some happiness and light to those young soldiers.

"I didn't come here to play it safe, colonel. When do I leave?"

The war movie I was in was about to become real.

[UNDER: sounds of helicopter rotors whining]

[CUT TO:]

MAMIE strapped in the seat of a Huey helicopter, her head wrapped in a scarf, wearing big sunglasses, her face taut with fear. The doors on each side of the compartment behind the pilots are wide open.

Though the chopper is still on the ground, the wash from the rotors kicks up wind and dust. Two soldiers carrying heavy machine guns climb into the compartment. Through the open door, we see another Huey warming up, and MAMIE'S orchestra conductor, BOBBY BENNETT, and her musicians climbing into it. MAMIE waves at BOBBY; he waves back.

MAMIE

[Shouting over the engine sounds]

Hey, guys! Is there any way we can close those doors?

SOLDIER #1

Sorry, ma'am, they've gotta stay open while we're in the air. If we crash, it'll be easier to get out.

SOLDIER #2

[Mounting his M60 machine gun on its pylon]

And the doors have to be open for us to use these babies.

[He caresses the gun fondly.]

MAMIE

How often do you have to shoot those things?

SOLDIER #1

[Shouts to the pilot]

We're good to go back here!

[The pilot throttles up the engine and the Huey lifts off.]

SOLDIER #2

[Gestures out the door to the landscape below]

We shoot 'em when we get shot at. There're folks down there that don't like us.

MAMIE

Yeah, that's what they tell me. How long does it take to get to Quang Tri?

SOLDIER #2

It's a long way. We'll stop in Da Nang to refuel. We'll stop over night in Phu Bai. Just a short hop from there to Quang Tri.

MAMIE

[Resignation on her face]

Right.

The two Hueys climb to altitude. Mamie gazes at the jungle below. She looks across the space between the two aircraft and sees Bobby Bennett standing in the open door. He waves. She waves back.

MAMIE

[Out loud but to no one in particular]

> Well, I'm sure as shit on my way now. That jungle down there looks like a tropical paradise—except for the craters from artillery shells—but it's full of people who want to kill us. I sure hope...what? Hope that I'll make it without getting shot? Yeah, Mamie, you should've thought about that a long time ago. Like when Perry was standing with your mother at the LAX departure gate, tears streaming down his face, begging you not to go. That would have been a good time to say, "Okay, Perry, I won't go." But I didn't do that.
>
> [Mamie looks at a snapshot of her son, Perry. She is nearly overcome with regret, tears in her eyes...]
>
> [FADE OUT.]

It was no longer a movie in my head.

***

The flight to the small airbase at Phu Bai was more than four hours—I lost track of the time. The hard upright seats in the Huey were unforgiving, and sleep was sporadic. By the time we touched down in Phu Bai in a driving rainstorm, my back and butt felt like someone had been beating me with a stick.

A soldier with an umbrella met me as I got out of the Huey. We jogged through the downpour to a little Quonset hut that was to be my quarters.

My first show was tonight here in Phu Bai, sort of a break-in for Bobby Bennett and the musicians. I was looking forward to a nap.

I asked the soldier if the show would be canceled because of the rain.

"Oh, no ma'am. These monsoon rains happen every year at this time. We're used to it. The whole base is really looking forward to your show. I'll go fetch your bags from the chopper."

My conductor, Bobby, came in and gave me the lowdown on where we'd be performing.

"It's just a little lean-to really. A plywood floor so we don't have to walk in the mud. And a canopy so we don't get rained on."

"How are the musicians?" Bobby had rehearsed with them back in Saigon for a few hours, teaching them my charts.

"They can play," he said. "They're a little green, but they'll be okay. You take a nap, Mamie. We'll get everything set up."

The rain had let up when I woke. I put on my makeup and selected one of the four gowns I had brought to perform in. They were all filmy and low-cut, front and back. Sexy. Hey, it's what I do.

The young soldier escorted me to the makeshift little stage. He carried me over a huge puddle so my shoes didn't get muddy and deposited me on the platform. There was a good-sized crowd of soldiers waiting. As soon as they saw me, they began cheering.

"Gentlemen," Bobby said into the PA microphone, "please welcome the lovely Mamie Van Doren!"

I took the microphone and launched into Three Dog Night's "Joy to the World." I no sooner got the first line out than the music stopped. The musicians had put down their instruments and were staring open-mouthed at me. I looked at Bobby, who was as dumbfounded as I was.

"C'mon, guys," he said.

"Bobby, what the fuck is going on?" I whispered.

He shrugged.

"Gentlemen," I said to the audience, "please excuse us for a moment." I motioned to Bobby. We turned our backs on the audience and gathered around the still befuddled musicians.

Bobby said, "Mamie, they've played your charts, but they've never seen you in person on stage. I think they were bowled over by the sight of you in person."

"Hey, what's going on guys?" I asked the musicians. "We've got a show to do."

"You made a movie with Chiquito!" the drummer blurted out. *"Arizona Kid!"*

The others chimed in, "Yeah! We saw you with him. He's cool and you're beautiful."

I had made a western called *The Arizona Kid* with an actor named Chiquito—a superstar in the Philippines, like Clark Gable or Steve McQueen. It suddenly all made sense—starstruck young musicians face to face with someone who had starred opposite their movie idol. Up to now, they'd only seen me with scarves over my head and wearing big sunglasses, never in makeup and costume. When I hit the stage in front of them, they just stopped in their tracks.

"Right! I did, boys. Chiquito's a great guy, by the way. But I'm just a regular person like all of you. We're out here to do a job, right? We want to put some smiles on the faces of those GIs out there. And I know we're going to do a great show together. Okay?"

They were all nodding now. I asked each one his name, where he was from, a little bit about his family. I told them a little about me—my movies; how I was raised in a farmhouse with no running water; Perry, my son. After a few minutes, everyone was more relaxed.

"What do you say, boys? Want to take another shot at it?" This time they all bobbed their heads enthusiastically. "Okay, Bobby, let's do it right."

I turned back to the audience of GIs.

"We're ready if you are!"

A shout went up, and they applauded like mad. Bobby coaxed the best out of the band for Three Dog Night's *Joy to the World!* The rain started again, but I did my whole show. When it was over, all of us were soaking wet. Everyone was grinning.

As the soldiers straggled back to their hooches, one stopped and said something that I would hear a lot in the next few months: "Mamie," he told me gratefully, "I can't believe you're here."

And there was a part of me that couldn't believe it either. Vietnam so far had been like a fever dream. I couldn't escape the alarming sense of being out of control, no longer in charge of my life, but at the mercy of authorities I didn't know, in service of a war I didn't understand. When I struggled to gain some perspective, there was the roar of helicopter engines, or the smell of gun oil, or the thud of distant artillery to shatter my concentration. And I hadn't even been here a month. But I touched on what each of those grunts in my audience must have felt—that their lives were commodities traded in quantity for an outcome they couldn't imagine.

I got into bed that night clutching my little brown Bible next to my heart, praying to somehow survive the forces swirling around me, praying that I would live to see my son again, and praying that I would manage to bring something worthwhile to the combat soldiers' dark world.

The next morning, we packed up the Hueys and flew north to Quang Tri on the southern edge of the demilitarized zone.

In 1954, the French gave up on colonial rule in Vietnam after a crushing defeat at Dien Bien Phu by Ho Chi Minh's North Vietnamese Army. The United States had long supported the French in attempting to suppress the rise of Communism in Southeast Asia. But resentment against colonial rule grew over the years and spawned open rebellion.

The Geneva peace agreement in 1954 partitioned the country into North and South Vietnam, separated at the seventeenth parallel by a demilitarized zone. Quang Tri was a major Marine outpost in Vietnam's central highlands—rugged, mountainous country on the edge of the DMZ. It is home to the indigenous Montagnard people, who have managed to survive despite centuries of colonial conflicts. It was the most dangerous place in the world.

We landed at Quang Tri in the late afternoon. It was cold and rain was threatening. I got out of the helicopter bundled up against the chill and waited on the edge of the helipad for my bags to be unloaded. Two men in civilian clothes and a tall striking woman wearing fatigues watched from a distance. The helicopter rotor blades were slowing to a stop as the woman approached me.

She extended a handshake. "Hello, I'm Françoise," she said in French-accented English. Tall and thin, she had dark brown hair cut in a mannish style, dreamy blue eyes, a lock of hair hung fetchingly over one eye, a wide smile, and straight white teeth.

"Hello," I answered, shaking her hand, "I'm Mamie."

"I know," she said. "We've been waiting to borrow your helicopter."

"Why?"

She smiled again. "To get the fuck out of Quang Tri and Vietnam. I've been reporting on the war for *Paris Match* magazine for two months. It's just too fucking dangerous. I need to get back to Paris to file some stories. General Hill, the commanding officer at this base, said we could borrow your helicopter. The sooner I get out of this God-forsaken place the better. What are you doing here?"

"I'm touring the firebases with my cabaret show."

Her eyes widened. "And they let you come *here*? Mamie, you are in great danger." She took me by the shoulders and gently turned me around. "That open space there," she said, pointing to the north. "That's the DMZ. The other side of that clearing is enemy territory. North Vietnamese troops are shoulder-to-shoulder in the bush. They're just waiting for orders to overrun this base."

"I came here to do a job. Like you did, Françoise. I've got to do it."

"I think you are braver than I am, Mamie Van Doren—or crazier. Or both. But you are certainly more beautiful than your photographs. You should leave while you can."

I shook my head. "Thank you, but I can't. Too many are counting on me."

She slipped a business card into my hand. "Well, if you run into anything the world should know about, get in touch. Information is hard to come by here. If you come to Paris, call me at this number. And this is my address. Just show up on my doorstep if you like, and you will be welcome." She shook my hand, and, for a moment our eyes locked.

"Until we meet in Paris, Françoise. Have a safe flight."

She turned and strode away toward her companions. She looked back and waved.

Our minder took me in tow to escort me to my quarters. Bobby and the rest of the musicians caught up with me.

"Who was that?" Bobby asked.

"Oh...some French journalist. She's borrowing our chopper to get out."

"Smart. And beautiful." Bobby couldn't suppress a smile. "Did you know her?"

"No. Why? What's that smart ass grin?"

"It just looked like you two were, um, getting well acquainted, that's all."

"Only a guy would say that. None of your beeswax, Bobby."

General Hill, Quang Tri's commanding officer, had generously loaned me his personal quarters—a quaint little villa, the improbable survivor of the French Colonial era, a little down at the heels to be sure, but with an air conditioner, a shower, and a flush toilet. It looked like heaven to me.

Instead of a show that night, there was a dinner in my honor. I showered and washed my hair. I wrapped my head in a towel and decided to take a quick nap.

I sat on the edge of the bed, turning Françoise's business card over and over in my fingers. It was interesting, our meeting. I have many gay or lesbian friends, but I've never really been tempted by their lifestyle or their sexual preferences. But this afternoon, being hit on by a dashing young woman, a war correspondent for *Paris Match* no less, that I had only known for, like, all of two minutes was titillating, not to say tempting.

Come see me in Paris.

What the fuck? My guilty Lutheran conscience wanted some answers. How did this happen? Was it the war effect? God knows Françoise was attractive. Was my libido bubbling because there were North Vietnamese soldiers half a mile away poised to attack? Sudden death being the logical product of all this, what was so terrible about exploring life's possibilities before the law of averages caught up with you?

Did I feel this way because of all the hard edges of life with the grunts? I was getting a crash course in the hardships of dirt, short rations, the impersonal voices of gunfire, artillery explosions, rain, mud, more rain, and diesel exhaust. The sight of Françoise—tall and sexy in such a casually bold way, at ease even here, had an impact on me.

And so it must be, I thought, for the soldiers watching my show. The sight of a woman in the midst of all this drab khaki green and gray, an island of softness, color, even perfume in a sea of brutality—it must be mind-blowing for a bunch of kids with little life experience outside of small towns, hayrides, and high school proms—kids for whom the most violence they've been exposed to is a Friday-night football game.

I told my Lutheran conscience to shut up. I didn't have any answers. I tucked Françoise's card in my Bible.

***

The dinner in my honor was also a send-off party for the next DMZ patrol leaving Quang Tri in the morning. It was a mission fraught with danger that the Marines called "walking the line." The North Vietnamese constantly infiltrated across the DMZ. Small patrols probed into the US side, mining the trails, setting booby traps, and stationing snipers in the dense mountain forest. Someone always died on these patrols.

A dozen or so of us were seated around a large table in the dining room of the general's quarters. I was flanked by General Hill and a young marine private named Charlie. Several officers and a scattering of non-commissioned officers were in attendance as well. The general had ordered up porterhouse steaks and French fries from his mess cooks. There was plenty of warm beer and sodas. Everyone was in high spirits.

"Charlie here," the general whispered to me, "volunteered to be point man for the convoy tomorrow. He's the one who leads the way at the front of the column, looking for trouble. He might run into land mines or booby traps, or maybe signs of North Vietnamese scouts. It's a dangerous job, but when I told the men that the point would have the honor of sitting next to you at dinner, Charlie stood up right away."

"My God." I asked. "How old is he?"

"Eighteen, I think," said the general.

"Do you think he'll see nineteen?"

The general turned his attention back to his steak without an answer.

I turned to Charlie and introduced myself. "Hi, Charlie, it's nice to meet you."

"Me too, Miss Van Doren," he answered shyly.

"Mamie. Call me Mamie. Where are you from, Charlie?"

"Toledo."

"Know it well. I was married there once upon a time."

He looked at me. "Are you still married?"

"Oh, no. That one dropped by the wayside quite a while ago. Are you excited about tomorrow?"

"Yeah, kinda. It's important."

Charlie was quiet for the rest of the dinner. The gathering broke up after a couple of hours. I went back to the general's quarters. I took another shower because who knew when I'd get another chance for a real shower. I climbed into bed and fell asleep.

A knock on my door woke me.

"Mamie," Bobby said from the other side, "somebody wants to see you."

I wasn't happy when I opened the door. "I need my sleep, Bobby. What's going on?"

"Sorry." He motioned to a figure standing in the shadows. "Charlie wanted to see you. He said he has a gift for you."

I nodded thanks to Bobby and wrapped my housecoat around me against the night chill. Charlie stood in front of me smiling sheepishly.

"Sorry I woke you, Mamie."

"It's all right, Charlie, I'm glad to see you."

"I just wanted to give you something…to remember me by."

He opened his hand and offered me a scratched and dented Zippo cigarette lighter. Engraved on one side was the Marine Corps Eagle, Globe, and Anchor; engraved on the other was: *I Walk the Line*.

"I know you don't smoke, but this lighter is my favorite thing. I've had it all through my hitch. It's kinda my lucky charm."

"I can't take it, Charlie. You don't want to give away your luck."

"I want you to have it, Mamie. You need all the luck you can get. This is a dangerous place."

"But what about you? What about your luck?"

Charlie grinned. "I got matches to light my smokes. And I got an M-16 for the rest."

I embraced Charlie.

He whispered, "I've got to go soon, Mamie. The patrol's assembling down at the camp perimeter."

"Are you scared?"

"A little. But we've got a good bunch of guys going out. We take care of each other." A pause. "Mamie, could I kiss you goodbye?"

I pressed my lips against his. The kiss deepened, and his tongue caressed mine. After a few moments, our lips parted.

"I love you so much, Mamie. I know it's crazy. Could I—I touch your breasts?"

I opened my housecoat, and he gently covered my breasts with his hands.

His palms were cold and sweaty.

"How old are you, Charlie?"

"I'll be nineteen in November. I know I'm probably too young for you."

"You're the perfect age. I'll make you a deal. When you get out of this, come see me. We'll go on a date, and I'll show you Hollywood. We'll make up for this interruption, and we'll make beautiful love. Will you do that?"

He smiled. "Oh, yes." Then his face darkened. "If I come back."

"We have a date, Charlie. You have to come back. Okay?"

He did his best to control his quivering chin. "Okay. It's a date. I will."

I kissed him again, and there were tears in his eyes. He walked away in the direction of the camp perimeter. I could hear diesel engines growling and the clank of tank treads as the patrol assembled.

I walked back to the general's quarters with an overwhelming sense of emptiness and dread. Bobby caught up with me.

"Seems like a nice kid."

"Yes. Too nice. Do you think the nice ones die first?"

Bobby shook his head. "I hope not. I dunno."

The next day I greeted the arriving patrol that had been relieved by Charlie's group. Tanks and personnel carriers lumbered through the sticky red mud into the compound, ridden by tired and skinny marines covered in dirt and mud. (All the grunts were skinny in Vietnam. It's hard to get fat on MREs—Meals, Ready-to-Eat).

A shout went up from the marines when they saw me. They carried me across the muddy track and deposited me on top of a tank. It was chaotic. Everyone was chattering, "Mamie! Mamie! Sign my helmet! Sign my shirt! Sign my arm!" By the time I was through hugging and posing for pictures, I was covered in mud too.

"Hey, guys!" I shouted over the din, "I gotta go take a shower. Everyone's going to be at my show this afternoon, right?"

The shout went up, "Right!"

***

John Huddleston

By accident, Rick and I wound up in Quang Tri Province. It was an area of operations for the marines, and we were army. We were but visitors.

I remember you that day. It was hot and humid, and when you started your show, beads of sweat had already formed on your forehead. Rick and I stood at the back of the crowd. We removed our helmets and put on our caps. The sun blazed down, and the humidity was in the stratosphere.

There you were, Mamie Van Doren, Hollywood movie star and sex symbol. The atmosphere was electric.

I remember your energy, and I thought, "If she could be anywhere on Earth at this moment, she would choose to be here with us."

You were tanned, dynamic, young, and radiant. You sang and joked, and the men hooted and laughed.

I noticed how Rick was so excited. You were the only celebrity he had ever seen in person. I had never seen him so happy. You were tired, but you soldiered on. The

GIs didn't want you to leave, and I could tell you didn't want to leave either.

Rick elbowed me and said, "She looked at me, John, she smiled and winked!" He laughed a joyful laugh.

"She couldn't have noticed you," I replied.

"I know she saw me, and you'll never convince me otherwise!"

"Okay. She saw you."

I remembered one moment in your performance when you shouted,

"Does anyone want to go home with me?" There was a loud roar of "Yes!"

Rick and I wanted to go home.

The next day we returned to the Central Highlands and rejoined our infantry unit. Rick told everyone, "We saw Mamie Van Doren!" You were the last American woman he saw. His mother sent movie magazines that featured you. It was one of the great joys of his life. We talked about you all the time.

Rick and I never went "home." We knew the American public had gone sour on the war and blamed us, but you were there, Mamie. You didn't give a damn what people thought. You stuck your neck out. Anything could have happened that day. We could have been attacked and all of us could have died. There is an intimacy that lasts forever between people who face potential death in the same moment. We shared that.

***

My show was a little home, a little sexiness, and music nice and loud. Smiles and cheers. The tent-pole song in the middle of my act was "Proud Mary." After I sang a couple of verses, the band would vamp while I looked over the audience.

"I feel so lonely up here," I purred. "I wish someone would come up and dance with me." A lot of foot stamping and cheering followed. "Any takers, marines?"

Several soldiers dragged a pimply young kid out of his seat and pushed him onstage. He had curly red hair and a shy smile. When I looked at him, he blushed as red as his hair.

"What's your name, honey?" I asked.

"Jeb."

"And where are you from, Jeb?"

"Hornbeak, Tennessee, population 328," he said with a proud grin. He had a soft Southern drawl.

"Have you got a girlfriend among that 328, Jeb?"

"No, ma'am."

"Well, you've got a girlfriend now, sweetie. Let's dance! Hit it, Bobby!"

Bobby gave the downbeat, and the band rocked into the chorus. Jeb and I bumped hips and danced while his buddies cheered. When the song was over, I kissed him on the lips to a chorus of whistles and shouts. I sang a couple of ballads and ended the show with a cover of Ray Charles's "What'd I Say."

I've performed for large and small audiences damn near everywhere—Las Vegas, New York, Chicago, in auditoriums, theaters, and nightclubs. Audiences have different personalities, some tough and reserved—*prove to me you can entertain me*—and some are generous and warm. But these audiences of service men were unique in my experience. Waves of delight and admiration washed over me while I performed. It was love of a sort I'd never experienced, mixed with gratitude that I had come to the worst place in the world for them. It was like a tonic to me. Addictive.

I was walking back to my borrowed quarters after the show when someone behind me said, "Hey, Mamie, did you know that John Russell in *Untamed Youth* was a decorated marine in World War II?"

I turned and saw two smiling young men in army uniforms. "Hi. One of my favorite movies. I knew he had been a marine."

"He was decorated for valor at the battle of Guadalcanal. Got a field commission. I hope we didn't startle you, Mamie." He extended his hand. "My name's John Huddleston. This is my friend Rick. Thank you for a wonderful show."

"Yeah," Rick added shyly, "it was really great!"

"Thanks, guys," I said.

"You winked at me tonight, right?" Rick blurted out.

"Aw, c'mon, Rick, give the lady a break."

I batted my eyelashes. "Well...maybe."

"I knew it. See, John, I told you she did, and you didn't believe me."

"You got me that time, Rick. Mamie, Rick and I are movie buffs. We know all about your movies. We even know all the words to 'Oobala Baby.'"

"I didn't know the words to 'Oobala Baby' when I sang it. That's a real accomplishment."

"I even know your character's name in *Francis Join the WACS*—Corporal Bunky Hilstrom. If we had more corporals like Bunky this would be a better place."

I shook my head. "Incredible. Okay, what was my character's name in *Teacher's Pet*?"

"Peggy DeFore!" they said in unison.

"You two are a regular vaudeville act. C'mon and walk me back to my quarters." They fell into step beside me. "How long have you been over here? And what are a couple of army guys doing in the midst of all these marines?"

John spoke first. "This is the second hitch for both of us. I'm a combat medic."

"And I'm a radioman," Rick put in.

John went on, "We get assigned to different commands if they need a medic and a radioman."

"And somebody most always need a couple of those."

We reached the general's quarters, and I turned to say goodnight. "Thanks for the escort, guys. I've got to turn in. I'm off to Dak To tomorrow."

"It was a pleasure, Mamie," John said.

"Yeah, Mamie, thanks so much," Rick said.

John's face got serious. "Be careful, Mamie. This is a dangerous place. And Dak To's even more dangerous."

"I'll be careful, thanks. Good night."

The next day, I gathered up my little gang, and we decamped for Dak To, a smaller, remote firebase about 140 miles to the south. The Huey that sexy Françoise had borrowed to get back to civilization hadn't yet returned, so General Hill kindly offered his personal helicopter to fly Bobby and me there. The musicians would follow in the other Huey.

I sat side-by-side with the pilot and Bobby in the cockpit of the little Bell 47 helicopter. The clear bubble canopy gave us a panoramic view of the jungle below—more than I really wanted to see. The rain forest was thick and deep. If we had to make an emergency landing, it would not be a smooth one.

Dak To is situated in a wide valley surrounded by low hills. In 1967, it had been the scene of some of the bloodiest fighting in the Vietnam War. The North Vietnamese held the base under siege for more than a month. Casualties were high. Now, four years later, there was still fighting in the area. Enemy troops continued to test the camp's defenses, and patrols into the bush often met with sharp fighting.

We arrived at Dak To in the early afternoon. The camp's commanding officer. Lieutenant Colonel Abbott met me at the helipad.

"Welcome, Mamie." He extended a handshake. "We're honored to have you here in Dak To." A couple of soldiers immediately took charge of my luggage. "The guys'll take your bags. You'll be staying in my personal quarters, so I want to escort you personally."

Lieutenant Colonel Abbott's hooch did not quite live up to the standard of General Hill's bungalow, but it was air conditioned and dry, and it had a private outdoor toilet nearby.

Our stage here would be on the bed of a truck used to haul munitions. Bobby and the musicians prepared as best they could. I put on my makeup and slipped into a gown. It was hot and humid. It felt like it might rain.

Two soldiers portaged me across the mud and onto the back of the truck. The show started, I sang, and everyone cheered.

Halfway through the show, I heard popping and crackling, followed by distant explosions. The soldiers began looking around, their faces suddenly serious. I stopped the show.

"That's small arms fire, Mamie," a marine shouted out.

Lieutenant Colonel Abbott rushed over and motioned me down off the truck. A couple of soldiers helped me down. The others gathered around me in a protective circle.

"Mamie, you need to get out of here *now*," Abbott said. "Scouts report there are NVA troops close by. This could be something bad."

"I'll need to get my things—"

"There's no time. I sent my aide to get some of my fatigues for you to wear. Put them on. It's going to be cold in that helicopter."

I pulled on the fatigue pants under my dress, slipped the top off and put on the shirt.

"Give me the dress, Mamie. I'll get it back to you with the rest of your belongings. Just get in General Hill's chopper and get the fuck outta here."

Bobby and the musicians sprinted toward their Huey, still carrying their instruments. Several soldiers shielded me as we rushed to the helicopter pad. The rotor was turning, the engine warming up. The sounds of gunfire were getting louder. I could hear men shouting. As soon as I got in the cockpit, the pilot opened the throttle and we took off into the gathering dusk. As we gained altitude, I saw muzzle flashes on a hillside near the base. A helicopter gunship began pouring fire into the location.

We circled away from the action and headed north in the direction of Quang Tri.

"You can relax now, Mamie. We're in the clear."

"What's going to happen to the men back there? I feel guilty leaving."

"That's no place for you, Mamie. They can take care of business. It's not the first time this base has been attacked."

"Well, it's my first time." I began to shake uncontrollably. "And I didn't like it."

The pilot grinned. "Hardly anybody does."

"What about Bobby and my musicians? Did they get out? Can you radio back there?"

The pilot shook his head. "They'll get out. We need to stay silent for now. The VC and NVA monitor our radio frequencies. That's most likely how they knew about your show."

That brought me up short. "You mean this attack was because of me?"

The pilot shrugged. "It's possible, Mamie."

"Holy shit."

General Hill met me at the helipad back in Quang Tri. He chuckled as he helped me out of the cockpit. "Nice uniform, soldier."

"Colonel Abbott loaned me his fatigues."

"Abbott always was the kind of guy who would give you the shirt off his back."

"I need to find out about my conductor and musicians, general."

He put a hand on my shoulder. "Their pilot radioed ahead. They're okay—on their way back here."

I leaned against the general for a moment. "Whew, that's a relief."

"I'll walk you back to your quarters."

I told the general what the pilot had said. "Yes, Mamie, it's likely they knew you were coming to Dak To. Headquarters Intel group monitors their radio frequencies, just like they do ours. They told me the enemy had been chattering about it for a couple days."

I looked at the general in disbelief. "And they didn't warn me? Or warn you to warn me?"

"All classified, Mamie."

"What the hell good is intelligence if you don't fucking use it?"

The general raised his eyebrows. "Good point. I agree."

When I got inside my room, I was weak from exhaustion and fear. Now anger was raging inside me as I got into the shower. By the time I got out, I was so pissed off I couldn't see straight.

Who had ignored the situation I was unwittingly in? Who in blooming hell didn't have the decency or just plain old good sense to see what was about to go down in Dak To and think, Hey, I'd better tell the unarmed, vulnerable entertainer who's going there risking her ass that some bad shit is brewing.

The answer is, of course, *no one*. For the headquarters intel folks, it was another day at the office. For the base commanders, it was an actress coming to entertain the troops—not routine, but they have a war to fight. For the grunts fresh in off the DMZ from walking the line, it was another lucky day that they were on the sunny side of a body bag zipper. They confronted the junction of life and death daily. The intel that NVA troops were massing for an attack was worth passing on. But the actress coming to sing some songs—she would just be collateral damage.

I sat on the edge of the bed for a long time, scared, homesick, mad, and crying, wishing I could talk to my mother, thinking of Perry's tearful farewell, feeling the guilt of leaving him behind. I was on the verge of shit-canning this whole trip. Better to chicken out now and go home standing up than to come home packed away in one of those tin-can coffins.

There was a knock at the door. "It's General Hill, Mamie."

I let him in and sat back on the edge of the bed.

"I wanted to let you know that your Huey is back. And I got all your belongings from Quang Tri by a special courier a little while ago."

He put my dress and makeup kit on the bed. My dress was neatly folded, and my makeup kit perfectly packed. The rest of my luggage had arrived safely too. The general handed me an envelope with my name hand lettered on it.

"Compliments of Colonel Abbot. I'll let you get some sleep now. You've got a long trip tomorrow to Chu Lai. We want you to dust off by oh-six hundred, just before dawn. It'll give you some cover to get to a safe altitude."

"What happened at Quang Tri?"

"Battle's over. They weathered the siege. A few casualties, not many."

"That's good to know. General, can you tell me about Charlie? Is he okay?"

He looked away and took a breath. "They were ambushed on the second day. We lost Charlie and three others. I'm sorry."

I gasped. "Oh, no!" I fished his Zippo out of my bag, flipped it open and lit it. I watched the flame for a moment, then closed the top. "Thank you for telling me, general."

"Look, Mamie, you were right about using intelligence. So let me tell you, the VC and NVA are aware of you. If I get any more info, I'll get it to you so you can be careful. If it looks too hot somewhere, you can cancel."

"I'm grateful to you for that. Thank you, general, for all your kindness." I jumped up and kissed him on the cheek.

"That makes it all worth it, Mamie. You may not know it, but you've made an enormous difference for our men. They talk about nothing else but you. Thank you for that."

"My pleasure, general."

When he left, I opened the envelope.

Dear Mamie,

I'm returning your dress. The color isn't right for me anyway. And you can you can keep the fatigues as a souvenir of your eventful visit to Dak To. Sorry that your show had to end so abruptly. I'm sure you're not anxious to return. We all understand. You can be assured that when the shooting started last night, there was not a soldier on this base who would not have willingly died protecting you. We all wish you Godspeed, Mamie.

Sincerely,
Col. Wes Abbott

I carefully folded the note and slipped it back in its envelope. I flicked Charlie's Zippo again and stared at the flame. I closed it and extinguished the flame. "Good bye, Charlie. May angels sing you on to heaven."

Chu Lai tomorrow. Not time to bail out. Yet. Of course, I would go.

I was packed and in my chopper with the rotors turning when the pilot got word to shut down. When I asked him what the problem was, he said, "Orders from General Hill, Mamie. He said *don't leave*."

I met General Hill on the helipad and he took me aside.

"I told you I'd let you know if there was a potential danger, Mamie. There is reliable intel that the VC are tracking your helicopters. An ambush is in the works, likely a hand-held rocket attack on your choppers. I've ordered in a C-47 transport to take you and your people to Chu Lai."

"Jesus, I came here to sing and dance, not to make this my personal war."

The general smiled. "It'll be okay, Mamie. The C-47 is the best I could get you on short notice. It's slow, but it flies at high enough altitudes to keep you safe."

"Okay," I said. "I'm grateful, general. I'd like to get going."

"Well, there'll be a bit of a wait for the aircraft to get here. Probably a couple of hours. You're welcome to rest in my quarters again until it arrives."

We cooled our heels for more than two hours before the airplane landed.

The C-47 was a vintage taildragger relic from WWII. We loaded up everything, took off, and climbed to a safe altitude. After a while, it seemed like we'd been flying forever. I stuck my head into the cockpit and asked the pilot, "Can't you make this thing go any faster?"

He grinned a big grin. "Sorry, Mamie, one hundred ninety knots is about all this old girl can do. But she'll get us there."

Chu Lai was an enormous marine base, a six-plus-hour flight from Quang Tri. In addition to elements of various marine fighting forces, the base provided support for naval forces. There were several venues where I was scheduled to perform.

A sergeant named Como met me at the helipad and drove me by Jeep to my quarters. He escorted me into a large recreation hall where a handful of marines were playing ping-pong and shooting pool. It grew quiet as we walked to the back corner of the room. Screened by some makeshift curtains, there was small corner with a cot, a couple of blankets, and a pillow.

"This is it, Mamie," Sergeant Como said quietly.

I looked incredulously at the cot and then at Sergeant Como. "This is where I'm supposed to stay? In the middle of a recreation hall? With no privacy?" My temper was smoldering! I could feel my face turning red. "What about a toilet?"

Sergeant Como pointed across the room. "There are toilets over there."

"You mean I'm supposed to sleep in the middle of a room filled with soldiers with these—these so-called curtains? And then walk across the room to use the toilet? Oh, no, sergeant, this is not going to do."

Sergeant Como looked chagrined. "I'm sorry, Mamie, this is where General Baldwin ordered you to be housed."

I was grinding my teeth. "You'd better take me to see General Baldwin, sergeant."

"I'm not sure he'll see you, Mamie. He's pretty busy."

"You just take me to him. He'll see me."

We got back in the Jeep and drove to the headquarters building. There was a small foyer outside the general's office.

"I'll see if the general's available."

The sergeant disappeared through a door labeled *Lt. General James Baldwin, Commanding Officer,* while I waited. I sat in one of two straight-backed metal chairs against one wall. My body ached for sleep. I hadn't eaten or had a drink of water since I left Quang Tri hours ago. I was in no mood to be trifled with.

After a few minutes, the sergeant came back. "Mamie, General Baldwin said he can see you in a day or two. If you'll just—"

"I'll be damned if I do!"

I shoved my way past the sergeant and through the door. The general looked up, startled. "What the—"

"General," I blurted out, "you and I need to have a serious talk."

General James Baldwin was smallish and bespectacled, balding with small mean eyes. His mouth was stretched in a grimace. He stood up from his desk.

"Just what do you think you're doing barging in here, madam? Who do you think you're talking to? I'm a general in the Marine Corps."

"I don't care if you're John Paul Jones. We need to have a discussion about my accommodations. I'm not going to live behind a curtain in a recreation hall."

"There's nothing to discuss, *Miss* Van Doren." He put a nasty emphasis on the word "miss." "There are no other quarters available on this base. This is not a luxury hotel, you know. We're fighting a war here."

My face was bright red, and my eyes were tearing up. I willed myself not to cry in front of this asshole.

"I was invited to this base, your base, General Baldwin, to do shows in several of your officer and enlisted clubs."

"I know. And you were allowed here against my better judgement. If there's one thing we don't need, it's another Hollywood type snooping around and undermining us when they get back to the states."

I shook my head in disbelief. "What on Earth are you talking about?"

The general held up two sheets of paper. "Do you know what these are?

They're letters of condolence. I just sent them to the families of two of our MPs, who were killed outside our camp perimeter three nights ago."

"I didn't know any of that."

"No, of course you didn't. And you also didn't know that the same three nights ago Jane Fonda gave a speech at an anti-war demonstration in San Francisco. Two of my soldiers got drunk and wandered outside the camp perimeter. Two MPs went out looking for them. They were hacked to pieces with machetes by two farmers jacked up on beer and Hanoi Hannah's descriptions of Jane Fonda's wild rally in 'Frisco." The general wiped his forehead. "She calls our soldiers baby killers—war criminals, for chrissakes. That's why I didn't want you here. Sergeant, please show Miss Van Doren out."

"General," I said, avoiding Sergeant Como's grasp, "I'm sorry for the loss of your men. It's tragic, and it's doubly tragic that their deaths were caused by that event. But that's on Jane Fonda, not me. I couldn't be more opposite from her. My whole reason for being here is because I saw our soldiers in tiger cages paraded through the streets in Hanoi. Jane Fonda hates the war and our soldiers. I'm not part of that group that believes the war is somehow the fault of the men and women doing the fighting. I hate the war, but I respect and admire our soldiers. I would never do anything to hurt them. They're just doing their duty."

"Well, you'll have plenty of opportunity to respect and admire them from your quarters in the rec hall."

I snapped.

"What are you trying to say, general? Are you actually implying that I'm here to be a whore? Why, you disrespectful son of a bitch. You don't even have the balls to say it to my face. Is that what it means to be an *officer and a gentleman*?"

I slipped my big satchel off my shoulders and rummaged around in it for a moment.

"That'll be all, Miss Van Doren. Show her out, Sergeant Como," he growled.

I took out the letter and slipped it out of its envelope. I tossed it on the desk in front of him.

"Not until you read this, *general*." I put an insolent sneer in his title. "That is a personal letter to me from President Richard Nixon. He is personally aware of my tour here, he personally encouraged it, and he offered to personally help me if I needed it."

He read the letter through with a scowl.

"I will need to make a call back to the states," I went on. "I have the president's private number. He may very well take a personal interest in the arrogant disrespect and lame-ass cooperation you have shown me so far." I gestured to the telephone on his desk. "If you'll let me use your phone, I'll get him on the line so you can explain why you're being such an unmitigated asshole."

General Baldwin handed the letter back and picked up his phone. I thought for a moment he was going to call my bluff. He spoke tersely into the telephone. "Tell Major Winestein he's going on R&R early. He will be out of his quarters in half an hour. And they better be clean. Sergeant, show Miss Van Doren to Winestein's hooch. You'll have a shower and air conditioning and a flush toilet, okay?"

"Okay, general. Many thanks."

He sullenly turned back to the papers on his desk. "Don't mention it."

Sergeant Como drove me to Major Weinstein's quarters. The major waved as he went out the door with his packed bag.

"Enjoy the place, Mamie," he shouted. "Sorry I'll miss your show. I'm off to Bangkok."

I waved back. "Wish I was going too, major."

Sergeant Como brought my bag inside and asked if there was anything I needed.

"Thanks, sergeant. Some fresh drinking water would be welcome."

"I'll bring some back for you." He walked to the door and turned back.

Mamie, you have to understand what's going on with General Baldwin."

"I understand he acted like a dick to me."

"I know he was bad. But he's been catching hell from his bosses for the loss of the MPs and the two soldiers they were looking for. It's not my job, but I apologize for my general."

"Why, Como?"

"Because what you're doing in this godforsaken nightmare of a country is so…important. General Baldwin's wrong to paint you with the same brush as Jane Fonda. He's got to live with his hatred of Jane Fonda, but the rest of us have to live with this war. And survive it."

"I don't stand for any of the things she does—except I'd like the killing to stop too. But she's not going to stop it by blaming the troops who're here because they have to be. She'll only create more hate. And I won't stop it by singing a few songs and vamping around the stage, but at least I'll leave a few smiles in my wake."

Sergeant Como grinned. "That you will."

"You know, sergeant, I was dog tired when I got here. My little tête-à-tête with the good general has left me desperate for ten hours of sleep and a good steak dinner. I'm probably not going to get either one. There are half a dozen enlisted men's and officers' clubs on this base where I'm going to perform. Thank God I don't have to work tonight."

"Get some sleep, Mamie. I'll go talk the general's stewards into making you some dinner."

When Sergeant Como got back with a steak and baked potato and some bottled water, I was asleep. I woke to the smell of the sizzling T-bone the sergeant had left on the bedside table. I wolfed down the steak and potato and guzzled some water. And went back to sleep.

It would be the last time I would get enough rest. From here on, I would be severely tested by my schedule. And the war.

***

John Huddleston

> It seems like a million years ago that I sat in a small bunker on a hot summer day with Rick. We were on a ridge overlooking the Dak To valley in the Central Highlands. We were playing double solitaire.
>
> Suddenly, without warning, a large explosion erupted on the other side of the firebase. Was it an RPG rocket or mortars? I didn't know. It happened in first platoon. I quickly heard the shout of "Medic!"
>
> I stood up and looked around to be sure there was no further incoming fire. I hurried to the opposite side of the firebase and ran into Hames, first platoon's medic. Hames was a no-nonsense experienced medic who had seen tons of shit over his four months in the field. His face was white, and his hands were trembling.
>
> He pointed to his right.

I saw what had been three human beings. Blood was everywhere. The bodies were so torn apart it was impossible to tell which parts belonged to which soldier.

Hames was in severe shock. He couldn't move. All three men were clearly dead. The only thing left to do was pick up the pieces.

My mind raced.

Sergeant Adams from first platoon approached me. "What do we do?"

I said, "Get the lieutenant and call in a medevac. Tell them we have three KIAs."

When I looked around, Rick and Garvin were standing next to me. Rick threw up.

We divided the remains into three piles, covering them with ponchos. When the medevac arrived, I talked to the crew chief and medic to prepare them for what they would see.

Together Hames, Rick, Garvin, the crew chief, and I put the remains into three separate body bags. I gave the crew chief each soldier's dog tags and rucksacks.

The medevac departed, and I walked with Hames back to his platoon.

He stood on the edge of the firebase perimeter, looking at the Dak To valley below. I put my hand on his shoulder. We stood in silence for the longest time. He looked at me.

Hames: "I know these guys. It was not my fault."

Me: "I know Jim. It was not your fault."

His platoon sergeant and lieutenant arrived, and he walked back to his platoon.

I returned to the little bunker that Rick and I shared. Garvin, Rick, and a new guy named Hogan sat with me. Hogan was fresh-faced and naïve, with a misdirected optimism that all would be well in the end. Garvin, Rick, and I had become very close. We all loved movies and talked about them constantly.

We began to talk about the movie *Madigan*, starring Richard Widmark. Madigan was a street-smart cop who felt intimidated by people of higher rank. We talked about how it was shot on location in New York. I mentioned Inger Stevens who played Madigan's wife.

After a few minutes Hogan interrupted, "Why are you talking about movies at a time like this?"

Garvin replied, "Because three of the actors in it died within six years of the movie being finished, and Inger Stevens, Michael Dunn, and Steve Ihnat were all under forty." For the rest of the day, we did not talk.

Before going to sleep, I turned over, looked at Rick and said, "This has been one fucking bad day."

Rick nodded. "I know, John."

***

The names of villages and firebases begin to sound alike after a while.

Flying from one to another in a Huey—noisy as a boiler room, torturous straight-backed seats, slow enough to be an easy target from the endless jungle below—takes its toll. As word spread about my show, more of the firebases—especially the remote ones—asked to be added to my schedule. Bobby kept up with the itinerary.

"They know you'll come to these little bases out in the boondocks," he told me.

I wondered out loud if the word had spread to the Viet Cong in the bush. Might there be a reception like Dak To waiting for me at one of those outlying bases?

"The dangerous ones."

"Yep, those. They really want to see you, but it's your call to go or not, Mamie."

"How're the musicians holding up?"

Bobby chuckled. "They're doing alright. They feel safe as long as they're with you. They think you're protected by an angel."

"Let's hope they're right. Sign me up."

I was doing my best to doze as we flew to the next gig. I jolted awake when I heard the "Ding da-ding! Ding!" of enemy rounds bouncing off the Huey's fuselage.

One of the door gunners shouted, "Enemy fire, left side!" and began firing into the dense jungle below. The pilot banked away and gained altitude. Both gunners were painting the trees with rounds.

"Ding, da-ding, da-ding!" Then it stopped.

We leveled off, and the pilot shouted back, "Sorry for the excitement, Mamie, looks like you've got some fans back there."

I waved at him but didn't answer. I was saving my voice, but that wasn't even funny.

When we got to our destination, I gathered the helicopter crew around me.

"Look, guys, I want you to make me a promise, okay? If we get shot down and it looks like we'll be captured, save a bullet for me. I don't want to be taken alive and tortured. I mean it. Deal?"

They all exchanged glances. "Mamie," the pilot said, "we've got the same deal among all of us. We'll take care of you too."

I clasped everyone's hands in mine. "Deal," we said in unison.

***

John Huddleston

When I was in the Central Highlands, around Dak To, Rick and I were close to the platoon commander, a lieutenant. We often shared the gallows humor common to those who face off with death on a daily basis.

For example, I'd say to Rick or the lieutenant, "Give me a cigarette or I'll kill ya!"

One day we flew in to replace another unit at a firebase. As the chopper landed, a sniper opened fire. Rick, the lieutenant and I dove into a nearby trench as bullets bounced all around us.

The following conversation ensued in the trench.

Lieutenant: "What kind of fucking place is this that they let bastards shoot at us like a shooting gallery!"

Me: "I don't know."

Lieutenant: "Is your pistol loaded?"

Me: "Yes."

Lieutenant: "Go down there and kill that lanky cocksucker!"

I slowly raised my head above the trench. In front of me was about fifteen yards of cleared area before the jungle line. I swallowed and took a deep breath.

Me: "Sir, how about you run the fifteen yards to that jungle line, and if you arrive with your head on your shoulders, I'll join you."

Lieutenant: "And if I don't arrive with my head in place, what then?"

Me: "Then I'll feel real bad, sir, but I'll join you anyway."

Lieutenant: "Why would you do that?"

Me: "To retrieve your carcass."

Lieutenant: "I always knew you cared."

Rick, the lieutenant, and I burst out laughing.

A new man in the platoon overheard us and innocently asked, "Do you guys think this is funny!?"

I stopped laughing long enough to say, "No, we're all scared shitless!"

***

As my little traveling road show worked its way south toward the Mekong Delta and Saigon, we were handed off to another helicopter squadron. The CO of the new squadron was Major James Scott. And because rank has its privileges, Major Scott chose to be my personal helicopter pilot. He had done several hitches in country and was wise in the ways of the war and Vietnam. He counseled me on which firebases might be too hot with enemy activity to visit. He was also a short-timer, scheduled to soon rotate back to the States.

We became better acquainted as time went on, and before long, we were lovers. I had no intention of becoming involved with anyone while in Vietnam. War zone romances may be a cliché, but the heart wants what the heart wants, even while it's ducking bullets.

There were only a handful of stops left when Major Scott flew me to My Tho. Huddled in a blanket against the chill air blowing through the Huey's side doors, I was thinking about Perry. As a child, I used to pretend if I thought of someone, they would think of me. I had occasion to practice it a lot when I was marooned on my grandparents' farm. I missed my mom and dad so much back then, I would pretend that when I thought of them, they would get the message and think of me, sending messages that they loved me and missed me too.

Now, I conjured up Perry's face and tried to make a connection with him. I told him I loved him and that I would be home soon. After My Tho, I only had a couple of gigs in Saigon for officers' clubs and a few at firebases in the south. I told Perry in my mind that I would be on my way home soon. I prayed he would get the message.

We landed at My Tho in a late afternoon downpour. I noticed an odd-looking helicopter on the pad near us. The seating was front-to-back, instead of side-by-side like our Huey. Head on it looked like an insect.

I asked Major Scott about it. "Huey Cobra," he replied with hushed respect in his voice. "It's a cousin of our Hueys but more powerful and faster and much better armed. It has rocket launchers and high-powered rapid-fire cannons. That is one badass chopper."

"Why's it here?" I asked.

"Probably refueling. Certainly it's classified. Command doesn't like to advertise where they are."

Bobby undertook locating whatever "stage" we'd be performing on and started setting up. In places like My Tho, it was simple: Our stage was little more than a lean-to with some plywood sheets for a floor so that my feet didn't get muddy.

The camp CO, Lieutenant Colonel Goodwin, came to my quarters and introduced himself. He explained that the area was swarming with enemy activity. Viet Cong raids and sabotage were a constant danger, but he was enthusiastic about having my show for his men.

"All my boys are gung-ho about your show coming here. They've heard about you from their buddies at other firebases, but just be prepared to make a quick exit. If it hits the fan, you'll want to be far away from here."

He glanced at the AK-47 lying on my bed. "I see you are prepared, Mamie. Do you know how to use that thing?"

"It's a souvenir from Pleiku. The night I was there the NVA started lobbing mortar shells into the camp after my show. I guess they didn't like the music. One of the grunts gave me this captured AK-47 and showed me how to use it in case they overran the camp."

Goodwin nodded appreciatively.

I put a brave face on it for Goodwin, but after he left, my hand was shaking as I put on my makeup. Strangely, I felt the kind of excitement you feel when you're a short-timer. I only had a few shows left. You feel the thrill of knowing that soon you'll be on your way home. And you try to ignore the fear that just a day—even hours—before you leave, you might get killed.

The soldiers from My Tho were noisy and approving. They had earned a good show, Goodwin had told me. After my last number, I spent some time with them just talking about home and signing autographs. Some wanted to know about the anti-war protests back in the States. I told them in no uncertain terms I was no Jane Fonda. One of the guys said, "It don't bother me if they protest. If it ends the war sooner and we get outta here, I'm all for it."

When I got back to my quarters, I was exhausted. I was dizzy and my knees were weak. I packed up my makeup and laid out some fatigues for the morning. I sent telepathic messages to Perry and my mom. I said my prayers and went to bed.

The first mortar explosion jolted me out of a deep sleep. It was at the edge of the camp, but the concussion made my ears ring. There was a lot of yelling, gunfire, and more explosions. I grabbed my AK-47 and fumbled the safety off. My panicked brain told me this must be the end. "Now let's see if I can shoot this son of a bitch," I muttered.

The door burst open, and I swung the gun toward it.

"Jesus, Mamie, don't shoot!" Bobby rushed in followed by Lieutenant Colonel Goodwin and Major Scott. "You've got to go," Bobby said.

Goodwin gingerly took the gun from me and flipped the safety back on. "Quickly, Mamie, we're under attack," Goodwin said.

Bobby gathered up my belongings. I quickly pulled on my fatigues, and the three of us rushed out the door. Outside soldiers were running to their battle stations. I could smell the explosives. Bobby joined the musicians and ran with them to our Hueys.

Goodwin turned to Major Scott. "You'd better get to your aircraft, major.

I'll help Mamie get into the Cobra." Scott trotted off toward his helicopters. The Cobra's rotor was turning. I could hear the engine whine over the din of gunfire and explosions.

"Mamie," Goodwin shouted over the noise, "this is Beau." He steered a tall, good-looking soldier next to me. "He's the Cobra pilot. He's going to fly you to Saigon. It's the fastest way to get you there. You'll meet up with your musicians at Tan Son Nhut airfield."

The pilot and Goodwin helped me climb into the front seat. Beau climbed into the higher seat behind me. Goodwin helped me into the helmet that would normally be worn by the front-seat weapons officer.

"Welcome aboard, Mamie," Beau said into my earphones. "Enjoy the ride."

I was too scared to answer. Beau throttled up the engine, and we lifted off. He banked sharply away from the firing and climbed. The acceleration jammed me back in the seat. My Tho disappeared into the night behind us. We climbed into the pitch-black sky. As my eyes adjusted to the darkness, I could make out stars. Without lights for landmarks, it was like floating in space. I wondered if it felt this way for the Apollo astronauts—minus the gravity.

My reverie was shattered by a sudden lurch of the helicopter.

"Damn! Incoming rocket! Hold on, Mamie!"

A red streak shot past our left side. The engine whined louder, and we went into a steep climb. I felt like I was strapped to a rocket.

"Wow! That left my stomach behind."

"Sorry, Mamie. Some of the VC have handheld rockets. This one probably heard us and took a wild shot. We're safe now. I'm radioing back to tell your crew to avoid this area. It's more dangerous for them 'cause they're lower and slower."

After we landed at Tan Son Nhut, I had to wait half an hour because the other choppers detoured around the hot spot. I was out on my feet by the time we got to our hotel in Saigon. I took a long hot shower and fell into bed and a deep troubled sleep.

The next morning, I ate a good breakfast and began to feel a little better.

***

My first show in Saigon was for officers and VIPs in a large auditorium. Someone backstage said that if a bomb went off in here, it would be the end of the war, because no one would be left alive to run it. The audience of top brass couldn't have been more different from the grunts in the field. They applauded and laughed in the right spots, but the raucous enthusiasm of the grunts was missing.

I felt alone and disoriented on stage, framed in a bright follow spot and unable to see the audience. Instead, I was staring into the darkened theater, with only the *exit* sign in the back to focus on.

Everything was going well when I got into the "Proud Mary" part of the show. After the first verse and chorus, I always stopped while the band vamped, and I asked for a volunteer to come onstage and dance with me. Blinded by the glare of the light, I could barely see a figure climb onto the stage and come lumbering toward me.

I extended my hand, but he grabbed my arm roughly and growled, "Come here, you little bitch."

I pulled my arm back, but he engulfed me in a bear hug, muttering, "You know you want it, baby."

Suddenly this was turning into a nightmare. "Help! Help me, please!"

He pinned my arms to my sides and tried to wrestle me off my feet. I struggled to stay upright. I felt one of his feet next to mine, so I jammed a stiletto high heel into the top of his foot.

"Arrgh!" he screamed.

Instead of loosening his hold on me, he squeezed tighter. I lost my balance, and both of us fell to the floor. He made snarling noises and clawed at my dress, exposing my breasts.

I yelled for help again. Everyone was frozen, staring. No one came to my aid. He was trying to tear my dress completely off. I struggled to fight him, my mind spinning in terror. I had the bizarre thought that my obituary would read, "She survived the Vietnam War only to be raped and murdered onstage by an audience member."

And that pissed me off. My ancestors were Swedes, Finns, and indigenous Samis from Lapland. Tough, strong warriors. Suddenly the Viking shield maiden in me erupted and I shouted, "Fuck you!" With all my strength, I freed my arm holding the microphone and clubbed him on the forehead with it as hard as I could.

"Umph!" he groaned. I hit him again on the temple and blood started to squirt. He went limp, and I rolled him off me. I gave him another shot to the head just for good measure. I dropped the bloody microphone, jumped to my feet, and covered my breasts as best I could as I dashed off the stage.

I ran into the backstage lady's room, locked myself in a stall, and sat on the toilet sobbing. I felt a stabbing pain when I urinated. When I looked there was blood in my urine. I gasped and looked closer, and there was blood in my stool as well.

Bobby burst in the door. "Mamie! Are you alright?"

"No, I'm not. I'm bleeding from my urine and stool. I'm scared!"

He opened the stall door and helped me up. "Let's get you some help."

I panicked. "No! I'm not going out if that crazy motherfucker's out there."

Bobby wrapped his jacket around me. "He's gone. The MPs took him away on a stretcher."

"I hope he was dead. Did I kill him?"

"No, he was alive."

"Too fucking bad. I wish I could've done a better job, but I was too scared."

I tried to walk, but my knees buckled. They brought a gurney for me and loaded me into an ambulance. When they closed the door, I must have blacked out.

The next thing I remember, I woke in a small hospital room, still on the gurney with an IV in my arm. As soon as I opened my eyes, I panicked again and cried out. The nurse in the room put a reassuring hand on my arm.

"You're safe, Miss Van Doren," she said gently. "You're in the base infirmary. We're giving you some IV fluids. You're going to be okay."

"What about the bleeding?"

"It has subsided. The doctor will be in shortly to explain."

The doctor arrived a few minutes later, looking barely old enough to be a high school senior, much less a medical doctor.

"You're fine, Mamie, you just need a long rest. You have some scrapes and bruises from your scuffle, but nothing's broken."

There was a patronizing note in his voice that made my hackles go up.

"Scuffle? That was an attempted rape, doctor, and he might have succeeded if it hadn't been for my microphone."

"I know you're upset—"

"Upset? Does anyone know that son of a bitch's name? I want to press charges. You have no idea how upset I am, doctor."

"I understand, Mamie. I only know what I've been told about the incident, and I've no idea about your attacker's name. I just know that from a medical standpoint, you're physically all right."

I didn't have enough energy left to be indignant. "What about the blood I was passing?"

"Most likely anxiety and fatigue and not a little bit of dehydration. You're going to need to drink a lot more water. I'm discharging you with some medicine to help you sleep. Take two teaspoons when you get to your hotel. Go to bed and get a good, long sleep."

Tears welled up. "I'm sick, doctor, and I want to go home."

The doctor smiled ironically. "You and everybody else over here. I can't help you with that, but I can help you get your sleep."

He put a small brown bottle on the bed tray. "I'll get someone to take you to your hotel."

Back in my room, I felt empty and alone. Never so alone. I longed to speak to my mother, hear her voice; and I longed to hold Perry in my arms and dry his tears and mine.

I shuddered at the recollection of last night's ordeal. I wondered what explanation there could be for an auditorium full of, maybe, five hundred military men, and not one was motivated to intervene in a rape and assault being carried out in front of them. My anger added to the hurt in my heart and the pain of my "scrapes and bruises." I began to cry again.

I took two teaspoons of the medicine in the brown bottle. The taste was bitter, and the aftertaste was as rancid as the Saigon street smells drifting in my window. As I closed my eyes and drifted into sleep, I made up my mind: No matter how many other firebases I was scheduled to visit, my time was up. I was getting the fuck out of Vietnam.

***

John Huddleston

In significant ways, Rick and I were an odd couple. Rick was from rural Idaho, and I was from the California Bay Area, but in many ways we were alike. We both loved movies. Seeing Mamie Van Doren perform fed our obsession with movies. We talked about movies even more.

We were both "street smart" about combat. Each of us had already competed one tour of Vietnam. We knew the score—what a firefight was like and what death was like too. We often talked of death. We both observed how death was a capricious visitor, how death could enter one man's life and leave another untouched. Why was that?

We often speculated about whether a man could know through intuition that he was going to die before it happened. Neither of us had a theory on that, but each morning we would reflect on how we felt and what we thought about the day. Could a man know the day he was going to die?

Rick and I were in high-risk roles. Rick was a radioman, and I was a combat medic. Our chances of survival were less than the average rifleman. Each day we'd wake up and ask each other how we felt facing the day. Did we feel ill at ease? Did something seem not right? Did we have a gut feeling that something was going to happen? Every day the answer was the same: "I'm okay."

It was a Friday. We had been choppered onto a hill the afternoon before. We dug in and set up defensive positions. A water tank arrived so that we could fill all our canteens.

The weather was cool. Like so many other mornings, we woke up at sunrise and asked each other how we felt. We felt nothing out of place.

During the day, two squads went out on short patrols. Rick and I did not participate. In the afternoon, I was checking my medical bag and drawing up a list of items I needed to order.

Thud…thud…thud.

I heard the sound of mortar fire. Like a reflex, I hit the ground. I heard three blasts on the hillside opposite me. Then I heard the sound of rifle fire—several shots in rapid succession. They came from the tree line, about a hundred meters from the perimeter.

First there was silence, then I heard shouting and the cry for "Medic!"

I grabbed my medical bag, and I rushed to where the commotion was. When I arrived, I saw the water tank and three bodies stretched out next each other.

"Are they dead?" I asked.

Lieutenant Manly said in a monotone voice, "Yes, they are."

When I saw their faces, I went into shock. One was Rick. His eyes were open, staring into infinity. I felt his carotid artery.

There was no pulse and no breathing. I tried external cardiac compression.

Manly pulled me back. "He's dead, Doc," he said gently.

I kept trying. *He can't be dead,* I thought. *Life wouldn't do this to him and me. I needed Rick to live. We had made plans. He had ninety days left in Vietnam and I had 110.*

When I returned to the States, I was going to meet Rick in Idaho. From there we would go to New York where neither of us had been. We were going to see Washington DC too. We had fantasied about starting some sort of business together. Maybe we would both go to Hollywood and become actors! We were war smart, but we were naïve about life and the "big picture."

I had told myself on this second tour I wouldn't let anything touch me or hurt me, yet I was devastated at Rick's death. I'd had enough of this fucking war and all the suffering.

I went back to the foxhole we shared and got Rick's poncho. I returned and covered him with it. Others covered the other two men.

When the medical "dust-off" chopper arrived, the medic onboard offered to place Rick and the others in body bags, but I refused. They were my men who died on my watch, and I had to do it.

I put Rick in his body bag last. I looked at Rick's face and recalled his laughter and innocence. I remembered how he always wore his Combat Infantry Badge, as I had always worn my Combat Medical Badge. I removed his badge and put it in my pocket. I intended to send it to his family. I touched his cold cheek and zipped up the body bag.

I retrieved their rucksacks and placed the three men on the chopper. The chopper left.

I walked back to my foxhole in a daze. I put my head in my hands. Why didn't I cry? Why weren't tears streaming down my face? Because the pain was more profound than mere tears and crying.

I felt a hand on my shoulder. It was Manly. He said nothing but sat with me. Later, Gavin came and sat next to me. I remembered how he had been moved when we talked about seeing Sidney Poitier in *Blackboard Jungle*, and I said I wished I was Black. When he had asked me why I said, "I think Black people feel more deeply than White people."

"Let's talk movies," he said.

As the sun went down, Garvin asked if we could share the same foxhole.

"You don't want me to be alone," I said.

"Absolutely," he replied.

I didn't sleep that night.

I woke from a terrifying nightmare to furious pounding on my door and someone shouting my name. I couldn't make myself move. The muffled shouting seemed far away and unimportant. I was sweating from the nightmare, but I drifted back into unconsciousness.

The pounding started again, louder. The door burst open and Major Scott was shaking me.

"Wake up, Mamie! Are you okay? C'mon, wake up!"

When I opened my eyes, I couldn't focus. Scott's face was a blur. His mouth was moving, I couldn't make out the words.

"Mamie, you've got to get up. I have to leave soon."

I was dizzy, but I managed to sit on the edge of the bed. "What's going on?" I mumbled. "I was dreaming that something terrible had happened, that someone I knew had been killed."

"I've been trying to find you for two days. I heard about what happened at the officers' club. You didn't answer your door here, so I thought you must be in the hospital. What have you been taking?"

I pointed at the brown bottle and fell back across the bed. He picked up the bottle and read the label.

"You've been taking opium, for chrissakes. How much have you taken?"

I shook my head. "I don't know. The doctor said to take it so I could sleep."

"Keep taking this you'll be sleeping forever." He poured the opium down the sink. "C'mon, I'm going to get you in the shower."

He undressed me and carried me into the bathroom. He eased me into the bathtub and turned on the shower. I screamed under the cold water. After a few minutes, he got me out, dried me off, gently slipped me back in bed, and tucked me under the covers.

"When's the last time you ate, Mamie?"

"I don't know. Day before yesterday?"

"You stay there. I'm going to get some food and drink for you."

"Okay," I whispered. I closed my eyes and went to sleep.

When I woke, Scott was standing over me with a tall glass of clear liquid.

"It's coconut water," he said. "Drink it. I bought a huge sack of them, and I want you to drink as much as you can. It'll hydrate you quicker than anything. And It'll raise your blood sugar too. I brought back some food. You need to eat and get your strength back."

I chugged down coconut water all afternoon. My blood sugar began coming around, and my dehydration began to ease. I ate as much as I could, and I started feeling a little better.

"Thanks for doing this, Jim," I said. "I appreciate it."

"I know you do, Mamie. Listen, I got my orders to rotate back to the States. And I'm leaving this evening. I'm not going to be here to help you. And you're in no shape to travel."

"What am I going to do?"

"I have a friend at the Field A Hospital. He'll try to get you admitted. They can give you the care you need so you can get back to the States. Rest while I pack your stuff. As soon as you feel a little stronger, we'll go."

A couple hours later, Scott stopped his Jeep in front of the Field A Hospital and took me inside. He introduced me to his friend, another young doctor. I explained my problems to him and he seemed genuinely concerned. He examined me briefly—blood pressure, temperature, listened to my heart.

"Mamie, your vitals are fine, but if you are consistently passing blood, that needs to be evaluated. If it was up to me, I'd admit you, but our CO, General Lombard, doesn't like admitting civilians."

I started searching though my satchel. For a terrifying moment, I thought I had lost my letter, but then I saw the envelope imprinted with the words "White House" and I breathed a sigh of relief.

"Doctor, please show this to General Lombard. It's a letter from President Nixon about my tour over here. He's fully aware of it and endorses it. And he asks that every possible assistance be extended to me if I need it. And if ever I needed assistance, it's now."

"Yes ma'am," he said, taking the letter.

Major Scott embraced me. "I've got to go, Mamie. You'll be in good hands here, you can be sure."

"Jim, I don't know how to thank you. But what if they don't admit me?"

"I'll wait. But I'm sure it'll be fine."

The young doctor came in a few moments later and handed my letter back. "General Lombard says he'll make an exception and admit you, Mamie."

I began to cry. "I'm so grateful, doctor. I want to get home so badly."

"We're going to get you well first. A nurse will be in shortly to prep you for admission."

The doctor left, and Scott gave me a kiss. "I told you it would be all right. Take care of yourself, Mamie. I'll see you stateside. Love you." He went out and closed the door.

***

My hospital room was in a surprisingly pleasant section reserved for high-ranking officers and VIPs. The only other patient in the section was the young daughter of the base commanding general, who I'll call General McKinley. She had been badly injured in a fall. Her mother was staying in the room with her.

I felt safer in the hospital, but I was still a long way from home with no clear path to get there. They sedated me with Valium to ease the nightmares. I was sensitive to loud noises—especially helicopters, which were constant. I cried at the slightest provocation, thinking of my son or my mother. I became nearly hysterical at the memory of my show at the officers' club.

The doctors subjected me to a battery of tests to locate the cause of my passing blood in my stool and urine. I was given a steady IV drip of antibiotics and fluids.

"The blood you're passing might be caused by dehydration and anxiety," Dr. Kent told me. "Your kidney function is down a little, but the IV drip should get that under control. I'm giving you antibiotics on the chance you might have amoebic dysentery."

"How on Earth could I have caught that?"

"It's common. Sanitation is not the greatest out where you've been traveling. Contaminated food or water is the usual cause. Those little single-celled bugs are all over in that environment. Antibiotics get rid of them pretty quickly if you are treated early. And you might not even have 'em. We'll know soon. We've got tests scheduled."

The thought of single-celled bugs swimming around in my gut made me feel sicker. "Let me know, okay?"

"Mamie, you'll be the first to know."

"Doctor, I know I sound like a broken record, but when can I go home?"

He looked away for a moment. "I can't say, Mamie. For sure you're not strong enough to fly commercial. And because you're a civilian, giving you a seat on a long-haul medevac flight puts the hospital in a difficult position. Those flights are always full. If you take a spot on one, a wounded soldier will have to wait."

"I understand, doctor."

"The top brass is trying to figure it out, believe me."

I was despondent after that conversation, even when my amoebic dysentery report came back negative. I had been asking myself why it was so difficult to transport one ninety-pound woman out of a place where she so clearly did not belong. Now I knew. For me to leave, some wounded soldier would have to stay behind.

Holy shit, what a dilemma, I thought.

I had wrangled a call back home to my mother when I was first admitted.

Now I managed to wrangle another.

"Mother," I said loudly down the overseas connection, "they can't seem to figure out how to get me out of here. If you haven't heard from me in ten days, contact the White House."

"Jo, I don't know how to—"

"Tell the White House operator you're my mother. Ask to get a message to the president that I'm ill in a Field A Hospital in Saigon and having a hard time getting home."

I struck up a friendship with General McKinley's wife, Beth, who was watching over her daughter's recovery in the room next to mine. She was very kind, and we each enjoyed having someone to talk to who was not a doctor. We traded stories about our children, and she was interested to hear behind-the-scenes Hollywood gossip. When I told her my predicament about finding a way to get home, she listened attentively.

"How long have you been in country, Mamie?"

"Four months."

And you've been hospitalized for how long?"

"Ten days."

She nodded and set her jaw. "Get your bags packed, Mamie."

"What do you mean?"

"I mean, I think I can help solve your problem."

The next morning the hospital's head physician came to my room.

"Mamie do you prefer Texas or Hawaii?"

"Easy one. Hawaii. Why?"

"We've found a way to get you back to the States. And Hawaii it is. You leave at oh-six hundred tomorrow."

"Thank you, doctor, thank you."

"Don't mention it, Mamie. You've got a friend in high places."

As soon as he left, I ran next door to Beth's room. She held up her hand when I walked in.

"No thanks necessary, Mamie. What good is influence if you don't use it?"

"There must be some way I can thank you, Beth."

"My daughter's on the mend, but you can pay me back in prayers for her.

We'll be leaving soon too. You get home to that boy of yours."

"Thank you. It's appreciated more than you can know."

I rushed back to my room and packed up my things. The telephone in my room rang. It had never rung before, in fact, I thought it was disconnected. I answered it.

"Mamie," the voice on the other end said, "this is John Huddleston. We met in Dak Tho."

"I remember you, John. You and your friend Rick were the movie buffs."

"That was…us." There was a long pause. "Rick was killed by a sniper about ten days ago."

"Oh, my God, John! I'm so sorry, *so sorry.*"

John's voice cracked. "Yes. Thank you. I know we didn't have much time to connect, but the little conversation we had with you meant so much…to Rick especially. He constantly talked about seeing you. He'd tell everybody. 'We saw Mamie Van Doren. She winked and smiled at me.' You were the last American woman he ever saw. You might have been in his very last thoughts."

"My God," I whispered. "I'm so sorry." After thought: "How'd you find me, John?"

He chuckled. "Grunts have a jungle telegraph. I heard what happened to you at the O club. A disgrace. If a few of us had been there, we'd have beaten the shit out of that no-good son of a bitch, officer or not. I heard you were sick and canceled some shows afterward. I've got a friend that's an orderly at the Field A Hospital. He let me know you were there."

"I'm leaving in the morning on a medevac for Tachikawa, then on to Tripler in Hawaii."

"Good! You'll get good care there. And you'll be safe from this…this monstrosity. I'm going back in ninety-nine days. My hitch is over, and I'm getting out. Rick had ninety days left the day he died. I'm going to visit his parents in Idaho—he was a farm boy." John stopped a moment to get his voice under control. "I'm going to give them his Combat Infantry Medal. And I'm going to tell them how he died and how brave he was."

Tears were streaming down my cheeks. "That's very kind of you, John."

"Rick and I were close. We went through a lot of bad shit together. I'd better go, Mamie."

"Wait, John. Contact me when you get settled back home. Got a pencil? Copy my number." I gave it to him and he read it back. "Get in touch, okay?"

"Okay, Mamie. Thanks for listening to me."

"Thank you for telling me about Rick. Stay safe. Bye."

The next morning, they put me on a stretcher and loaded me into the belly of a huge transport plane. My stretcher was snapped into metal racks along with scores of wounded. There were moans of pain and despair from them as we waited for the orderlies to load everyone. Nurses moved among the racks giving sedative injections. The moaning quieted. When my turn came, the nurse smiled at me.

"You'll have a good snooze all the way to Japan."

"Thank you," I said. "I can use it."

The needle went in, and I closed my eyes.

I woke as they wheeled me into my room at the Tachikawa hospital. The doctor in charge advised me that it would be a week before there was space for me on a medevac bound for Hawaii. I got permission to phone my mother and let her know.

"I'm out of Vietnam!" I shrieked as soon as she came on the line. "Wonderful, Jo! Perry, your mother's out of Vietnam and on her way home!"

Mom was sobbing, and I could hear Perry cheering in the background.

"I don't know exactly when I'll leave here. They say sometime in the next week. Get plane tickets for yourself and Perry and leave as soon as you can. Book a room at the Moana. Call Tripler Hospital and tell them who you are and where you're staying. They'll notify you when I arrive."

"Jo, we're all so happy!"

"Me too, Mother."

Five days later, I was loaded onto another medevac plane and strapped into place. My sedative shot was given by a lovely Japanese nurse. "You'll sleep all the way through," she reassured me. And she added with a sweet smile, "Sayonara, Mamie."

I didn't even wake up when the plane touched down in Hawaii. I was groggy as they transferred our stretchers from the plane to an army bus. They took us off the bus when we arrived at the hospital.

It was like a dream as they wheeled me into the hospital. I could smell Hawaii—flowers and warm breezes—and someone was calling, "Mom! Mom!" And, "Jo! We're here with you." I opened my eyes and my mother was leaning over me. Perry was next to her tugging my arm.

Everyone was crying, even the hardshell orderlies who were pushing my stretcher. They stopped for a moment to give us a chance to embrace. Bystanders looked on and smiled.

I thought my Vietnam was over. I felt like I could breathe for the first time in months. Engulfed in love, showered by tears of joy, it was almost as if the past four months had never happened. Almost.

Coda

Zen Master Thich Nhat Hanh was once asked what kind of bad karma could have caused the Vietnam War to happen to the Vietnamese people. He replied, "Did the Vietnamese War only happen to the Vietnamese? Isn't it still here in this room with us? The karma of Vietnam is the karma of the world." This seems so true. The United States I returned to in 1972 was forever warped by Vietnam. As the war's utter futility became increasingly obvious, Americans in droves turned against it. The sight of young men returning home with catastrophic wounds or in flag-draped aluminum caskets fueled the opposition. Every nightly newscast bore witness to the carnage in body counts and numbers wounded. And for what reason? Policy boiled down to fighting communism to make the world safe for democracy. With 1950s McCarthyism still fresh in their minds, politicians swore to stop the spread of communism in Asia. Privately they whispered that *they* wouldn't be responsible for losing a war to the reds. But really, what was our skin in the game for a small Asian country halfway around the world?

The unscrupulous and misguided soon jumped on the opposition bandwagon and shifted the blame for the war to the soldiers themselves. Many became famous for their opposition, but none more so than Jane Fonda. "Hanoi Jane" as she became known was infamous for labeling our soldiers as war criminals and by suggesting they should be executed for their crimes. She used her celebrity to gain access to TV talk shows and magazine interviews. Her antics sparked outrage and disgust, particularly her widely publicized trip to Hanoi where she posed on an anti-aircraft gun. Later in the war, she made radio broadcasts from North Vietnam praising the North Vietnamese and the Viet Cong.

Since Vietnam, she has done her best to rewrite history and redeem her traitorous behavior, but almost without exception, the grunts who fought in the jungles and rice paddies, or in villages barely on the map, have a special, finely tuned loathing for Jane. They refuse to forgive and forget her betrayals and smug pronouncements at the expense of soldiers whose only sin was trying to survive a nightmare from which they could not wake.

John Huddleston, who has contributed so much to this chapter, was a decorated combat medic, one of the grunts who made the war go 'round. As a medic, John witnessed the worst that war had to offer. When he came home, he witnessed the worst his fellow citizens had to offer. He was spat upon, shunned, and scorned as the reward for his service. John decided to permanently leave the country he fought and nearly died for, but first he had one last mission.

***

John Huddleston

> I went to Idaho and met Rick's mother, father, and sister. I sat in their living room. His father was very stoic. His sister looked at me with intense narrowed eyes. His mother was very distressed and said she appreciated me coming all the way to see them.
>
> I reached into my pocket and pulled out Rick's Combat Infantry Badge. His dad told me the army had given them all his medals. I told them that this one was the Combat Infantry Badge that Rick had actually worn. His mother grasped it in her hand and cried. Like Rick's dad, I was stoic too.
>
> I shared with them how in the evenings we'd sit at a firebase and talk about our lives. He'd tell me how much he

loved Idaho and how he would return. If I ever needed a home, he would say, I could stay on the family farm with him.

I told them about a day in Pleiku when Rick and I ate Vietnamese food and he got very drunk on Vietnamese 333 beer. I helped him back to basecamp, and he kept me awake laughing and talking nonsense all night. It was a special day we shared.

I told them about Mamie Van Doren and how happy you made us feel in those moments. I mentioned how Rick and I were outsiders that day. We were army, surrounded by marines, but the marines respected us.

I said that listening to your voice, hearing your accent, and looking at your glistening skin took both of us home. You took Rick back to Idaho and me back to the nightclubs of North Beach in San Francisco.

His father said something like, "So Mamie Van Doren was part of a big tour like the *Bob Hope Show*?" I told him you had come with your own musicians, that there were not a bunch of TV or movie cameras. I told them that the event was intimate and rewarding and dangerous. I told them how Rick had laughed, and that we both had tears in our eyes because you had brought "home" to us.

I mentioned how my view of you had changed. That you were so much more than a sexy movie star, and Rick and I knew you had taken your life into your hands by coming there.

They wanted to know how Rick had died.

I stood up, walked to the living room window, and stared at the flat Idaho landscape.

There was silence. I cleared my throat.

"He went to fill canteens with water. When the mortar attack hit, snipers in the bush outside the camp perimeter started firing. Rick was one of three men hit. He had felt no pain. His face was peaceful. I sat next to him and held his hand. I loaded him into the helicopter. I have never felt the same about anything since that day."

Rick's mother sobbed. His father asked if his son was brave. I told him he definitely was. "He saved my life more than once."

I felt exhausted and empty. I told them I had to go, and they said I could spend the night with them.

"Thank you, but no," I said. They asked where I was going and I said, "Away from America."

They asked about my family. I told them I was alone. As I walked toward their front door, his mother cried and gave me a big hug. She said, "John, I'll never get over this!"

"Neither will I," I said.

I walked to the car and opened the door. Rick's father called out to me to wait. His mother and father walked to me and took turns hugging me and crying.

"John, Rick told us all about you in letters. We want you to know that if you ever need a home...you can always stay with us."

Someone once said, "Even a grain of sand thrown into the ocean changes the ocean forever."

As I drove back to Boise to catch a plane to San Francisco, I thought about how Rick's life had changed me. I smiled remembering his boyish crush on Mamie Van Doren.

Where is Mamie now? Does she have any idea of the lasting impact her tour of Vietnam had? It revolves around a woman who loved her country and cared about those who served.

She entered the hell of war to visit those that felt forgotten and scorned, even by some members of their families.

I thought, *Where do women like this come from? What touches their hearts in this way, that they seek those who have been ostracized and let them know they are important?*

They announced boarding for my flight. My last task in America was over. I would leave it forever.

Mamie Van Doren was so much more than a grain of sand in the ocean.

***

Today John calls Sydney, Australia, home. Of course, he lost my phone number. It was disconnected long ago anyway. John and I crossed paths many years later on Facebook. His friendship, help, and encouragement with this chapter have been invaluable. Writing this chapter has been difficult for me. Certainly dredging up memories of the war for his contributions was difficult for him. I'll let John's words conclude it.

***

John Huddleston

Many years in the future, someone will pick up a copy of *You Thought I Was Dead* in a used bookstore and thumb through it. They'll stop on the Vietnam chapter and read about Rick and me seeing you. In that moment, the years will dissolve and reveal you, Rick, and me forever enjoying a moment under the Southeast Asian sun.

***

A Final Postscript

It was surreal for a little farm girl from Rowena, South Dakota, to be seated at a table in the White House State Dining Room, across from Robert Evans, listening to Happy Rockefeller tell a dirty joke and realizing that Henry Kissinger, Secretary of State and National Security Advisor to President Nixon, was feeling me up under the table. But it was real.

I was only a few months back from my Vietnam ordeal. I still jumped when I heard a car backfire. My nights were still haunted by the sounds of helicopters and the smell of cordite, gun oil, and death.

I brushed away Henry's hand and laughed at Happy's punchline.

When I accepted the invitation from President Richard Nixon asking for my presence at a White House State Dinner for German Chancellor Willy Brandt, I told myself that I would get my shit back together, stop being frightened of my shadow, and make a dramatic appearance.

And I looked pretty damned good. When I arrived, I discovered that I was Henry Kissinger's date for the evening. I was not altogether unhappy. He had lately gained a reputation for dating glamorous actresses, as well as negotiating with the North Vietnamese to end the Vietnam War. Not a bad résumé for a fancy dinner party escort.

White House State Dinners pull out all the stops. Stewards keep bringing course after course, each complete with its own wine and tiny pallet-clearing dish of sherbet. And they keep pouring the champagne.

During dinner, Henry remarked that he had just returned that afternoon from the Paris peace talks.

"The peace accords were signed in January. We've finally ended this thing."

"You deserve congratulations," I told him, taking hold of his wandering hand and squeezing it.

After dinner, we listened to Chancellor Brandt and President Nixon speak, then adjourned to the East Room for a concert by The Carpenters. When the concert was over, everyone filed out and headed for the lobby to get to their cars.

Henry took me by the arm. "Mamie, would you like to see the Oval Office where the president works?"

"Sure!" By then, I was pretty much game for anything. The champagne had taken over, and I was feeling no pain.

We followed the hallway to the Oval. Henry nodded to the marine standing guard at the door. I sat on the edge of the president's desk, then spun around in his big swivel chair, while Henry and I both giggled like naughty children. The marine stoically took it all in, staring straight ahead.

I was still pretty tipsy. In fact, I was one glass this side of drunk. So was Henry.

"I think it's time I got back to my hotel, Henry."

"But you haven't told me what it was like for you on your Vietnam tour."

"That would take longer than we've got tonight," I said. "Besides, I have a limo waiting."

"Nonsense, let's go to my place and have a nightcap. I'll have one of my aides dismiss your limo. We can take my car, have a quick drink, and I'll drive you back to your hotel."

"Are you inviting me to see your collection of etchings, Mr. Secretary?"

He grinned. "No, my dear, but you can look at some Chinese art I still have to declare to the National Archives."

We rode to his Georgetown flat in the back seat of his car, his two aides in the front.

"So, you were in Vietnam for three months? You must have gone to many out-of-the-way places."

"Four months. I don't think I missed a firebase. Some were so remote, I don't think the army even knew they existed. There were times when

I was ducking bullets. I had to helo out of a base just ahead of being over run."

"You must have been frightened, Mamie."

"Scared shitless is more like it. But tell me, Henry, now that the peace agreement's been signed, why do I keep hearing about casualties? Is the war over or not? Because I can tell you, Henry, it doesn't take an international statesman to see that we're losing the war."

"Mamie, have you ever met a man smarter than you?"

The question stopped me for a moment. "Yes," I replied, "you."

"I doubt it," he said. "Mamie, keep this conversation in confidence, please." He shook his head gravely. "Stopping a war is like trying to stop a tsunami. It has a powerful momentum all its own that needs to run its course. Politicians can issue orders to generals, who issue orders to colonels, who issue orders to junior officers, who issue orders to petty officers, who tell the troops to stop shooting. If we're lucky, they stop."

"And if they don't?"

Henry shrugged. "Then people continue to die. The North Vietnamese are reluctant to give up the ground they've gained. So far, they have ignored the cease-fire we agreed upon. President Thieu's government in the south will ultimately collapse."

"And more grunts will die."

"Wars are easy to start but hard to end."

We arrived at Henry's apartment. The place was messy because he had just returned from a trip to Paris. He showed me his Chinese art and did his very best to convince me to go to bed with him. He pushed me onto the bed. I pushed him away.

We were more than a decade early for the Dead Kennedys punk band, but the fact is we were "Too Drunk to Fuck."

Finally, Henry delivered me back to my hotel, exhausted from grappling with him and a hangover already coming on. I got to my room and collapsed on the bed. In seconds, I fell into a deep sleep.

The telephone jolted me awake at 5:00 a.m. I fumbled it off its cradle and said, "Mmurruf."

"Mamie, it's Henry! Are you still sleeping?"

"I just got to sleep, Henry. Why are you calling me so early?"

"Get dressed, Mamie, and come have breakfast. I have five Russians who saw you last night, and they are all mad to meet you. Come join us. I'll send my car."

"No, Henry, no. You'll have to deal with the mad Russians alone. I'm going back to sleep."

"Mamie, please! It's the least you can do for Soviet-American relations."

I was getting really annoyed. I've always been a girl who needs her sleep, and I do not suffer gladly people who disturb it. Even a secretary of state.

"Why are you not hungover, Henry?"

He chuckled. "Years of practice."

"What the hell kind of champagne do they serve at the White House anyway? I feel like a mugging victim."

"Schramsberg," Henry said without hesitation. "It's a small vineyard in Calistoga, California. It's a sparkling Blanc de Blancs made by the champagne method used in France. The president and Chinese Premier Zhou Enlai toasted with it when the president made his trip to China. It packs a punch. It made Zhou's eyes cross."

"Powerful stuff," I muttered. "Sorry, Henry. I'm going back to sleep for a couple more hours before I catch a plane back to LA. Washington makes Hollywood look positively tame."

"The Russians will be desolate at not seeing you. And so will I."

"Maybe next time, Henry."

"I'll call you, Mamie."

I never saw or spoke to Henry Kissinger again. Henry Kissinger died in November 2023 at age one hundred. In spite of all the criticism leveled at him over the years, I have always felt that he was an honorable man who accomplished remarkable things and who, for better or worse, changed the course of history.

***

On June 15, 2015, the Hollywood American Legion Post 43 honored me at their annual Commander's Ball with a promotion to the rank of honorary colonel. The commendation was in recognition of the two tours I made in Vietnam to entertain the troops. As you read in the chapter above, it was a demanding and often arduous tour—a personal crusade, really—made virtually alone, accompanied only by a small group of musicians, at my own expense, to the most remote and perilous firebases in Vietnam. The things I experienced there are indelibly etched in my memories, as they are in the memories of the grunts who were my fans, companions, and protectors.

This honor was bestowed upon me by those who served in Vietnam. Their gratitude means everything to me. I cherish this award more than any other I have ever received.

Chapter Fourteen

The Man in the Moon—Buzz Aldrin

"Bravery comes along as a gradual accumulation of discipline."

"One truth I have discovered for sure: When you believe that all things are possible and you are willing to work hard to accomplish your goals, you can achieve the next 'impossible' dream. No dream is too high!"

"Remember, your mind is like a parachute: If it isn't open, it doesn't work. So keep an open mind!"

—BUZZ ALDRIN

"Good afternoon, Miss Van Doren," the voice on the other end of the phone said. "This is Rose Mary Woods, secretary to President Nixon."

"Hello, Rose Mary, it's good to hear from you again."

"And you too, Mamie." Rose Mary replied. "I'm calling with an invitation from the president. The Committee to Re-elect the President is putting on a gala evening fundraiser next weekend in Dallas, Texas. The president would love for you to attend. We'll send a limo for you to and from the airport on each end, courier a first-class ticket over to you, and we'll put you up in a luxury suite at the Fairmont in Dallas. Everything's on the house, first class all the way as usual, Mamie."

"That sounds like fun," I said.

"I'm sure it will be," she replied. "Chuck Connors, Chad Everett, and Buzz Aldrin have committed to go. You'll arrive in Dallas in the morning, and a limo will take you to the hotel. The event begins at 8:00 that evening, so you'll have the rest of the day to rest up. You can make your appearance for as long as you like, just mingle with the donors, and enjoy yourself."

I had met Chuck Connors (*The Rifleman* TV series) and Chad Everett (Dr. Joe Gannon on the *Medical Center* TV series) at parties and such over the years, but I had never met Buzz Aldrin, command pilot of Apollo Eleven. Along with Neil Armstrong, the mission commander, they were the first men to set foot on another celestial body. Since that historic mission in the summer of 1969, Armstrong and Aldrin had become two of the most famous men in America.

"Count me in, Rose Mary. I'd love to attend."

I was an Eisenhower Republican back then. I had worshipped Ike since his heroic generalship of the allied forces in the 1944 invasion of Normandy. It was the beginning of the end of WWII. His bold leadership began the liberation of France and Western Europe from the Nazis. Besides, when Universal changed my name, they gave me his wife's first name—Mamie. It seemed only fitting that I become a Republican.

Nixon had been a senator from California before being elected as Ike's vice president. After Ike's second term, Nixon ran for president against

John F. Kennedy and lost. By 1968, when Nixon ran against Hubert Humphrey and won, I had become active in the Republican Party and Nixon was aware of me. He had encouraged and even facilitated my two tours in Vietnam. Ultimately, his letter of support got me out of the war zone when I fell ill.

It's worth noting, however, that as I write this, today's GOP is unrecognizable from the party I knew in 1969. The kinky Republican fascination with controlling women's sexuality is appalling to me. Limiting contraception and abortion rights, and the party's overall misogynistic attitude drove me out. I figured out that the Republicans ain't no party—they're not even a coffee klatch—so I kicked them to the curb years ago.

I packed a slinky gown and a toothbrush and caught the flight to Dallas. I checked into the Fairmont and ordered lunch, washed my hair, put it up in curlers, and slathered some moisturizing cream on my face. I closed the blackout drapes, turned the air conditioning down to arctic against the blazing Dallas heat, and climbed into bed for an afternoon nap.

I had just snuggled comfortably under the covers when the telephone rang. A man's voice said, "Hi, Mamie, this is Buzz Aldrin."

Okay, you might call it wish fulfillment, or you might call it kismet, but somewhere in between was this phone call and cheerful baritone greeting.

"Buzz! How great to hear from you. Are you here at the hotel?"

"Yes, just got here. In fact, I think I'm just one floor above you. Why don't I come down and see you?"

"No, you don't want to see me now, Buzz. I'm covered in beauty cream that's not very beautiful, and with a dozen curlers in my hair, I look like a Martian."

"You sure I couldn't drop in for just a minute?"

"I'm sure, Buzz. But I'm looking forward to meeting you tonight. We'll talk then."

"Okay, Mamie, see you tonight."

I hung up the phone and settled myself back under the covers, smiling at the memory of July 20, 1969. On that night, like hundreds of millions of people in America and around the world, my parents, Perry, and I gathered around the television to watch one of the great historic milestones of the twentieth century: the landing of Apollo 11 on the surface of the Moon. Neil Armstrong cautiously climbed down the ladder of the lunar lander, Eagle, followed a short time later by Buzz Aldrin. The first two men to set foot on the moon kicked up moondust and planted the American flag.

And, holy shit, one of them just called and wanted to meet me. You've come a long way since Rowena, kiddo.

The fundraiser gala was in the Fairmont's enormous ballroom. It was wall-to-wall with tables, overflowing with would-be campaign donors. There was a brightly lit dais on the stage where the celebrities and GOP dignitaries were to sit.

The moment I stepped into the ballroom, I was blinded by flashbulb bursts from newspaper photographers and the glare of TV camera lights. I could make out the dais on stage, but I kept bumping into people and chairs trying to get there. Finally, someone from the fundraiser staff took my arm and guided me to my seat on the dais.

The dais was crowded with politicians and hangers-on wanting to press the flesh. I caught glimpses of Chad Everett and Chuck Connors shaking hands like crazy with prospective donors. Buzz was deep in conversation at another table, no doubt with someone wanting to know what it was like on the Moon. I caught Buzz's eye, and he waved back, but we didn't have a chance to talk. I was quickly surrounded by paunchy men introducing their beehive-haired wives and swearing that, "Me and Beth here are yer biggest fans, Mamie."

We raised a couple of million seventies-era dollars that night. I excused myself after an hour or so. When I looked in Buzz's direction, he was gone. I headed for my room and a hot shower. I packed the few things I had brought, left an early wakeup call to catch the CREEP limo to the airport, and went to bed.

The next morning, I was at the airport departure gate reading a magazine when a voice said, "Hey, lady, can you give me a lift?"

I looked up and Buzz Aldrin was grinning down at me. "Buzz!"

"Hi, Mamie! Going to LA?" "Yes, you too?"

"Sure am. Do you mind if we sit together?" "Not at all, if the stewardesses will let us."

"Oh, don't worry, they will."

Other travelers at the departure gate quickly recognized Buzz and gathered around to shake his hand. As the crowd grew, it began to clog the departure area, and the gate crew became increasingly nervous. Finally, the flight purser whispered something in Buzz's ear. He nodded and held out his hand to me.

"C'mon, Mamie. They want me to board so they can get rid of this crowd."

Buzz took my hand, and we followed the flight purser down the jet way into the aircraft's first-class section. She examined our boarding passes. Our seats were across the aisle from each other.

"We'd like to sit next to each other," Buzz said.

"Go ahead," the flight purser said. "The flight's not full."

I settled into the window seat, while Buzz sat on the aisle. The flight attendant brought champagne. We made small talk.

"Some shindig last night, huh?" Buzz said.

"The place was packed. How long did you stay?"

"I hung on until I saw people starting to leave. Then I bailed out. You?"

"I stayed an hour or so."

Buzz nodded. "Right. I looked for you when I left, but you were surrounded by fans."

"Does everyone ask you what it was like on the Moon?"

"Not if you don't," Buzz quipped. We both laughed. "But seriously, Mamie, it's difficult to describe. The Moon's gravity is one-sixth of Earth's, so it's easy to get this childish giddiness over being able to jump higher and run faster—not that easy in one of our spacesuits. And yet we're supposed to be scientists—no nonsense, intent on the mission. And it's hard to take it all in while you're there. We were loaded down with experiments and observations and gathering Moon rock samples. There just wasn't time to absorb it and reflect. But I can say that though I was the second man to walk on the Moon, I have the distinction of being the first man to *pee* on the Moon."

Somewhere out over Lubbock, Buzz took his briefcase from the overhead compartment. He removed a large manuscript and began thumbing through it. When I asked about it, he said, "It's the galley proofs of my book. It's just about to be published. Would you like to read it?"

"Yes, I'd love to."

He handed the sheaf of pages covered in blue pencil marks to me, and I dove in. Occasionally, I looked up and asked a question. Buzz would answer, and I'd go back to reading. By the time we were landing in Los Angeles, I knew a lot about Buzz Aldrin.

"It's a wonderful book, Buzz," I said, handing the manuscript back to him. "I know it'll be a bestseller."

He grinned. "I hope so."

We made our way through the airport to the baggage claim area. I was traveling light and only had one small suitcase, but Buzz carried it to the curb where my mother was waiting. I introduced Buzz to my mom. She was driving my Bentley Mulliner, a giant 1962-vintage beast the color of vanilla ice cream.

"I'd like to see you sometime, Mamie," he said, putting the suitcase in the boot of the Bentley. "You said you live in Newport Beach, right?"

"I have an apartment at the Balboa Bay Club. It's lovely down there. Give me a call."

He reached into his briefcase and jotted my number on the front page of his book galleys. I got behind the wheel, and Mom and I drove away, leaving Buzz waving at the curb.

A few days later, Buzz called and asked me to dinner.

"I got a room at the Bay Club where you are. Think of someplace really nice. You'll have to drive."

I made reservations for us at an upscale little place called Ambrosia, tucked away in a corner of Newport Beach's Cannery Village. By candlelight, we had a pair of martinis and a Caesar salad, then moved on to prime rib and a bottle of good Pinot Noir. It was romantic. By the time we had shared a Crêpes Suzette, I was feeling overfed but warm, cuddly, and amorous.

Back at the Bay Club, we sat in the Bentley and necked like teenagers for a while. When things began to get serious, I suggested we adjourn to my apartment, since it might be too shocking if the staid Balboa Bay Club citizens caught the Second Man on the Moon shagging the Girl Who Invented Rock and Roll in the front seat of a Bentley.

Buzz and I captured a little bit of magic that night. Maybe it was the wine and the Crêpes Suzettes; maybe it was the softness of the spring night and the fullness of the westering Moon. Or it may have simply been a man and woman finely tuned to each other's passion, intent on mutual fulfillment. Say it was this: one of those rare moments when the universe conspires with your own heart to bestow the unforgettable.

Afterward, Buzz and I watched the Moon set from the balcony of my apartment. The lights of Newport Harbor shimmered with the fading moonlight as we held each other. I looked at the Moon and then to him.

"Tonight, you made me a space traveler too, Buzz. You sent me to the Moon and back. Wonderful."

"It takes two to be wonderful, Mamie."

We kissed again and said goodnight. Buzz stopped and turned back.

"Mamie, I'd like to give you my jacket." Buzz had arrived that night wearing a white silk bomber jacket, embroidered with NASA logos and medallions commemorating the Apollo 11 mission and moon walk. It was a handsome jacket.

"I couldn't do that, Buzz. I don't want you to feel that you have to give me something, but thank you. It's a gorgeous jacket."

Now, why on Earth (or the Moon) did I do that? I would love to have that jacket today.

Buzz and I dated a couple more times over the next couple of months. A part of me that I barely gave voice to felt that this could develop into something serious. I was rebounding from a romantic crash-and-burn with another fighter pilot. My nesting instincts were kicking in. Occasionally, I was finding it hard to get through the nights when the visions of what I'd seen and been through in Vietnam flooded into my mind. But I had been independent and unattached for a long time, and I was not quite ready to give it up. I didn't make any of this known to Buzz.

When an offer came along to do a long run of *Gentlemen Prefer Blondes* in New York, I took it. It was a lot of money, and, after all, I'm an actress.

That's what we do. We did good business, and I was held over a couple of times.

When I got back to LA eight months later, Buzz was dating Lois, who would become his third wife. I often ran into the two of them at the Playboy Mansion and parties around Hollywood, and we were always the best of friends. Buzz and Lois divorced in 2012. Lois died in 2018. in 2023, Buzz married his fourth wife, Anca Faur, who died in 2025.

Coda

Buzz has been a lightning rod for conspiracy theorists and moon-landing deniers. He was harassed by a conspiracy dingbat named Bart Sibrel, who lured him to a fake interview at the Luxe Hotel in Beverly Hills. Sibrel shoved a bible in Buzz's face and told him to swear on it that he had landed on the moon. When Buzz refused, Sibrel called him a fraud and liar. Buzz settled the matter by punching Sibrel in the face. When Sibrel tried to sue, the judge dismissed the case saying that Sibrel provoked the attack.

Then Buzz made some remarks in public appearances that went viral. The conspiracy mongers claimed that Buzz had admitted that he never set foot on the moon. In fact, Buzz's words were shown to have been taken out of context and misquoted.

Though the romantic relationship between Buzz and me was destined to be short-lived, we've remained friends for more than fifty years. I've always been proud of my fellow Swede, Buzz Aldrin, who, in the great tradition of the Vikings, dared to explore the unknown, then return to talk about it, and defend his adventure with his fists.

Chapter Fifteen

Embracing the Rainbow

Shortly after midnight on July 23, 1983, the Roxy Theatre on Sunset Boulevard was still filling up. As the capacity crowd settled into their seats, you could feel their nervous anticipation, the thrill that something vaguely illicit yet important was about to happen.

History was being made. The first shot in the battle against HIV/AIDS in Los Angeles was about to be fired. The curtain was about to go up on a benefit performance of Tom Eyen's *Women Behind Bars,* directed by Ron Link. The A-list celebrities who had been invited to attend didn't show. Notable by their absence were household name gay icons from the movie and music industries. They were afraid.

On the sidewalk outside the theater, reporters from local independent TV stations, Channels 11 and 5, CNN, and Entertainment Tonight were interviewing attendees as they entered the theater. No network affiliates would cover the event. They too were afraid.

This benefit performance had been orchestrated by Alan Eichler, New York theater producer and Los Angeles public relations man, Eichler had been working with AIDS Project Los Angeles (APLA) to promote public awareness of HIV/AIDS and to raise money to care for indigent AIDS victims.

Public perception of HIV/AIDS was critical at the time. The Reagan administration had initially ignored the disease and the alarming rise in cases in America. Mainstream media was largely dismissive of the disease's impact on the "straight" population, labeling AIDS as a so-called "gay disease."

Almost no information was available to the public about AIDS. No one knew how it was transmitted—a cough or sneeze might be deadly, a mere kiss could be suicidal, even a handshake was believed to be risky. The first signs of the illness were often flu-like symptoms, followed by grotesque opportunistic infections, such as Kaposi sarcoma, where sores and purple patches appear on the skin; and pneumocystis jirovecii, a rare pneumonia strain that was unresponsive to treatment. Then, there was rapid weight loss, resulting in wasting and weakness, opening the patient to further infections. The medical community was desperately casting about for effective treatments, but in those early days of uncertainty, infection with HIV/AIDS was a death sentence.

When Alan Eichler approached me about attending the *Women Behind Bars* benefit, I discussed the risks with my husband, Thomas, who would be attending with me. In spite of the uncertainty, we agreed that someone needed to step up and champion the cause. If not me, who? If not now, when? If I was afflicted with this mysterious ailment, what would I want? Would I not want someone to stand beside me and help? Regardless of the unknown dangers of HIV/AIDS we all might be facing, the audience at the Roxy that night had weighed the human costs of the HIV/AIDS crisis and concluded that standing on the sidelines in the face of suffering was, well, bullshit. When someone says "Help!" you extend a hand, and you bear witness.

The celebrities in attendance that night—all women—came onstage after the curtain call: Sheree North, Marie Windsor, Adele Jergens, Terry Moore, Virginia O'Brien, Betty Garrett, Vivian Blaine, Patti Page, and me. We received an enormous ovation. Indeed, it felt like the beginning of something important.

I really had no idea of my popularity with the gay community when I got involved. But at Alan's urging, I agreed to appear at a gay nightclub for another HIV/AIDS benefit.

It was the eighties and disco was king. Alan urged me to record a disco single written for me by a talented songwriter, Rob Simpson. Befitting of the times, it was titled, "State of Turmoil." Here's how Alan described my first outing:

> Mamie had never been in a gay bar, but it was time to perform "State of Turmoil" in the clubs, and the first one I booked was the heaviest leather-oriented disco called Probe, where guys danced all night till daylight, most likely on some form of drug. Mamie now represented APLA, and all of her appearances were fundraisers for them. Tony Carroll, a Black Mr. Universe who had carried Eartha Kitt on stage in my Broadway show *Timbuktu!* was now living in Los Angeles, and I got him to carry Mamie through the screaming throng of hot, bare-chested men at two in the morning! She performed "State of Turmoil" accompanied by a young break dancer and the crowd went wild.
>
> She followed with performances at the Revolver, Gazzarri's and the Palomino. *The Los Angeles Times* ran a front-page story by Robert Hilburn with the headline, "The Return of Bimbo Royalty." Mamie also judged a

body builder contest at the Hollywood Palladium called "Super-Men 85."

"State of Turmoil" went to the top of the disco club playlists. Rob Simpson was inspired to write more songs for me: "Young Dudes," "Queen of Pleasure," and "Act of Submission" also enjoyed popularity in the clubs. Shortly after my appearance at Probe I received a letter from Max Drew, then the president of APLA, informing me that I had raised the first $30,000 AIDS Project had received.

In 1984, I rode in a convertible in the Gay Pride parade. The parade route through West Hollywood was lined three-deep with cheering spectators.

Word got around that Rock Hudson was ill. When photos of him began surfacing, it was obvious that he had AIDS. Thin and gaunt, his voice weak and reedy, Rock was a shadow of the tall, handsome movie star I had dated and been friends with at Universal Studios. Though it was common knowledge in the movie business that Rock was gay, it was not widely known to the public. Rock remained steadfast in his public denials about being gay.

I wrote in *Playing the Field* about my first studio-arranged date with Rock at the Golden Globe Awards. I had been assured by friends at Universal that Rock was gay and that I would have no worries about unwanted advances from him. Truth be told, Rock was devastatingly handsome and I was not unhappy to receive his advances when I invited him into my parents' kitchen for coffee after our date. We got amorous while the coffee perked and tussled around on the kitchen floor trying to have sex. Unfortunately, he prematurely ejaculated on the crinolines of my studio-provided skirt. (At that stage of my career, the studio thought I should look like a teenage prom queen. Come to think of it, there are probably a lot of teen prom queens with stray semen on their underskirts.)

In 1985, Rock at last disclosed that he had been diagnosed with AIDS. It set off a panic in the movie industry. At the time, it was incorrectly believed that the AIDS virus could be transmitted by saliva and tears. Rock's guest appearance on *Dynasty* in which he kissed Linda Evans caused an uproar. Linda never contracted the disease.

Rock's death emboldened Elizabeth Taylor to become a very public advocate in the fight against HIV/AIDS. She organized a large fundraiser in her name. I was glad to see someone of her stature also lending her name to the cause. It would certainly increase public awareness of AIDS and boost donations, which, in turn, would make the suffering of the victims more bearable.

As the date for the fundraiser approached, I prepared to attend. My first reaction to almost any occasion is to buy a new dress, so I bought a new frock and some Christian Dior shoes. Then, a few days before the event, I got a call informing me that I was *not* invited, nor was Vivian Blaine, nor were any of the early celebs who had lent their names to the cause. I was told that Elizabeth wanted none of the original group to show up. Those who had taken all the risks to lay the foundations of change to public perception of AIDS were callously shunted aside. Elizabeth would pretend that she alone had discovered the scourge of AIDS and was ordained to be its savior.

I felt a twinge of hurt at being snubbed, but when you've been in Hollywood as long as I have, you get used to it. You can always count on someone claiming credit for something they didn't do. To this day, Elizabeth's foundation claims that she was the first actress to raise money to fight AIDS.

I created a cabaret act featuring many of Rob Simpson's songs and continued making appearances to raise money and awareness of AIDS. Alan Eichler booked me in the Trocadero Transfer, a heavy leather club in San Francisco, and in the Limelight in New York City.

Friends kept on dying—playwright Tom Eyen, who not only wrote *Women Behind Bars* but *Dreamgirls*, *The Dirtiest Show in Town*, and many others passed; Larry Evans, a video producer and deejay, succumbed; and APLA president, Max Drew, contracted the virus and died. A main feature of life became the growing stream of AIDS-related casualties.

With Max Drew's death, APLA drifted away. Newer, younger movie and television stars got onboard the AIDS crusade, and the trailblazers in the movement were largely forgotten.

In 1987, the organizers of the Gay Pride parade named me grand marshal of that summer's Gay Pride parade in West Hollywood. That parade showed me beyond a doubt how much love and support I was given from the gay community.

It took a long time for HIV/AIDS to be understood. Methods of transmission eventually became known. Sexual contact, blood, and sharing needles were ultimately recognized as the prime mediums of infection. The early days of violent discrimination against AIDS victims faded, but the stigma still remains, even though drugs that are capable of suppressing the AIDS virus are widely available by prescription and are advertised widely on network television.

It is not my intention to cast shade on the Elizabeth Taylor AIDS Foundation. The work they did and the funds they raised were vital to the fight against AIDS, and they deserve credit for it. However, I do think it's important to get the history straight. Many people in the early shoestring days of the cause supported me in my appearances. I traveled and stayed in hotels at my own expense, but many, many volunteers lent a hand to make sure the event went off as scheduled. They showed me love and never got the credit they deserved. And sadly, many died unsung before anyone could figure out a way to save them.

Coda

The response to the HIV/AIDS epidemic became normalized in the public consciousness. The disease was just as deadly, but the perception was that if you followed the rules and took adequate precautions, you could avoid the disease. Over time, much of the mythology surrounding infection and transmission was dispelled. With Elizabeth's organization doing good work and saving lives, I and my fellow pioneers from the Women Behind Bars era took comfort in the realization that we started the ball rolling on something important.

That changed in September of 2025. AIDS Project LA honored me with their APPL Award for my volunteer work in the early days of the epidemic. It's an award I'll cherish always.

Epilogue

Under the Dome

If you are still reading this, I am grateful. You have stuck with me on this journey, and we are now almost at our destination. You've laughed and cried in all the right places, and you've appreciated Stephen B. Whatley's brilliant cartoons. Mind you, there was trickery. You were unaware that you were becoming part of the story. Whether it's a play, a painting, or a book, if there's no audience, no viewer, or no reader, there's no show, no uplift, no story. You flawlessly brought your own magic to the experience, playing all the parts, painting in all the scenes, filling in your own details. My deepest thanks—you've been one helluva collaborator.

There are still some loose ends to tie up. Like, I was the first sex kitten in cyberspace when I launched my website, mamievandoren.com, in 1998. It was early in the internet revolution and many people said, "Why would you waste your time on the internet?" Or, more often they actually said, "What's the internet?" Back then nobody really knew.

For me, the internet was a publishing revolution, a way to instantly communicate with my fans in a totally unfiltered way, without editors or producers second-guessing me. I wrote about pop culture, politics, sex, sports, my experiences in Vietnam, movies—did I mention sex? Anything that caught my fancy was fair game.

When I first launched the site, I posted many pictures. I've probably been photographed more than any other actress in history. A day doesn't go by that I don't see a photo of myself that I've never seen before.

Name the movie star: Marilyn, Harlow, Bette Davis, Joan Crawford, Carole Lombard, Rita Hayworth, Shirley Temple—I don't believe any of them were photographed more than I was. Many of those photos of me became content.

I trace my life from the earliest pictures of me posing in a yellow party dress on the farm, to snapshots my dad took outside our little flat on Harvard Boulevard in LA, to my first publicity photos when I got my contract at Universal Studios, to endless press photos of me at movie premieres, parties, and appearances—you get the idea. (By the way, I have total fashion recall: I can calibrate my outfit to the era and identify when the picture was taken.)

The most important pictures of me were shot by my dear friend, the late Julie Strain. Before I tell you that story, I need to backtrack.

My father died from a heart attack in 1992. He was in robust health, a man who truly never had a sick day in his life. It took all of us by surprise.

My father and mother lived near Palm Springs in the California high desert town of Yucca Valley, in a home on a golf course. A month after he died, Thomas and I made the ninety-minute drive to Yucca Valley on a Saturday to finish some business related to his death. That night the whole house shook every few minutes with small earthquake tremors.

"There's going to be a big earthquake," I predicted.

"Naw," Thomas groused. "These are probably just normal aftershocks from the quake back in April."

I ignored him and walked around the house putting breakables on the floor.

At 4:58 the next morning, the record-breaking 7.3 magnitude Landers earthquake hit. Hard. A mere mile from the epicenter, the violent shaking jolted us out of bed and sent everyone in the neighborhood running into the street. Mom's home was severely damaged, but we got out alive and uninjured.

The loss of her husband of sixty-some years, followed by the loss of her home, left her grieving and in shock. She moved in with me. After a short time, some lingering health issues began to worsen, and ultimately, she was diagnosed with ovarian cancer. Her doctors agreed it was terminal, and she entered hospice care in my home. As we both got used to the idea that her time was growing shorter, we talked about what her death might be like.

"Mother, if there's a way you can get in touch with me from the other side, please send me a sign to let me know you're all right."

"What kind of a sign?" she asked skeptically. Never one to have serious religious beliefs, she humored me. "Sure, I'll come back and let you know."

"Why don't you come back as a bird so I'll know you are okay?"

She was not really crazy about birds. We have two large loud Moluccan cockatoos in our home that annoyed her to no end. Finally, she relented, "Okay, I'll come back as some kind of a bird."

When she died in 1995, her death left an enormous void and spiraled me into a deep depression. I wouldn't leave the house, and I barely spoke to anyone. Finally, my husband Thomas shoehorned me out of the house to have an early dinner at our favorite little Japanese restaurant in nearby Corona Del Mar. We were the first customers, alone in the dining room except for a small preschool-aged girl at a table by the window, surrounded with crayons and colored construction paper. We ordered our dinner and sipped tea, talking quietly.

Our conversation was interrupted by a flurry of movement. The young girl suddenly ran to our table, placed a small object in front of me, and dashed through the double doors into the kitchen.

I picked the thing up with trembling fingers—bright purple construction paper folded into a shape—an origami bird. The hair prickled on the back of my neck as I stared at it through tears.

"It's Mom," I whispered to Thomas. "She's all right."

Children are somehow closer to the spirit world. This little one had brought a message from another side of consciousness, telling me it was time to move on. From that moment, though the grief persisted, I knew I had turned a corner. It was time to start living again.

When I was invited to a party at the Playboy Mansion, I jumped at the chance. I had known Hugh Hefner since Playboy purchased a photo layout of the infamous beer bath scene from my movie, *Three Nuts in*

Search of a Bolt. Husbands and boyfriends were not invited to the mansion, so Perry went along as my escort. Hef and I got reacquainted, and before long, I became a regular at the mansion soirées.

It was at one of the mansion parties that I met Julie Strain, a gorgeous, tall brunette who had been *Penthouse* magazine's Pet of the Year. "Six foot one, and worth the climb," Julie always said. In addition to being a model and sometime actress, she was a photographer. During the course of the party, she mustered the courage to ask if I would do a photo layout with her—glamour shots, even nudes.

Here's a goddess secret: I'm very shy about shooting actual bare-assed nude pictures. Up to that time, I had done very few. It goes back to my Lutheran upbringing, as inconsistent as it was. I certainly wasn't inclined to shoot nudes with a photographer I didn't even know. And anyway, I was getting close to seventy. I assumed I was a few decades past taking nude pictures. Julie, however, was very persuasive.

"Mamie, you don't understand!" She pointed around the room at the young, scantily clad girls dancing and drinking. "There's not a girl in this room who doesn't know who you are and who doesn't envy you that body! I'm serious. Your breasts are unbelievable. Most of the ones you see here are silicone."

"Mine are real," I said, taking her hands and placing them on my breasts. "See for yourself."

She gave them a gentle squeeze and laughed out loud. "Oh, yeah! There ain't no oranges in there! Look, Mamie, I've got a big backyard we can shoot in. We can do all kinds of scenes. You bring clothes you want to use, and I've got tons of costumes and crazy outfits you can try. I promise it'll be fantastic."

I said yes.

Over the next several years, we shot many Saturdays in the backyard of Julie's big, rambling house on Coldwater Canyon. Those were some of the most fun times of my life. Often, Julie would also be nude as she shot pictures of me. Thomas did not object. He brought along his new high-end video camera and recorded everything, edited the footage into short videos, added music, and posted them online. Some of the photos from the Julie sessions appear in this book. If we have a little luck, others will appear in a coffee table book I'm planning. Julie's untimely death several years ago from chronic traumatic encephalopathy (CTE), caused by a serious concussion she received falling off a horse, haunts me still. She was a talented photographer, fun to be around, and a great friend. She brought me out of my cocoon. Thanks to her, I realized that at seventy and beyond, I was just beginning.

I'm fortunate to have lived in Newport Beach, California for many years. I first came to Newport Beach with my best friend Verna Doyle when I was thirteen. It was called Balboa back then. Verna was the daughter of a circuit judge. Her mother had died young, and Judge Doyle raised Verna by himself. They had a vacation cottage on Balboa Island, and I was invited to join them on holidays. I loved Newport Beach from the start. I always told myself that was where I wanted to live.

In the 1960s when I was trying to bring up my young son, Perry, Hollywood became increasingly too weird and drug-ridden. It was not the place to raise a young child. I had divorced Perry's father, band leader Ray Anthony, when Perry was quite young. I was a working single mom rearing a youngster long before it became the routine parenting role it is today. Perry and I pulled up stakes and moved to Orange County and Newport Beach.

Orange County was (and is) known for its staunch conservatism. I felt differently about many things, so sometimes it wasn't easy for a sexy blonde actress to fit in. When I appeared in *Playboy* magazine, it became tough on Perry too. Kids teased him because of his sexy mom. He bounced from military academies to private schools to public schools, even attending one while living with my mother and dad in Yucca Valley, while I was working out of town. He finally found comfort at a Christian school and went on to graduate from a Christian college. His journey was at times complicated. Perry is a fine man. He is, and has always been, the light of my life.

My husband, Thomas Dixon, and I celebrated our fifty-first anniversary this year (2025). I never imagined I would be married to the same man for half a century. That was complicated at times too. You don't live with someone for fifty years without a few bumps in the road. I have always stuck to the contract when I got married, but there are times when, well, temptation might come knocking. 'Nuff said. Even a goddess needs a secret or two.

Thomas is fourteen years younger than I am. When we first started going together, it was seen as a huge difference. "It'll never last," people criticized. But we have stood the test of time. I used to call him my "toy boy." Now, fifty years later, he has a shock of white hair, all his own teeth, and qualifies as a hot-looking senior. He now jokes about being a "toy geezer."

Fortunately, Thomas and I laugh at the same things and enjoy the same quiet routines. We love adopting dogs. I look forward to meeting them all at the Rainbow Bridge when I die.

I like to walk the same beaches I did when I was thirteen. Now, we walk the dogs there or watch the surfers and skateboarders on the boardwalk. I sit on the same stretch of sand and let the waves wash over me, or I sit on the same rocks and dare the spray to wet me. It all connects me to who I was and who I am. The beach doesn't change, really. Sand, sky, and Pacific. Uncomplicated.

If you want advice for longevity, it's this: don't look back. The view in the rearview mirror is mostly dark. Look forward toward the light.

There is a concept in Buddhism of the Pure Lands. It is the place where enlightenment is achieved and where time is reduced to an all-encompassing present. All things happen at the same moment. Past and future fuse into a singularity where all things happen at once. It is sometimes called the Golden Dome of Eternity. I'm no Buddhist scholar, but it seems to me, if you can get there, that is enlightenment.

So, now it's time to say goodbye. Jack Kerouac once said of life and stories, "It all ends in tears anyway." Though my stories contain plenty of tears, as well as laughter, I wanted to avoid a tearful memoir farewell, striding off into the Newport Beach sunset. So, I decided to steal an ending from the Bard. (Hey, if you're going to steal, steal from the best.)

One of my favorite endings is Puck's speech at the end of *Midsummer Night's Dream*. It's humble and funny, and, best of all, clues the audience in that they've been part of the play.

Puck says, "If we shadows have offended, think but this and all is mended. That you have but slumbered here, while these visions did appear."

What a wonderful idea: the audience—or, in this case, you, the reader—has fallen asleep and dreamt the trials, tribulations, and joys, as well as the deep dark secrets of this goddess. For you, it was a dream; for me, I lived it.

And, since we now must part for a while, let me end by paraphrasing Puck:

> Give me your hands, if we be friends,
>
> And Mamie shall restore amends.

THE END

Acknowledgments

Heartfelt thanks to John Huddleston who was a Combat Medic in Vietnam. John saw me perform there all those years ago and generously contributed his own recollections of the war to the Vietnam chapter.

Special thanks to the brilliant artist, my dear friend, Stephen B. Whatley, who created the illustrations that open each chapter. And thanks to photographer and longtime friend, Alan Mercer, for his cover photo. No one does a cover picture better than Alan.

Many thanks to Post Hill Press for taking on this unusual memoir, and to managing editor Caitlin Burdette, and my manuscript editors Lexi Merring and Sophie Jefferson for their sharp eyes, good judgement, and unflappable patience.

And thank you Alan Nevins, agent, advisor, and keeper of the wisdom.